SCOTTISH LITERATURE INTERNATIONAL

Gael and Lowlander in Scottish Literature

Cross-currents in Scottish Writing in the Nineteenth Century

EDITED BY
CHRISTOPHER MacLACHLAN
and RONALD W. RENTON

Occasional Papers: Number 20
Association for Scottish Literary Studies

Published by
Scottish Literature International
Scottish Literature
7 University Gardens
University of Glasgow
Glasgow G12 8QH

Scottish Literature International is an imprint of
the Association for Scottish Literary Studies

www.asls.org.uk

ASLS is a registered charity no. SC006535

First published 2015

Text © ASLS and the individual contributors

All rights reserved. No part of this book may be
reproduced, stored in a retrieval system, or
transmitted in any form or means, electronic,
mechanical, photocopying, recording or otherwise,
without the prior permission of the
Association for Scottish Literary Studies.

A CIP catalogue for this title
is available from the British Library

ISBN 978-1-908980-10-6

ALBA | CHRUTHACHAIL

ASLS acknowledges the support of Creative Scotland
towards the publication of this book

Contents

Introduction		v
Acknowledgements		ix
One	Contacts and Tensions: Highlands and Lowlands in the Nineteenth Century *Allan I. Macinnes*	1
Two	The Poetry of Ailean Dall *Ronald Black*	22
Three	Cultural Crossings and Dilemmas in Archibald Maclaren's Playwriting *Ian Brown and Gioia Angeletti*	41
Four	What Walter Scott Can Offer Us Today *Christopher Whyte*	56
Five	James Hogg and the Highlands *Suzanne Gilbert*	72
Six	The *Noctes Ambrosianae* and the Highlands *David Manderson*	88
Seven	'That Fairyland of Poesy': The Highlands in Early Nineteenth-Century Women's Fiction *Pam Perkins*	104
Eight	The Unknown William Livingston (Four Songs) *Christopher Whyte*	121
Nine	Gaelic Periodicals in the Lowlands: Negotiating Change *Sheila M. Kidd*	143

Contents (continued)

Ten	Màiri Mhòr – Victim of Circumstance or Self-Made Celebrity? *Mark Wringe*	159
Eleven	Niall MacLeòid, Bard of Skye and Edinburgh *Meg Bateman*	172
Twelve	Robert Louis Stevenson's Highlanders *Christopher MacLachlan*	190
Thirteen	Art, the Highlands and the Celtic Revival *Murdo Macdonald*	203
Fourteen	From Celtic Revival to Scottish Renaissance? *Douglas Gifford*	216

Introduction

CHRISTOPHER MacLACHLAN AND RONALD W. RENTON

The collection of essays here presented derives from papers given at a conference entitled 'Crossing the Highland Line in the Nineteenth Century: Cross-currents in Scottish Writing', held from 8 to 10 June 2012 at Sabhal Mòr Ostaig, Isle of Skye. This was a sequel to an earlier conference with a similar title on eighteenth-century Gaelic and Scottish literature held in May 2005 at the same venue. Though the weather in 2012 was not quite as good as in 2005, the second conference was as successful as the first, affording the opportunity for scholars of all aspects of nineteenth-century Scottish literature, in the Highlands and the Lowlands, to meet and learn about their colleagues' work, compare and contrast their research and opinions and produce lively discussion of books and authors for a large and appreciative audience in very congenial surroundings, and with splendid views of lochs and mountains.

Thanks to the success of the conference and of the volume of papers from the first conference, *Crossing the Highland Line: Cross-currents in Eighteenth-Century Scottish Writing*, published by ASLS in 2009, it was easy to decide to produce a second volume devoted to papers from the second conference. We are grateful to the speakers at the conference for contributing their work, suitably revised for publication, to appear in this volume. The arrangement of the papers here is roughly chronological, which has the effect of interleaving the various strands of the discussion, notably the Gaelic and the Scots, and also promotes a strong sense of the change and development of Scottish writing (and not only writing) about the Highlands in the course of the nineteenth century.

The collection begins, then, with Allan Macinnes's masterly survey of social and political change in the Highlands in the period, and in the range and nature of the contacts between Highlands and Lowlands. With a breathtaking command of a multitude of sources and a mass of information, Professor Macinnes presents an authoritative and often corrective view of developments that have sometimes been too easily summarised under simple notions of clearances and romantic tourism. The urge to look more closely and offer more detailed and more nuanced appraisal, set in this opening essay, is a keynote of many that follow and of the collection as a whole.

This is certainly true of Ronald Black's scrupulous and systematic appraisal of the poetry of Ailean Dall, the second paper in this volume, which sets out in detail a critical survey of the poet's work, supported by attention to his life and the detail of the texts, which are copiously quoted. The roots of Ailean Dall's technique in traditional forms are shown, as are also his departures from them, serving to highlight the continuity of nineteenth-century Gaelic poetry with that of the previous century, and so taking up the link between this volume and its predecessor. The same is true of Ian Brown and Gioia Angeletti's examination of the plays of Archibald Maclaren, a fascinating example of a Gaelic man of the theatre, who both exploited and adapted his Gaelic background at the time when the Highlands, thanks to Macpherson's Ossian, had become prominent in the culture of Scotland, and the United Kingdom, and before Sir Walter Scott had begun adding his massive weight to the impression they made on European culture.

It is with the issue of Scott and how he is dealt with in the twenty-first century that Christopher Whyte deals in the fourth paper here. Whyte asks for, and makes a start on demonstrating, fresh approaches to Scott, setting aside the embarrassment with his achievement that has characterised much of the twentieth century's attitude to him as not suitable either in critical or political terms to the orthodoxies of academic criticism. Too much of modern opinion on Scott is driven by a sense that Scottish literature and the image of the Highlands has to be considered in spite of him. Whyte wants to set that aside and look at what he wrote and how intriguing and subtle it actually is. In a way that is to do to Scott what has so successfully been done for his contemporary, James Hogg. In two fascinating studies by Suzanne Gilbert and David Manderson we see Hogg's response to the Highlands used to explore the image of the Highlands themselves, and, as importantly, their treatment outside the Highlands. Suzanne Gilbert leads us through an account of Hogg's journeys in the Highlands to theoretical questions about the geographical modes his responses exemplify, and David Manderson, in widening the focus to how the authors of the *Noctes Ambrosianae* treated both Hogg and the Highlands, opens up the question of how the Highlands were viewed in the nineteenth century, the theme of several later papers in this volume. Pam Perkins considers this from the perspective of several lesser-known women writers of the early part of the century. What she shows is both how strong, but also how varied, was the impact of the idea of the Highlands on fiction in the first quarter of the century.

Christopher Whyte's second contribution to this volume, 'The Unknown William Livingston (Four Songs)', is a magisterial consideration of this very significant Gaelic poet. What is brought out is not just, as in Ronald Black's discussion of Ailean Dall, the way in which a nineteenth-century poet built on tradition while contending with change, but also how Livingston's life and work are a fascinating response to his times and his society. The bardic clichés give way to a recognition of the true complexity of a poet who is a witness to the nineteenth century. Something of what this means in terms of the changes in the readership of the first half of the nineteenth century and of the methods of publishing literature, particularly in Gaelic, is shown in Sheila Kidd's paper. The first-hand research here gives us an insight into the ferment of activity that is the background to the literary productions of the first half of the century, and into the growing interweaving of Highland and Lowland factors, not least the movement of people from one to the other. The impact of change, personal and cultural, is of course the background of Mark Wringe's discussion of the life and work of Màiri Mhòr MacPherson, focusing particularly on the question of her bilingualism. The subject of Meg Bateman's essay 'Niall MacLeòid, Bard of Skye and Edinburgh' offers further examples of the cross-currents between Gael and Lowlander that Sheila Kidd highlights. The work of Niall, and his father and brother, shows how Gaelic poetry developed in the latter half of the nineteenth century, and indeed into the next.

Christopher MacLachlan's contribution also begins to look forward into the next century, if only in offering a reading of some of Robert Louis Stevenson's Highland characters that tries to shift out of the shadow of Romanticism towards a more sceptical, if not astringent, modern view. By focusing on the unprepossessing figure of Catriona's father, James More, in the sequel to *Kidnapped*, MacLachlan tries to bring out the queasy balancing of glamour and grimness in Stevenson's Highlanders. Murdo Macdonald, in a paper devoted to fine art rather than literature, then takes us into the final phases of the nineteenth century and the movement towards Celticism and the Celtic Twilight. The volume ends with Douglas Gifford's opening out of the question of the relationship between the Celtic Revival and its sequel, the modernism of the early twentieth century that so violently rejected it. Undaunted by the critical mauling meted out to William Sharp, notorious under his pen-name of Fiona Macleod, Professor Gifford asks awkward questions about what the Celtic Revival means in the history of Scottish literature and culture and gives some challenging answers. Thus he brings this collection of essays to a climax by facing us with the way crossing the Highland Line in the nineteenth century affected the process in the following century, and down to us today.

Acknowledgements

The Editors would like to thank Jim Alison, for his help in planning the conference from which this book of essays derives; Michel Byrne, for assistance in organising the conference programme and with Gaelic language issues; Ian MacDonald, who also helped with the Gaelic; and Margaret Bennett, whose recordings of the conference proceedings were an invaluable resource.

C.J.M.M.
R.W.R.

1. Contacts and Tensions: Highlands and Lowlands in the Nineteenth Century

ALLAN I. MACINNES

From the late middle ages, poets and chroniclers usually propagated antipathetic relationships between Highlanders and Lowlanders. Government officials, intent on punitive military and legislative offensives, claimed the cultural gap between the *Gael* and the *Gall* was that between barbarity and civility. The 'Highland problem', however, was primarily an issue for intrusive central government rather than for the clans whose engagement in feuding and the lifting of livestock was never an everyday occurrence.[1] Certainly, there were linguistic differences that continued into the nineteenth century. But no matter how culturally nuanced, other differences between *Gael* and *Gall* were more of degree than of kind in relation to political and religious affiliations, landholding, imperial engagement, agrarian transformation and industrialisation.

In the civil wars that scarred early modern Scotland, the clans tended to be on the side of the Royalists against the Covenanters in the seventeenth century and for the Jacobites against the Whigs in the eighteenth. But a minority of clans fought for the Covenanters and the Whigs. Highlanders as well as Lowlanders were complicit in the carnage inflicted on the clans at the behest of William, Duke of Cumberland, in 1746. Religious commitment rather than opportunities to commit atrocities was the principal motivation for Presbyterian clans to side with the Whigs. But again the clans were divided confessionally. The majority of those favouring the Jacobites were Episcopalians with Roman Catholics constituting a no less committed minority. While the feudal components of landholding were more pronounced in the Lowlands, occupation and settlement depended on binding ties of kinship and local association that were bound up with clanship whose ruling elite were viewed as trustees as well as landlords. But the landed elite in the Lowlands were also expected to offer kindness and paternalism to their tenantry.[2] Clannish ties of kinship and local association were also integral to the capacity of Scottish commercial networks to sustain and expand the country's trade from the Baltic and the Mediterranean to the Caribbean and on to the Indian Ocean and the South China Seas, particularly as Union with England in 1707 opened up new global horizons. Albeit not as numerous, Highlanders, like Lowlanders, were to be found among the ranks of the tobacco lords, sugar barons, African slavers, Indian nabobs and China tea traders by mid-eighteenth century.[3]

As well as repatriating capital from Empire, Highlanders were in particular demand in the colonies as frontiersmen and indentured labours. Their transoceanic relocation was expedited by wholesale agrarian transformation promoted as improvement but accomplished by Clearance. In the first phase of the Clearances from the 1730s to the 1820s, communal townships were broken up in favour of single-tenant holdings for cattle and sheep farming, while retained tenantry were removed into crofting communities, rural ghettos geared to fishing, burning of seaweed for kelp, illicit distilling, slate and lime quarrying, charcoal burning and timber extraction. Crofting facilitated the retention of labour pools of soldiers and sailors for imperial service. Subsistence agriculture was a secondary pursuit. But the Lowlands no less than the Highlands suffered Clearances. The one perceptible difference – with the north-west rather than the Highlands as a whole – was that removed tenantry tended to be relocated in planned villages that diversified from agriculture into textiles, fishing and distilling. Planned villages, in turn, served as a bridge between town and country.[4]

The replacement of customary by commercial relationships on the part of the clan elite, no less than their Lowland counterparts, transformed all of Scotland, albeit there were considerable regional and local variations with respect to time and achievement. The majority of those removed were obliged to relocate into villages, towns and cities, primarily to participate in the first phase of industrialisation from the 1770s to the 1820s. This first phase, which is most notably associated with textiles and chemicals, involved Highland entrepreneurs as well as migrant workers, but rarely was industrialisation pursued within the Highlands beyond the primary level of extractive products.[5]

Notwithstanding Scotland undergoing both agricultural and industrial revolutions at the outset of the nineteenth century, the transfer of people, goods and ideas between Highlands and Lowlands diminished rather than aggravated the purported longstanding tensions between *Gael* and

Gall. More mutually supportive contacts can now be explored through 'Highlandism', further Clearances, evangelical religion and urbanisation. No social contacts are without tensions, but those between Highlanders and Lowlanders in the nineteenth century were creative as well as exploitive.

I

'Highlandism' is the association of tartan with military prowess and imperial service, a peculiar weave that came in the course of the nineteenth century to represent Scotland's distinctive presence within the British Empire. Responsibility for this fabrication has been laid at the door of Sir Walter Scott for stage-managing George IV's visit to Edinburgh in 1822 as a tartan extravaganza. However, the association of 'Highlandism' with kitsch 'Caledonianism' requires qualification.[6]

Notwithstanding the role of the clans as the front-line troops in the Jacobite risings, the rehabilitation of the Highlander through imperial service dates back to the Seven Years War (1756–63), in the course of which the Glasgow Highland Society made much of former Jacobite clansmen serving loyally in North America as light infantry in the British Army.[7] This rehabilitation was furthered by the notable contributions of Highland regiments as the most reliable light infantry in the service of the British Empire on a global scale from the American Revolutionary Wars (1776–83) to the Napoleonic Wars (1793–1815). Indeed, in the immediate aftermath of the latter, Alexander MacDonald of Glenaladale, a Highland laird from a family with a long Jacobite pedigree, felt sufficiently confident in the process of rehabilitation that he erected on his Lochaber estate the Glenfinnan Monument to the raising of the standard by Prince Charles Edward Stuart at the outset of the '45. The Monument was designed by the leading Scottish baronial architect James Gillespie Graham, who had played a prominent role in developing the New Town of Edinburgh as a monumental tribute to Hanoverian monarchy and British Union. Making the Monument even more remarkable was the confessional affiliation of the MacDonalds of Glenaladale as staunch Roman Catholics. Glenaladale's initiative took place fourteen years before he and his co-religionists were accorded full religious and civil liberties by the Catholic Emancipation Act.

In addition to imperial service, the rehabilitation process had been facilitated by another prominent Scot with a Jacobite pedigree, James 'Ossian'

Macpherson. His rich embellishment of Gaelic oral tradition relating to the classical heroes of Celtic mythology had provided a Scottish template for Romanticism. Macpherson was a formidable archival historian and a noted polemicist opposed to the East India Company's regressive and lax running of imperial enterprise. His lament for the passing of a warrior society can be viewed as a coded elegy for the Jacobite Highlands. But, at a time of major agricultural and industrial transformation along capitalist lines, his Romantic appeal to the past carried echoes not just of epic heroism but of a moral economy. The need to conserve a virile past in association with social benevolence found lasting local expression in the year following George IV's visit. The Lonach Games and Friendly Society, founded in 1823 by Sir Charles Forbes of Newe and Edinglassie, in the Episcopalian and Jacobite heartlands of Aberdeenshire, sought to preserve the Highland dress and the Gaelic language while promoting competitive games that would provide funding for distressed members and their families in Strathdon. On the one hand, The Lonach was drawing on the community self-help initiatives through savings banks and friendly societies pioneered from 1812 in the Lowlands by the Rev. Henry Duncan in Ruthwell parish, Dumfriesshire. On the other hand, The Lonach was instrumental in developing Highland games as a tartan spectacle that would carry professional sports from Scotland to North America.

As a promoter, antiquarian and novelist, Sir Walter Scott strove to restore an appreciation of the enduring validity of the essentially rural community values of Scotland. A Jacobite by inclination if not by intellect, Scott, through his history and his historical novels was concerned to give equal prominence to Highlanders as to Lowlanders. As evident from his *Tales of a Grandfather* (1828), Scott offered a version of Scottish history from the Wars of Independence to the last Jacobite rising that was rooted in civic humanism and adventurous patriotism that celebrated rather than anaesthetised heroic traditions. Scott was no prototype for a Hollywood director with a distorted view of Scottish history. He welcomed the accomplishment of Union in 1707 for its validation of Scotland as a partner in Empire. On no account did Union justify the provincial relegation of Scotland or the subordination of Scottish political, commercial and ecclesiastical interests to those of England.[8] He certainly took considerable dramatic licence in his sympathetic portrayal of Rob Roy MacGregor, which took little account of the bandit proclivities of his immediate family and clan. But his primary interest was to rehabilitate the Highland clans that had been the military bedrock of Jacobitism and were now at the beck and call of the British Empire. Notwithstanding his glossing of the Highland Clearances, he began a rich tradition of historical novels involving clanship, Jacobitism, political ambivalence and moral ambiguity that was taken up by Andrew Lang, Robert Louis Stevenson, John Buchan and Neil Munro. Only the latter, himself a Highlander, was a contemporaneous social commentator in both urban and rural settings.[9]

The artistic contribution to social realism was no less notable for its omissions than its commissions. Sir Henry Raeburn's portrait of *Colonel Alasdair MacDonnell of Glengarry* (1811) darkly shadows this kilted promoter of 'Highlandism' with the moral ambiguity appropriate for a foolhardy and mendacious martinet who instigated swingeing Clearances of his erstwhile clansmen in Lochaber at the outset of the nineteenth century. The Romantic magnificence of landscape as initiated by Alexander Naismith was notably developed in a Highland context by John Knox in *Landscape with Tourists at Loch Katrine* (1820) and his subsequent work on Loch Lomond, which appealed to the more leisured classes. But only David Wilkie, in his *Distraining for Rent* (1815), dealt directly with eviction for Highlander as for Lowlander. Edwin Landseer, particularly through his *Monarch of the Glen* (1851), came to glorify the recreational use of Highland estates for hunting, shooting and fishing. Horatio MacCulloch painted *Glencoe* (1864) as a wilderness with no acknowledgement that this wilderness was man-made, an omission only passively acknowledged in *The Emigrant's Dream of His Highland Home* (1860).[10] Notwithstanding the emptying of the glens, recreational landlordism received a major boost when Victoria and Albert acquired and developed Balmoral on Deeside during the 1850s. But again, some caution must be exercised in negating 'Highlandism' by royal warrant. Queen Victoria, especially as a widow, found not only solace but inspiration in the Highlands. She so immersed herself in its history, natural history and culture that she, perhaps, can even be depicted as the only Jacobite monarch to reside by choice in the Highlands![11]

II

Imperial service, at best, was no more than a temporary check to Clearance in the Highlands, especially after the first phase, associated with the creation of crofting communities, gave way to a second phase, marked by the removal of these communities for commercial pastoralism and recreational land use from the 1820s to the 1880s. With the industrial production of inorganic salts and alkalis leading to a collapse in demand for organic kelp, with the distilling of malt whisky being legitimised and with diminishing calls on manpower for imperial service by land and sea, the parlous state of crofting communities was increasingly exposed. The contrary nature of herring shoals affecting the viability of those communities engaged in fishing, the only relatively buoyant aspect of crofting was working with such extractive industries as slate, lime and timber. Crofting communities in general were over-reliant on potato cultivation and seasonal or episodical migration to the Lowlands to find employment in arable agriculture, heavy industries or construction work. But here again Highlanders faced stiff Irish competition as casual labourers. The critical condition of crofting was first exposed by the potato famine of 1836–7, which was relieved largely through relief funds raised in British cities, with relief being co-ordinated from Glasgow under the energetic and committed leadership of the Rev. Norman MacLeod of St Columba's (the city's pre-eminent Gaelic kirk) and C. R. Baird, the city's chief medical officer. For his endeavours, MacLeod earned the epithet *Caraid nan Gael* (Friend of the Highlanders). However, MacLeod's solution to endemic destitution was wholesale migration, having lined up the shipping company Pollok, Gilmour and Co. to transport thousands of Highlanders to Canada. He considered that at least a third of a notional crofting population of around 80,000 should be removed. The principal concern of C. R. Baird was the proneness of destitute Highlanders to disease in urban ghettos. Accordingly, he wanted a greater emphasis on education rather than emigration in order to equip Highlanders with the technical skills to gain meaningful employment in the heavy industries of iron, coal, steel and shipbuilding, which dominated the second phase of industrialisation in Scotland from the 1820s.[12]

Neither MacLeod nor Baird sought to criticise landlords either for creating or clearing crofting communities. Landlords' general, but by no means universal, reluctance to finance adequate work programmes was combined with their particular aversion to the Poor Law Amendment Act of 1845, which they feared would give the able-bodied poor a right to claim relief at the expense of the landed interest. In marked contrast to the contemporaneous Irish situation, the Great Famine did not become a demographic disaster in the Highlands. Again relief funds were mobilised through British cities and supplemented by contributions from the Scottish diaspora in North America. A Central Board of Management, based in Glasgow and Edinburgh, sponsored destitution roads and other infrastructural developments that enhanced the value of landed estates. By 1851 'no sensible progress has been made and the state of the population continues to decline' according to Sir John McNeil from Colonsay, who made his career as a diplomat serving in India and Persia. McNeil was reporting to the Board of Supervision which had overall responsibility for the secular administration of poor relief in Scotland since 1845. His report, the first of many compiled by the Board on the limited prospects for crofting, came down firmly in favour of assisted emigration rather than state intervention in land management. On the one hand, sheep farms as well as crofting communities were losing out to deer forests for sporting purposes. On the other, the Board's parsimonious administering of poor relief was geared more to an urban rather than a rural context.[13]

The positive case for state intervention through the promotion of infrastructural projects had been made eloquently at the outset of the nineteenth century by the Scottish engineer, Thomas Telford. Reporting to the British Parliament in 1802, Telford claimed that the interests of the Empire, in terms of the free rein of market forces, could be served by having the Highlands produce as much food as possible at the least possible expense. But this would lead to the Highlands being stocked chiefly by sheep rather than people, who would be obliged to remove to other parts of the country to engage productively in agriculture, fisheries or manufactures. However, it could be countered 'that it is a great Hardship, if not a great Injustice, that the Inhabitants of an extensive District should all at once be driven from their native Country, to make way for sheep Farming, which is likely to be carried to an imprudent Extent.' If no remedial action was taken the Highlands would soon be depopulated. His diagnosis was accurate if apocalyptic. It was the duty of government to consider the Highlands as an extraordinary case by curtailing the excesses of estate management as practised by those landlords who preferred profiteering to enlightened planning. This prognosis fell on deaf ears, but Telford was employed to direct the imperial government's programme of road, bridge and canal construction to stem what had become a tidal flow of emigration from the Highlands.[14] Telford's flagship project, the Caledonian Canal, primarily served to expedite the access of more highly capitalised and technologically advanced north-east fishing fleets into west coast waters. The Crinan Canal did directly benefit the penetration of urban markets in the central Lowlands by Argyllshire slate quarries and Islay distilleries, but led to no overall transformation of crofting or any halt to emigration. Joseph Mitchell, a later if less celebrated engineer, who worked primarily on public and private projects in the Highlands, astutely observed in 1879 that improved infrastructure in terms of roads and harbours had actually accelerated the migration of Highlanders to Lowland towns and cities regardless of any prompting by landlords, whom he was not averse to criticising for their extravagant tastes and absenteeism.[15]

Nevertheless a pronounced feature of public discourse in the Highlands in the later nineteenth century was that of landlords on the defensive. In part, this can be attributed to the astute use of the English language by Highland polemicists and of British newspapers by crofting sympathisers. *The Gloomy Memories* (1857) by Donald MacLeod, a former crofter cleared to Canada, provided an evocative riposte to the whitewashing of the Sutherland Clearances by the American novelist, Harriet Beecher Stowe. Alexander MacKenzie collated powerful eyewitness testimonies on the harrowing process of removal and relocation in *The History of the Highland Clearances* (1883). But perhaps the most powerful indictment of landlords' conduct came during the Great Famine from front-line accounts of destitution and limited resistance to evictions by the journalist Robert Somers. The adverse publicity generated for landlords during the 1840s was sustained, though not indiscriminatingly so, in the British press for the remainder of the nineteenth century and was not abated by the trenchant defence of the landed interest by George Douglas Campbell, eighth Duke of Argyll.[16]

Visual representations of the Highlands sent out mixed messages in their endeavours to inform, educate and entertain. Artists, particularly those with studios located in London, had a limited capacity to change public perceptions. Thomas Faed's *The Last of the Clans* (1865) is certainly poignant in its treatment of Clearance but rather lacking in perception with respect to their causes. Robert Pettie condoned the march of civility by portraying kilted Highlanders as bandits given to looting in *Disbanded*

(1877) or illicit distilling in *The Tussle for the Keg* (1868). However, the new art form of photography offered more realistic, even if at times staged, depictions of Highland life from the pioneering work of David Ocatavius Hill and Robert Adamson from St Andrews in the 1840s and the prodigious output of George Washington Wilson in Aberdeen from the 1850s to the 1890s. The pictorial postcard, a vacational spinoff from vocational photography, gives a less engaged but more familiar perspective on the Highlands for Lowland consumption. The Highlands may have missed out in the second phase of industrialisation, but they were profoundly impacted by two technological advances in transport associated with heavy industry. The steam ship and the railway opened up tourism and consumerism in the Highlands not just for the aspiring middle but the skilled working classes from the Lowlands with increased leisure time. Tourist towns spread from Rothesay and Dunoon in the Firth of Clyde to Oban, Fort William and Ullapool in the West Highlands and on to Tobermory, Portree and Stornoway in the Hebrides. Package tours by steamer, train and even charabanc expanded from the staples of Loch Lomond and the Trossachs, Glencoe, the Great Glen, Iona and Staffa to the exotic St Kilda in the course of the later nineteenth century.[17]

The appeal of tourism notwithstanding, the urban Lowlands was increasingly moved to support land reform in the Highlands. In part this can be attributed to committed leadership, in part to the example of the Land League Movement in Ireland but, above all, to changing perceptions towards customary rights on the part of the imperial government, particularly when led by William Ewart Gladstone, whose family origins were Scottish and who acquired an estate in the Braes of Angus. Land reform attracted varied support from individuals operating mainly in Glasgow and Edinburgh. They included W. F. Skene and Charles Fraser-Mackintosh, antiquarians with a commitment to public service; Professor John Stuart Blackie of Edinburgh University, a classical intellectual; Angus Sutherland, a radical schoolteacher; Dr G. B. Clarke, a pioneer socialist; and John Murdoch, an exciseman turned campaign journalist. However, the main activist body, the Federation of Celtic Societies founded in 1878, was more notable for disseminating the need for land reform than effecting its accomplishment. Indeed, the Federation had limited influence over landed agitation which was spreading from Lewis to Skye by the outset of the 1880s. Here, the grass-roots influence of the Irish Land League was undoubtedly inspirational but not necessarily an exemplar given sectarian tensions between Irish Catholics and Scottish Protestants in Highlands and Lowlands.

The Irish Land League certainly demonstrated how imperial government could be moved by direct action. But Gladstone was primarily influenced to promote legislation rehabilitating customary rights by prior initiatives to this end in the Punjab promoted by George Campbell, a colonial official with landed connections in the Highlands. The first response to accommodate the pressure from committed Lowlanders in the cities and crofting activists on the ground was the Napier Commission of 1883–84, led by the former Indian career diplomat and Borders landowner, Francis Napier, Lord Napier and Ettrick.[18] Influenced by antiquarians and intellectuals, the Napier Commission favoured the rehabilitation of communal townships to promote agricultural viability. This was not acceptable to crofting activists whose prescriptive rights of possession would be subordinated thereby. Following further pressure from the Highland Land League, supplemented by the return of a handful of Crofting Members of Parliament in the general election of 1885, the Crofters' Holdings Act was duly passed the next year. The Act granted security of tenure but not security of income to crofters. Nothing was done to promote the interests of those not conceded or able to attain crofting statues.

A third phase of Clearance duly ensued. This was most powerfully depicted in *The Storm* (1890) and *The Sailing of the Emigrant Ship* (1895) by William McTaggart. Rooted in the fishing communities on Kintyre, McTaggart portrayed an authoritative testimony to the continuing heartbreak of Clearance. His paintings, populated by indigenous Highlanders not tourists, were realistic portrayals of the hardships endured on land and sea. No less realistic was the constricting of crofting ambitions that can be attributed to the Crofters Holdings Act. For subsequent protests and land raids by those seeking land from Lewis to Lochaber were no more than heroic gestures. The creation or concession of further crofting communities neither guaranteed agricultural sustainability nor halted the haemorrhage of people from the Highlands. At the same time, commercial landlordism and the primacy of individual rights of property were checked but not seriously challenged. The nineteenth century closed with the growing separation of city based Land Leaguers and crofting activists.[19]

III

While religion was a divisive influence between Irish and Highland Land Leaguers, it was by no means a force for unity of purpose or radical solidarity for Highlanders in town and country throughout the nineteenth century. There was distinctive Highland engagement with evangelical Presbyterianism, but evangelical Presbyterianism was not necessarily a distinctive aspect of Highland identity.[20] Although Roman Catholics, especially their clergy, were subject to penal laws from the Reformation in the mid-sixteenth century until the Catholic Emancipation Act of 1829, Catholicism continued to survive in discreet pockets from Barra and South Uist to the Small Isles of Rhum, Eigg and Muck into Stratherrick and Strathglass and on to Glenlivet and Strathavon. Episcopalians, who were also subject to punitive penal laws for their association with Jacobitism until the death of Prince Charles Edward Stuart in 1788, continued to flourish in Lorne, Wester Ross, Caithness, Strathdon, Deeside and the Braes of Angus. In the vast and rough bounds of Lochaber, Catholics and Episcopalians more than held their own with Presbyterians.[21] Certainly missionary endeavours in support of Presbyterianism had been directly sponsored by royal bounties from 1724. Successive British governments also looked favourably on the educational initiatives of the Scottish version of the Society for the Propagation of Christian Knowledge (SPCK) that promoted basic literacy in English, Presbyterian catechising and loyalty to the Hanoverian dynasty through ambulatory schooling in normally extensive Highland parishes. These oppressive endeavours of the SPCK – rendered appropriately in Gaelic as CCCP – were gradually relaxed once the perceived political threat from Jacobitism was terminated. The Scottish Society went on to promote Gaelic as a medium of instruction in 1766. In the following year they published the first Scottish Gaelic version of the New Testament and then of the Bible in 1801. They subsequently won deserved commendation as the major publisher of Gaelic religious texts in the nineteenth century. But their missionary and educational policies remained markedly denominational. Nevertheless, ambulatory schooling was furthered on a notably non-denominational basis throughout the Highlands by the Gaelic Society Schools established by public subscription in Edinburgh (1811), Glasgow (1812) and Inverness (1818). Their promotion of basic literacy and bilingualism actually accelerated emigration by the time public funds were running short in the late 1820s, after which time ambulatory schools increasingly became the province of evangelical Presbyterian initiatives funded from Lowland towns and cities.

One hundred years after the award of the royal bounty, parliamentary funding was secured to further Presbyterian missionary endeavours through the building of churches to supplement existing parish churches. Not only were Highland parishes usually extensive but one parish church, even if centrally located, could not effectually serve dispersed populations; a situation compounded by the removal and relocation of people to coastal districts by the Clearances. The erection of Parliamentary Churches from 1824, basically a task of kit-building that was initially entrusted to Thomas Telford, set benchmarks particularly in relation to narrowing windows for churches subsequently erected by evangelical Presbyterians no longer content to remain within the orbit of the established Kirk of Scotland. In Highlands as in Lowlands divisions over the appointment of ministers by landlords as lay patrons were compounded by theological concerns about the dilution of orthodox Calvinism and the failure to promote adequate spiritual missions at home and abroad during the Moderate ascendancy in the Kirk from the late eighteenth to the early nineteenth century. After ten years of legal conflict, a substantive minority left the Kirk at the Disruption in 1843 to constitute themselves as the Free Church, whose strength lay among the urban middle classes and the crofting community. Three significant influences promoted widespread support for the Free Church within the crofting community: the spread of spiritual poetry through Gaelic oral tradition; the charismatic leadership provided by *na daoine* (the men) usually in defiance of Moderate ministers; and the evangelical endeavours of the teachers in ambulatory schools. However, the Free Church did not sweep the board in the Highlands. Moderate Presbyterianism still retained a dominant presence in the southern and eastern Highlands. The strongholds of evangelical Presbyterianism were to the west and north of the Great Glen. In turn, the role of the Free Church as a vehicle for anti-landlord protest and, indeed, as a radical political entity in the Highlands must be questioned, particularly in the light of the Site Controversy occasioned by the refusal of landlords to grant land for churches to their tenantry who adhered to the Free Church.[22]

The Site Controversy was not characterised by endemic class conflict. The general consensus of those testifying before the parliamentary inquiry of 1847 was that localised tension along class lines was more the product than the cause of landlords' refusal to grant sites; a situation analogous to the discriminatory application of poor relief by landlords during the contemporaneous famine of 1845–50. There was no unreserved condemnation of landlords' conduct in the findings of the Select Committee's report in July 1847, which noted with satisfaction that in many cases where sites had been refused in 1843, landlords' objections had subsequently been waived and sites granted. That this was not a black and white issue of class conflict can be illustrated from three salutary examples. Sir James Riddell of Ardnamurchan's refusal of a site at Strontian led to his tenantry building a floating church in Loch Suinart. But Riddell had already proved his generosity in providing sites and maintaining Parliamentary Churches from 1825 in the most extensive parish in Scotland. A Skye landlord, MacDonald of Skeabost, not only granted a site but joined the Free Church. But he was rapidly disillusioned by the sectarian intolerance of the evangelical Presbyterians who propagated the view that to remain or even to attend divine service in the established Kirk was sinful. His neighbouring landlord, Rainy of Raasay, who remained a staunch supporter of the Free Church, actually refused the minister of the established Kirk access to his island charge.[23]

The Free Church's call to the crofting community to abstain from acts of violence during the Site Controversy was in keeping with its determination to give institutional respectability to evangelical Presbyterianism. Its principal constituency, the urban middle classes in the Lowland towns and cities, were not intent on challenging the social order or threatening rights of property. Notwithstanding the anti-establishment ethos of the Disruption and the Site Controversy, the Free Church was not inherently opposed to landlordism. Its religious leader at the Disruption, the Rev. Thomas Chalmers, eulogised the benevolence of John Campbell, second Marquess of Breadalbane, to the general assembly at Inverness in 1845 for his defence of the Free Church in the House of Lords and for his provision of timber from his yards at Perth and slates from his quarries in Argyllshire to advance church building. The schooner chartered every summer to take Gaelic-speaking ministers around the Western Isles to spread the evangelical gospel in the five years following the Disruption was named *The Breadalbane*. During the summer tour of 1846, the schooner made a voyage of inquiry to ascertain areas of greatest want and duly carried meal to the destitute that was financed by Lowland congregations and distributed on a commendably non-denominational basis.

Intent on containing the spiritual enthusiasm of Gaelic bards, the men and itinerant schoolteachers, and simultaneously seeking to impose temperance on crofting communities, the support of the Free Church for crofting agitation in the later nineteenth century was not unequivocal. Certainly Hugh Miller from Cromarty, a prolific journalist and lay leader of the Free Church at the Disruption, was intent on translating crofting grievances into English to ensure their wider currency in the Liberal as well as the Evangelical Press. But the political alliance of the Free Church with the Liberal Party served principally to embroil the crofting community in the protracted debates on union among overwhelmingly Lowland churches who had seceded from the established Kirk in the eighteenth century. A further distraction was the issue of church disestablishment. The collective nature of the crofters' struggle against evicting landlords was not advanced by the ethos of individualism which imbued the Free Church and the Liberal Party. The most radical minister who supported land agitation was the Rev. Donald MacCallum, both as a poet and preacher. But as a member of the established Kirk he usually preached to an empty church in Skye. Certainly James Cumming, Free Church minister of Melness, made one of the most elegant submissions to the Napier Commission. In calling for the resettlement of deserted glens he pointed out that between seven to eight thousand people in the Reay country of Sutherland had only about a thirteenth part allocated for their settlement, 'the rest is under sheep, under rabbits, under hares, under deer, under grouse, and other unprofitable occupants of the soil.'[24] Yet Hector Cameron of Back, the Free Churchman revered as the 'Tory Pope of Lewis' was an uncompromising opponent of land reform. At Barvas in 1887, he sought to debar crofting activists from the sacrament of communion and railed against land reform as the Devil's work. Moderates no less than Evangelical ministers tended to publicise the predicament of Highland communities by providing casual testimony to agricultural journals and topical magazines on the predicament of the crofting community. Alexander MacGregor, writing from the manse of Kilmuir on Skye to the *Quarterly Journal of Agriculture*, not only analysed the impact of destitution in 1836–37, but also identified structural weaknesses within the crofting community: notably, an excess of population, early and improvident marriages, rampant subdivision of lands among cottars and squatters, and bad husbandry. At the same time, he discounted the fashionable panacea of emigration in which the young and able left behind aged and helpless dependants.

Evangelical Presbyterianism gave a sense of dignity not dialectic to crofting communities. Its emphasis on enduring the travails of this world – life was a 'glen of tears' – in the hope of spiritual reward in the next was a barrier to crofting radicalism, as recognised by the Gaelic poets. Mairi Mhor nan Oran (Big Mary of the Songs), alias Mary Macpherson, was a leading propagandist of land reform who claimed that the people of Skye had been so affected by evangelical preaching that sorrow was like wheat for them. She went on to condemn evangelical preachers for their manifest lack of care for the oppressive conditions under which the crofting community laboured. Moreover, evangelical Protestantism offered no politically realisable redress this side of the grave. John Smith of Iarsiadar in Lewis made perhaps the most penetrating criticism of Highland landlordism. Yet it was God not man who would redress the oppressions of Sir James Matheson, the opium trader who had acquired Lewis.[25] Evangelical Protestantism fostered a politically regressive passivity in keeping with its cardinal purpose of spiritual awakening and individual conversion. But the evangelical mission was also afflicted from the 1860s by a legalistic approach to ecclesiastical procedure adopted by a vocal minority of Highland ministers to oppose union among Seceders from the established Kirk and to contest any moves towards disestablishment of the Kirk.

The Evangelical ascendancy of the Free Church in the Highlands was breached irreparably in 1892 when its general assembly passed the Declaratory Act which made orthodox Calvinism optional. A mainly Highland minority seceded to form the Free Presbyterian Church in the following year. The overwhelming decision of the general assembly in 1900 to unite with the United Presbyterians (the eighteenth-century Seceders) in the United Free Church was not accepted by a 'Wee Free' rump dominated by Highland congregations. Despite limited numbers and even more limited means, the Free Church continuing was determined to maintain its national pretensions by appealing through the civil courts to secure the landed and financial resources of the pre-union church, a course upheld by the House of Lords in August 1904. However, both secessions had lost considerable moral and financial support from the Lowlands. Notwithstanding internecine legal actions, rival church building and even the seizing of churches from denominational rivals, evangelical Presbyterianism never degenerated into an introspective Highland activity. Evangelical Presbyterianism was sustained by transatlantic exchanges and by outreach from the Highlands to urban migrants particularly in the Clyde shipyards and to seasonal workers in the herring industry around the British coasts. Evangelical Presbyterianism never lost touch with its support base in the Lowlands.

IV

Highlanders in an urban context have been extensively studied. Census returns, kirk session records, membership of clubs and societies, and recruitment patterns for a range of employment from merchants and craftsmen to the police have all contributed to a picture of a distinctive, even ethnic, grouping akin to the no less thoroughly researched urban Irish but apparently with very little in common with the relatively understudied English migrants to Lowland towns and cities.[26] However, the drive for distinctiveness tends to underplay those urban migrants who chose not to remain distinctive and actively sought assimilation into the Lowland middle and working classes. No less underplayed is the fissiparous nature of Highland associations. Both these features are notably evident in Glasgow, the largest receptacle for migrant Highlanders in the nineteenth century.

A Highland Society was established in Glasgow in 1724, with Argyllshire landowners prominent among its founding members. Operating formally as a charitable body intent on promoting apprenticeships and educational services, the Highland Society brought together aspiring and established entrepreneurs among the commercial and professional as well as the landed classes. Entrepreneurship was to the fore in 1760, when the Society purchased lands on Argyle Street, the main thoroughfare into the city from the West Highlands, with profits raised from the preaching at Glasgow Cathedral by the noted English evangelical, George Whitfield, two years earlier. The Society went on to erect the Black Bull Inn, which allowed Highlanders and their Lowland associates to drink freely in furtherance of its charitable objectives. The Black Bull Inn was subsequently expanded into a shopping complex; augmented income was primarily invested in schooling. Having worked in association with the SPCK from 1773, the Glasgow Highland

Society moved to expand day and evening schools between 1788 and 1820, with a specific day-school for girls opened in 1827 for basic literacy, sewing and knitting. All schooling was brought under the one roof at Montrose Street (now the present site of Strathclyde University) in 1831. By this juncture the Society was increasingly coming under evangelical control and the Black Bull Inn was converted into warehouses by 1849.[27]

On the initiative of George MacIntosh, a Highland entrepreneur specialising in the production of dyes and mordants for the textile industry, the Glasgow Highland Society had developed a socially elite offshoot, the Gaelic Club of Gentlemen in 1780. Originally, members of this elite offshoot were expected to be of a Highland landed or military background and be able to converse in Gaelic. However, membership criteria were relaxed from 1798, which served to make the Club one of the most socially and politically eminent in Glasgow by attracting landowners, industrialists, West Indian traders and city financiers. Among its leading lights were Henry Houldsworth, the textile industrialist who had relocated from Lancashire and David Dale, the founder of New Lanark who went on to sponsor ill-fated linen and cotton mills at Oban in Argyll, at Corpach in Lochaber and at Spinningdale in Sutherland. Also to the fore was another textile entrepreneur, Kirkman Finlay, who became first provost of Glasgow, then MP for the city. He furthered his tenuous Highland ties by acquiring Castle Toward estate in Cowal, a move which set exemplary standards for the establishment of landscaped coastal retreats from 1816. The Gaelic Club was particularly noted for its balls, its lavish turtle dinners and its entertaining of Highland Regiments. The Club worked in tandem with the city council to raise the Glengarry Fencibles in 1793, a largely Catholic regiment recruited by the erstwhile clansmen of MacDonnell of Glengarry who had been displaced and then abandoned. Ten years later, the Gaelic Club was the driving force in raising the 3rd Regiment, Highland Volunteers, a kilted contingent around 900 strong. But its social pre-eminence did not continue easily into the second phase of industrialisation. The Club was wound up in 1841.[28]

Notwithstanding the prominence of evangelicals and a declining appeal to industrialists, the Glasgow Highland Association continued to operate until 1876. By this juncture, Highlanders were long becoming assimilated in the city, as is evident from the testimony of John McLaren as part of the deputation from a public meeting of the working classes in Glasgow to the touring Commission for Religious Instruction in 1836. He reported that he had come to Glasgow in 1828 and had attended a Gaelic Church until 1834. He left when he got what he considered to be a good knowledge of English. He claimed never to have known a Highlander in Glasgow who could not speak English, usually within six months, twelve at the most. He was certain that at least two-thirds of the city Gaels understood English better than Gaelic after being five years in Glasgow. His wife was also from the Highlands and was in the same linguistic position as himself.[29]

At the same time as large scale migration of destitute crofters into Glasgow was beginning to stretch the city's coping mechanisms, territorial associations independent of the Glasgow Highland Association began to proliferate, such as the Kintyre Club (1825), the Glasgow Northern Highland Benevolent Society (1836) and the Glasgow Caithness Benevolent Society (1837). The formation of the Glasgow Celtic Society in 1856 suggests an attempt to promote a degree of urban co-ordination. But this Society was closely associated with St Columba's, which had remained within the established Kirk at the Disruption. The first codification of shinty, which can be attributed to the Celtic Society in 1878, was actually accomplished by the eldership of St Columba's intent on regulating the drunken recklessness that was associated with the annual New Year's Day shinty match, with legions of caman wielding Gaels on rival sides. Five years earlier, a Glasgow Gaelic Society was constituted for the promotion of the culture as well as the welfare of the Highlander as land agitation was again taking off. But this Society actually folded without attaining any social or political momentum. When the Glasgow Gaelic Society was refounded in 1887, the year following the Crofters' Holdings Act, it was essentially cultural – for the promotion of the Gaelic language, literature and history – and it accordingly thrived. This Society recognised that there was less emphasis needed on schooling as the Education Act for Scotland of 1872 had made universal schooling a state rather than a charitable objective. There was still a recognised need for welfare provision, as Highlanders continued to migrate, permanently and episodically, to the city. However, the territorial associations increasingly saw their remit as sporting and recreational, in sponsoring shinty and dances for the weekend entertainment of Highlanders who were increasingly assimilating as state schooling inculcated the belief that English was the language of progress.[30]

V

Notwithstanding the burgeoning, global reputation of Highland regiments in imperial service, the nineteenth century saw a marked shift to the periphery of the Highlands in the social, economic and religious development of Scotland. Assimilation rather than distinctiveness was becoming the more pronounced feature in town and country. The Highlands were as noted for their recreational uses as the Lowlands were renowned for commerce and industry. Lowland perspectives on the Highlands, where not shaped by tourism, were increasingly derived as much from the music hall as from any widespread appreciation of history and culture, as was particularly evident when the Highland Clachan became a major feature of the Scottish Exhibition of National History, Art and Industry held at Glasgow in 1911. The money raised from this pastiche of life in the Highlands before the rising of 1745 did, however, fund the Chair of Scottish History and Literature at the University of Glasgow![31]

Notes

1. For a realistic picture of clanship see A. Cathcart, *Kinship and Clientage: Highland Clanship, 1451–1609* (Leiden: Brill, 2006).
2. For the convulsive impact of civil war on clanship see A. I. Macinnes, *Clanship, Commerce and the House of Stuart, 1603–1788* (East Linton: Tuckwell Press, 1996).
3. An overview of Scottish engagement with Empire can be gleaned from T. M. Devine, *Scotlands's Empire, 1600–1800* (London: Allen Lane, 2003); M. Fry, *The Scottish Empire* (Edinburgh: Birlinn, 2001). For more detailed studies see J. M. Mackenzie and T. M. Devine (eds), *Scotland and the British Empire* (Oxford: OUP, 2011) and A. I. Macinnes and D. Hamilton (eds), *Jacobitism, Empire and Enlightenment* (London: Pickering & Chatto, 2014).
4. For comparative Clearance see T. M. Devine, *The Transformation of Rural Scotland* (Edinburgh: John Donald, 1994).
5. For the linkage between agricultural and industrial revolutions see C. A. Whatley, *Scottish Society, 1707–1830: Beyond Jacobitism, towards industrialisation* (Manchester: Manchester University Press, 2000). The best collection of essays on the transformation of Highlands and Lowlands remains T. M. Devine and R. Mitchison (eds), *People and Society in Scotland, vol. I, 1760–1820* (Edinburgh: John Donald, 1988).
6. T. M. Devine, *The Scottish Nation, 1700–2000* (London: Allen Lane, 1999), pp. 241–45, 292–95; C. Kidd, *Subverting Scotlands's past: Scottish Whig Historians and the Creation of an Anglo-British Identity* (Cambridge: CUP, 1999), pp. 263–67.
7. Huntington Library, San Marino, California: Loudoun Scottish Collections, box 29/LO 8936, /9937.
8. C. Kidd, 'The Rehabilitation of Scottish Jacobitism', *Scottish Historical Review*, 74 (1998), pp. 58–76.

9. See R. W. Renton and B. D. Osborne (eds), *Exploring New Roads: Essays on Neil Munro* (Colonsay: House of Lochar, 2007).
10. For more forensic studies on visual representation see M. MacDonald, *Scottish Art* (London, Thames and Hudson, 2000), pp. 69–129, and J. D. Macmillan, 'Art, Gaelic, in modern times' in D. S. Thomson (ed.), *The Companion to Gaelic Scotland* (Oxford: Basil Blackwell), pp. 11–14.
11. I owe this suggestion to Fiona Armstrong, the broadcaster and currently also a graduate student at the University of Strathclyde.
12. Testimonies of C. R. Baird and Rev. Norman MacLeod, in *First Report from the Select Committee on Emigration from Scotland* (Parliamentary Papers, 1841, VI (i)), pp. 48–86.
13. For a magisterial account of Highland destitution see T. M. Devine with W. Orr, *The Great Highland Famine: Hunger, Emigration and the Scottish Highlanders in the nineteenth century* (Edinburgh: John Donald, 1993); still the best account of state intervention in the Highlands is that by J. P. Day, *Public Administration in the Highlands and Islands of Scotland* (London: University of London Press, 1918).
14. Thomas Telford, 'Survey and Reports of the Coasts and Central Highlands of Scotland in Autumn 1802' in *Reports of the Select Committee on the Survey of the Central Highlands of Scotland* (Parliamentary Papers, 1832, IV), pp. 15–17.
15. Joseph Mitchell, *Reminiscences of My Life in the Highlands*, 2 vols (1883 edition, reprinted Newton Abbot: David & Charles, 1971).
16. Robert Somers, *Letters from the Highlands on the Famine of 1846* (1848, reprinted Inverness: Methven Press, 1985). The two most notable contributions by John George Campbell, eighth Duke of Argyll, were 'On the Economic Condition of the Highlands of Scotland', *Journal of the Statistical Society of London* (1866), pp. 503–34 and *Crofts and Farms in the Hebrides being an Account of the Management of an Island Estate for 130 Years* (Edinburgh, 1883).
17. For the full range of tourist travel see *Murray's Handbook for Scotland* (1894, reprinted Newton Abbot: David and Charles, 1974).
18. For wider discussion on the imperial context see C. Dewey, 'Celtic Agrarian Legislation and the Celtic Revival', *Past & Present*, 64 (1974), pp. 30–70.
19. The best treatment of crofting agitation is I. M. M. MacPhail, *The Crofters' Wars* (Stornoway: Acair Press, 1989) and for legislative reform E. A. Cameron, *Land for the People? The British Government and the Scottish Highlands, c1880–1925* (East Linton: Tuckwell Press, 1996).
20. This section draws heavily on A. I. Macinnes, 'Evangelical Protestantism in the nineteenth-century Highlands' in G. Walker and T. Gallagher (eds), *Sermons and Battle Hymns: Protestant Popular Culture in Modern Scotland* (Edinburgh: Edinburgh University Press, 1990), pp. 43–68.
21. For a religious snapshot see Anon., *An Account of the Present State of Religion throughout the Highlands of Scotland* (Edinburgh, 1827).
22. J. Hunter, 'The Emergence of the Crofting Community: The Religious Contribution 1798–1843', *Scottish Studies*, 18 (1974), pp. 95–116.
23. *Select Committee on Sites for Churches, Scotland* (Parliamentary Papers, 1847) *passim*.
24. *Royal Commission on the Condition of Crofters and Cottars, Evidence* (Parliamentary Papers, 1884, II), questions 25, 256–351.

25. For poetry in depth see D. E. M. Meek, *Tuath is Tighearna - Tenants and Landlords: An Anthology of Gaelic Poetry of Social and Political Protest from the Clearances to the Land Agitation* (Edinburgh: Scottish Gaelic Texts Society, 1995).
26. The most comprehensive study is that by C. W. J. Withers, *Urban Highlanders: Highland-Lowland migrations and urban Gaelic Culture, 1700-1900* (East Linton: Tuckwell Press, 1998).
27. *Glasgow Highland Society, Regulations Thereof and Lists of Members* (Glasgow, 1861); National Records of Scotland, General Assembly Papers, CH 1/2/116, ff.480-83.
28. John Strang, *Glasgow and its Clubs* (London & Glasgow, 1856), pp. 128-51; James Cleland, *Annals of Glasgow*, 2 vols (Glasgow, 1816), I, pp. 223-24, 283-84.
29. *Commissioners of Religious Instruction, Scotland* (Parliamentary Papers, 1837, IV), pp. 707-08.
30. *The Gaelic Society of Glasgow Centenary Brochure* (Glasgow: Comann Gàdhlig Ghlaschu, 1988); *Transactions of the Gaelic Society of Glasgow*, I (1906): Papers on the Old Highlands, 1895-1906.
31. D. N. Mackay (ed.), *Homelife in the Highlands 1400-1746* (Glasgow: Highland Village Association, 1911).

2. The Poetry of Ailean Dall

RONALD BLACK

The Gaelic poet Allan MacDougall (*Ailean Dall*, 'Blind Allan', c. 1750–1828) was born in Glencoe.[1] He was apprenticed to a tailor, but lost his eyesight, turned to playing the fiddle for a living, became dependent on charity, and was given a house and a little land by a benefactor in Inverlochy. His songs becoming popular in Lochaber, he obtained the help of Ewen MacLachlan (1773–1822), a young academic and himself a Gaelic poet of a very different kind, to write them down. Following their publication in 1798, both men fell under the patronage of one of the greatest hypocrites of this hypocritical era, Sir Walter Scott's friend Alexander Ranaldson Macdonell of Glengarry (1773–1828), who was busy raising his people's rents to levels which they could not afford while ostentatiously strutting the part of an old-style Highland chieftain – a guise in which he was famously painted by Sir Henry Raeburn.[2]

There is no modern edition of Allan's songs, and very few have ever been translated. With regard to commentary, Derick Thomson failed to mention him at all in the body of his *Introduction to Gaelic Poetry*, but begged forgiveness for the omission in his 'Introductory Note'. Anja Gunderloch made up for this in her essay 'Imagery and the Blind Poet' – her purpose, to compare the visual and non-visual imagery of three Gaelic poets known for their blindness, disguises the fact that she provides a review of Allan's work which is both objective and comprehensive. She includes much interesting detail on his steamboat songs in particular.[3]

The following general survey of Allan's work is an attempt to build upon Gunderloch's paper. I will assess the size of his surviving output and the precise nature of his subjects, then consider what he tells us about himself, how in my opinion his blindness is reflected in his work, what light he sheds on his times, where he stands on the spectrum of tradition and innovation, and, finally, what is his greatest achievement.

First, then, how can we measure Allan's output? Precisely one copy survives (Edinburgh University Library JA3625) of the 1798 edition of his work, *Orain Ghaidhealacha: le Ailein Dughallach, fear ciuil ann an Ionbhar Lochaidh. Maille ri Co'-Chruinneachadh Oran is Dhan, le Ughdairibh Eile.* It contains twenty-five of his songs (including most of the best ones, in my opinion). The 1829 edition, published the year after his death (*Orain, Marbhrannan, agus Duanagan, Ghaidhealach*), added another twenty-nine, totalling fifty-four in all, ranging in length from forty lines to over two hundred and occupying 215 pages. Thanks to the two editions, we can neatly divide his oeuvre into an eighteenth-century half and a nineteenth-century half. Nearly all the 1829 songs look dateable to me, so ultimately we should have a corpus consisting of four or five dateable eighteenth-century songs, about twenty other songs made at an unknown date before 1798, then nearly thirty dateable songs ranging through the first three decades of the nineteenth century. There are also two songs attributed to Allan in MacPherson's *Duanaire* of 1868, giving a total of fifty-six.[4] No doubt there are also some items that I have missed; there always are.

Next, however, what are Allan's subjects?

There are twenty-nine elegies/eulogies, ten songs about men's relationships with women, five in praise of groups of people (clubs, clans, regiments), six about ships, two on drink, two on snuff, and two that cannot be categorised – his well-known song on the Lowland shepherds, which is his only known satire, and his much less well-known song on the making of his book. Total, fifty-six.[5]

Now to provide a little more detail on some of these.

Of the elegies/eulogies, eight are to Glengarry himself, three are to other members of his family, two are to Glencoe MacDonalds, one is to a Keppoch MacDonald, eight are to Camerons, two are to MacLachlans, one is to a MacRae, one to a Chisholm, one to a MacDougall, one to a MacFarlane, and one to a Lochaber lady married to a farmer called Rankin in Glenelg. Total, twenty-nine. There is nothing surprising about this distribution, given that Allan lived most of his life among Camerons (in what we now call Fort William, but which was then Maryburgh, or as Allan calls it, *Bruach Màiri*).

In social terms most of the people to whom Allan addressed these songs were well above him: chiefs, sons of chiefs, lairds, tacksmen, army officers. The only exceptions seem to be the lady in Glenelg, John MacFarlane who was Glengarry's piper, Alexander MacRae (a native of Strath Cluanie who had a tack of Glenquoich), a Donald Cameron who died in Leckroy in Lochaber (widely known as Dòmhnall Mór Òg), and the two MacLachlans, who are perhaps the most interesting cases. One was Ewen MacLachlan the young poet and scholar, who was his *real* friend and his *real* patron; unfortunately Ewen was much put upon by his fellow academics in Aberdeen and had no money, or very little.[6] The other was the subject of the song 'Òran do Dhùghall Òg MacLachainn, mar gum b'ann le 'Leannan' ('A Song to Young Dugald MacLachlan, as if Made by his Sweetheart'). Allan does not keep up the pretence of a woman's song very well – he says that he would like to sleep with Young Dugald, then speaks of his prowess as a seaman and a hunter, ending with a passage on gun technology. As very often happens in these songs, there is obviously a story behind it, and in the ceilidh-house when the song was sung that story would have been told, but now it is lost.

Of the five songs in praise of groups of people, one is to the Lochaber Volunteers who were raised in 1795, one is to the Black Watch following their campaign in Egypt, two are to *Comunn nam Fìor Ghaidheal*, Glengarry's 'Society of True Highlanders' who met at Inverlochy, and one is Allan's *Smeòrach* on the Clan MacDougall, in which he says a little about himself and a good deal about the history of the MacDougalls. A *smeòrach* is a thrush or mavis, and the main point about the song for us is that it reveals the influence of the great Jacobite poet Alexander MacDonald, Alastair mac Mhaighstir Alastair, who was the first to make a *smeòrach* in the shape of 'Smeòrach Chlann Raghnaill' ('The Mavis of Clan Ranald'). Allan may perhaps have met the older poet, who died about 1770.

Of the two poems on snuff, one is actually about a powder-horn used for keeping that substance. I would call it a 'museum song', a loving description of an item that today would belong in a museum, so the best use of the text now would be to reunite it with its artefact. Of the two songs on drink, one is for it, one is against it.

What does Allan tell us about himself? The quick answer to this question is that he is a native of Glencoe, he spent part of his childhood at Callart on the north shore of Loch Leven, he lives in Maryburgh, he dislikes Lowlanders and sheep but likes steamboats, he has been to Islay and Glasgow, he likes drink, tobacco and women, and is married, perhaps to a woman from Knoydart. Whether they have children is unclear.

The evidence implied by the eulogies, elegies and drinking songs is that Allan spent a great deal of time in taverns and ceilidh-houses, making his songs known, being paid in food and drink for the entertainment he provided, then presumably going to seek payment in cash or kind for his songs at the doors of the great houses of the district. The boat-songs, too, show him plying his trade on the ships that ran between Inverness and Glasgow following the opening of the Caledonian Canal in 1822. He was clearly a poet of celebration. Of the twenty-nine, twelve are elegies. That is twelve big funerals at which we can be pretty sure that Allan was present and made his voice heard. In the beginning of his song to MacRae, however, he comes across as something little short of a beggar.

> Turas dhòmhsa mach air chuairt
> Thachair mi air Gleanna Cuaich,
> An làmh a dhìoladh dhomh duais
>   'S bho'n d'fhuair mi rud an latha sin.
>
> *Once when out upon a jaunt*
> *I chanced to bump into Glenquoich,*
> *The hand whose wont was to reward me*
>   *And from which I got a bit that day.*⁷

The closest he comes to describing his relationship with Glengarry is in a song first published in the 1829 edition, entitled (I translate): 'The poet denying the allegation that Mac 'ic Alastair had abandoned him, and praising Glengarry for his tenacity in getting back the arms that were removed from his castle in the year 1746.' The allegation is that he is like a midwife, cast away once his services are no longer required. He says: "S nan deanadh iad rìgh dhiot, gheibhinn fhìn bhith air caisteal, / 'S gum falbhainn do Shasann gu siùbhlach leat' (*'If they made you king, I'd get a castle to myself, / And I'd go with you speedily to England'*).

No doubt there are elements of autobiography in Allan's ten songs to women, if only they could be teased out. I will describe these songs briefly in the order in which they were published. The 'Òran Leannanachd' or 'Sweethearting Song' does not come easily to him. There is too much in it about *him* and not enough about *her*. At the end the girl looks like marrying a shepherd, of all things, but the poet hopes that he will be invited to the wedding. In 'Òran don Mhaighdinn Cheudna' ('A Song to the Same Girl') he is off to Islay and missing her. Again it is not very passionate. The 'Òran Gaoil' ('Love Song') is better, more original and touching, though moved a little too much by lust. The 'Òran do Chéile Nuadh-Phòsta, air Dhi Dol air Thuras' ('Song to a Newly Wedded Spouse, when She had Gone on a Journey') is very touching, which is why I chose it as the representative song by Allan in my eighteenth-century anthology *An Lasair* (pp. 338–41) with the new title 'Bantrach an Duine Bheò' ('The Widow of the Living Man'), taken from the third of the five stanzas.

> Tha mi fo ghruaman gach oidhch' a' bruadar,
>   Tha m' inntinn luaineach 's mi air do thòir,
> Gach là fo chianal a' bagradh liathaidh
>   'S mur tig thu 'm-bliadhna chan fhiach mo dhòigh;
> Chan fhaigh mi t'eile théid 'nighe m' éididh
>   Ged bhiodh mo léine mar bhréid am bròig—
> Nach fada 'n geamhradh gun laighe teann riut,
>   Tha mi mar bhantraich an duine bheò!

> *I'm sunk in gloom every night in my dreams,*
>   *My mind is restless as I pursue you,*
> *Each day of depression brings threat of grey hairs*
>   *And if you don't come this year my life is worth nothing;*
> *I'll get no other who'll go washing my clothes*
>   *Even were my shirt like a patch in a shoe—*
> *The winter's so long without snuggling up close to you,*
>   *I'm like the widow of a living man!*

The 'Òran don t-Suirghe' ('Song to Courting') is clever, amusing and tongue-in-cheek in the style of the great Sutherland poet Rob Donn, though never quite beyond the bounds of propriety, despite the opinion of an anonymous reader of the 1798 edition who scribbled in pencil: 'Clever in composition – verses 14 & 16 might have been omitted.' Strangely, this annotator did not express a view on 'Òran anns a bheil an t-Suirghe air a

Samhlachadh ri Sgibeireachd' ('A Song in which Courting is Compared to Seamanship'), which is full of *doubles entendres* and goes on to assemble a whole collection of metaphors for sex. 'Comhairle do Chloinn Òig Shuirghich Theisteil' ('Advice on Courting for Well-Behaved Youngsters') shows Allan taking on an educational role, no doubt having been paid to do so as someone to whom young people might listen. He finds it hard to take the role seriously. The last song in this group in the 1798 edition is 'Òran air Trod Mnà an Taighe ri 'Fear air son a bhith 'g Òl an Drama' ('The Goodwife's Scolding of her Husband for Drinking Whisky'), a dialogue which ends in compromise.

Of the two women's songs first published in 1829, 'Gearan na Mnà an Aghaidh a Fir' ('The Wife's Complaint against her Husband'), another dialogue, portrays a husband who does not work hard and has a taste for the lassies. It works through all the issues, contains some sexual *doubles entendres*, and once again ends in compromise. 'Òran mar gun Deanadh Duin' Òg e 's e Pòsta ri Caillich' ('A Song as would be Made by a Young Man Married to an Old Woman') is misogynistic: in a clever last stanza the poet distances himself from any idea that the subject is himself and his wife, and it is true that in 'The Widow of the Living Man' he says that he married her young, *fhuair mi òg thu*. But there are hints about whoring in the songs to drunkenness and snuff: Allan fantasises about getting '*a girl under my wing*' (nam faighinn caileag am' sgéithidh), and his friend Ronald winds him up about '*A virgin coming to your bed / As was practised by your forebears*' (Maighdeann thigeadh air do leabaidh / Mar a chleachd do dhaoine).

How is Allan's blindness reflected in his work? The first thing to say on this is that the existence of a well-established set of visual motifs, what Dr John MacInnes has called the 'Panegyric Code', made it easy for a blind man to be a poet.[8] The traditional view of poetry did not prize originality so much as the clever reordering of existing tropes. Older poets such as mac Mhaighstir Alastair and Rob Donn had broken through this and produced works of startling originality. Allan references their work, particularly through his choice of tunes and structures, but mainly sticks to the old guidelines.

As I have already pointed out, Allan was not blind from birth. In 'Òran don Mhisg', his song on drunkenness, first published in 1798, he seems to blame his blindness on alcohol: 'Gun d'fhalbh mo neart gun léirsinn cheart, / Gun chaill mi 'm beachd bha m' shùilibh' (*My strength has gone, I can't see right, / I've lost the sight from my eyes*'). In his song on snuff, first published in 1829, he says, ''S ged bha mise dhìth mo léirsinn, / Bho chionn ochd bliadhn' deug is tuilleadh (*'And though I'd been deprived of sight / For eighteen years and more*'). If we were to assume that this song was made fairly soon after the publication of the first edition, it would date his blindness to the 1780s, when he was probably in his late twenties or early thirties. This helps us understand why in his song to John MacFarlane, the piper, we are confronted with a whole series of images that are both visual and original. This song appears early in the first edition and perhaps it was made before 1780. Research on MacFarlane's biography might help, if such a thing is possible.[9]

That song is the exception however. Over and over, the poet's blindness is reflected in his use of sound and of dreams. Sound is especially prominent in Allan's song in praise of whisky and his 'Òran Gaoil'. 'Dh'aithn'inn faram do bhuinn air a' chlàiridh', he says of the girl's dancing: '*I would know the sound of your soles on the floorboards*'. In his sweethearting song, where he talks mainly about himself, it seems to me that his lack of sight is the problem, then in his second song to the same girl it comes across that he sees things in dreams. In his elegy for Cameron of Glen Nevis he empathises with the widow: 'Chan eil aice chùis aiteas / Ach bhith gad fhaicinn am bruadair' ('*She has no cause to be happy / Except seeing you in dreams*'). And in his elegy to MacDougall of Dunollie he pointedly uses the word *sealladh* (vision) in its abstract sense: 'Fhuair thu sealladh ceart mar dhìlib / 'S cha b'ann le innleachd na speuclair' ('*You had true vision by inheritance / And not by contrivance or spectacles*').

What light does Allan's work shed on the times in which he lived? I think this can be summed up under four heads: sheep, ships, people and events. 'Òran do na Cìobairean Gallda' ('A Song on the Lowland Shepherds'), first published in 1798, conveys a visceral sense of disgust at the coming of sheep-farming.

> Is olc a' chuideachd do chàch
> Neach nach àbhaist a bhith glan:
> Cha chompanach dhaoine as fiach

> Fear le fhiaclan a' spoth chlach
> Ann an garbhuaic air a ghlùinean,
> Le chraos gan sùghadh a-mach—
> 'S ma leigeas tu an deoch ri bheul
> 'Na dheaghaidh na feuch a blas.

A poor companion for anyone else
  Is a man unaccustomed to be clean:
Unfit to consort with people of worth
  Is one who castrates balls with his teeth
In slimy sheep-dirt upon his knees,
  Sucking them out with his wide-open mouth—
And if you then let him have a drink
  Don't try and taste it when he's finished.

There is strong social comment in it, along with praise of Glengarry for his dislike of sheep. The song has been published in full, with translation, in Donald E. Meek (ed.), *Tuath is Tighearna: Tenants and Landlords* (Scottish Gaelic Texts Society, Edinburgh, 1995), pp. 47–50, 186–89, and in Hugh Cheape (ed.), 'A Song on the Lowland Shepherds: Popular Reaction to the Highland Clearances', *Scottish Economic and Social History*, vol. 15 (1995), pp. 85–100. There is also a eulogy to Chisholm, first published in 1829, very traditional, in which Allan praises him for *not* bringing in sheep, dogs and shepherds. The sting is not in the tail but in the title: 'Òran do Shiosalach Shrath Ghlaise, romh Theachd nan Caorach Móra d'a Dhùthaich' ('A Song to Chisholm of Strathglass, before the Coming of the Great Sheep to his Estate').

Now ships. Allan celebrates five paddle-steamers and Glengarry's *birlinn* or yacht. One of the steamers is unnamed, Allan's only interest being in praising the crew, but I can name the others. The steamers are the *Chieftain*, the *Ben Nevis*, the *Maid of Morvern* and the *Ben Lomond*. No two of these songs are the same. One describes the marvels of new technology and praises the skipper in terms of hunting and fishing; another concentrates on the ship; another is equally good on the ship, but mention of the skipper's name sends Allan off on a panegyric of the Mathesons, whom he has never thought of praising before; the fourth concentrates on the people on board, presumably the crew. There is nothing about scenery, for three excellent reasons: Allan was blind, landscape and seascape played no particular part in Gaelic poetic convention, and Allan was uninfluenced by Romanticism. The yacht was the *Emerald*, built at Invergarry in 1824, and the song is heavily influenced by MacDonald's 'Birlinn Chlann Raghnaill'. The song to the *Chieftain* is published with translation in Donald E. Meek, *Caran an t-Saoghail, The Wiles of the World: Anthology of 19th Century Scottish Gaelic Verse* (Edinburgh: Birlinn, 2003), pp. 130–33.

People now. Obviously Allan's elegies and eulogies tell us something about the great men of the West Highlands in general, and Glengarry in particular. One good example is 'Òran don Chòirneal Mac 'ic Alastair Ghlinne Garadh, air dha bhith Tinn' ('A Song to Colonel Macdonell of Glengarry after he had been Sick'). It begins very factually, telling us that Glengarry is in London; Allan mentions some recent deaths, and worries about his own position. Then suddenly he declares that Glengarry is well again and treats us to a controlled flood of conventional motifs, especially social ones – as good a collection as there is. Another good example is 'Òran do Thighearna Ghlinne Garadh, air dha dol don Ghearmailte' ('A Song to the Laird of Glengarry, after he had gone to Germany'). Allan is so bereft since his patron went away that he has become addicted to tobacco. There is a stanza which goes exactly with Raeburn's famous portrait.

> Fhir 'gam math dha'n tig deise,
>   Is cùmbach deas thu fo t' armachd:
> Gunna caol a' bheòil shnaidhte
>   'S paidhir dhag nam ball airgid,
> Lann thana 'n deagh fhaobhair
>   'S làmh mo ghaoil-sa 'na ceannabheairt—
> Is mairg a thigeadh air t' aodann
>   Nuair a mhaomadh an fhearg ort.

> *O man who fits well your clothing,*
>   *You're neat and shapely when armed:*
> *A slender gun with carved muzzle*
>   *And a pair of silver-trimmed pistols,*
> *A thin razor-edged sword-blade*

THE POETRY OF AILEAN DALL

> *With my love's hand in its hilt—*
> *Woe betide him who'd challenge you*
> *When you rose up in a frenzy.*

There is a passing reference to some event in the parish of Petty involving a MacLeod – by no means the only instance in Allan's work where we are left wishing that we knew what he was talking about. He acknowledges that some people bear ill-will towards Glengarry, which is an understatement. This poem is *not* a collection of images but a contemporary document that requires commentary.

The same applies to the events category, which consists of the five songs on clubs, clans and regiments. The best example is the first song to the Society of True Highlanders, which opens and closes with Allan displaying awareness of the need to argue the value of the Gaelic language. It contains his fundamental *Weltanschauung*: that is, the Society consists of gentlemen who will open their purses and everyone will have a drink. But every so often Allan goes off into heroic, even violent, motifs and praise of Glengarry. And in his other song to the Society, addressing Glengarry, he says of the Royal Family: 'Chum thu ri chéil' iad' ('*You held them together*'). Either Allan believed that Glengarry enjoyed an astonishing degree of influence in the highest circles, or it may be seen as an interesting extension of the traditional *sàr chùirteir* ('great courtier') motif.[10]

Where does Allan stand on the spectrum of tradition and innovation? I will try to answer this question by running through the elements that we could hang on the pegs marked 'tradition' and 'innovation', then I will identify a song that challenges those concepts.

Allan works very effectively within the demands of tradition. Right at the beginning of the first edition, his elegy to MacDonald of Keppoch reads like a rehearsal of the panegyric code with scarcely a motif omitted. Much later in time, a piece with the interesting title 'Òran do Mhac 'ic Alastair, air dha Bheannachd a Thoirt don Ùghdair' ('A Song to Glengarry, on his having Greeted the Author') disappoints because it is pure old-fashioned eulogy. In between, we notice Allan selecting from the code as appropriate to his subject. When the heir to Glengarry dies in infancy there are two requirements, dignity and sympathy: the dignity comes through in conventional motifs, the sympathy comes across best in the women's stanzas – mother, nurse, keeners. When an officer returns from the war against Napoleon in Egypt, Allan celebrates him almost exclusively with martial motifs, and where there are direct echoes from earlier poets these are from the war-torn seventeenth century. Similarly, the second song on the Society of True Highlanders consists almost entirely of 'allies' motifs.[11]

Generally speaking, the higher the proportion of social motifs in one of Allan's songs, the lower is the social status of the person addressed. This is actually a perversion of the tradition. A hundred years earlier, Gaelic poets were forcefully reminding the chiefs of their social responsibilities to the whole community; now this is often reduced to the need for generosity to poets. The most extreme example is a song to a young member of the Glengarry family on the occasion of 'thu thigh'nn foghlaimte dhachaigh á Sasann a-nall' (*'your coming home educated from England down there'*), which consists basically of only two motifs: hunting and wearing Highland dress. So tradition and reality entered into a grotesque conspiracy to justify each other.

Still on tradition, there are some motifs which Allan is so fond of deploying that they become his signature. One is the disparaging description of Lowlanders as 'luchd adan', 'luchd chleòcan', 'luchd nan casag', wearers of hats, cloaks or coats. He is keen on hospitality motifs and toasts but twice takes the latter so far as to curse those who would refuse to drink his hero's health. Significantly perhaps, he describes one of the gentlemen who receive this rather doubtful compliment, Alexander MacRae, as a ladies' man and an enthusiastic hunter, in that order. The other is – surprise, surprise – Glengarry.

Two motifs are even more remarkable. One which occurs three times is 'chan éisteadh iad caismeachd', literally *'they would not listen to an alarm'*, that is, Highland warriors in battle are praised for ignoring signals. To understand this properly one would need to excavate the earlier tradition, but it is certainly not a common motif, which is probably just as well for the reputation of Highland troops in battle. Finally, there is a consistent fiction in Allan's mindset which we can call 'the independence of the chiefs', very well summed up by the line to Glengarry 'cha d'thoir luchd nan currac cìs dhiot' (*'you don't pay tax to those who wear skullcaps'*, that is, clerks and lawyers). Down to a hundred years earlier the poets put it more simply by calling their chiefs kings. Nowadays chiefs like Glengarry were in debt up to their eyeballs but either Allan was in denial or, more probably, he was anxious to remind them of their traditional status.

So much for the box. What evidence is there that Allan could operate outside it?

It is noticeable that some of Allan's elegies and eulogies are more innovative than others – more *ad hominem*, or in one case *ad locum*. The man, or his estate, comes across more strongly than the motifs. None of these are to Glengarry. Three are to Camerons, one is to MacDougall of Dunollie. The MacDougall elegy has some original-sounding metaphors, tears being 'mar uisge nan gleann bhon fhireach' (*'like the water of the glens off the hill'*), and MacDougall's gentle side 'mar aoibh an t-sìoda' (*'like the cheerfulness of silk'*). Unfortunately Allan never knows when to stop, and the second half is conventional. The elegy to John Cameron of Callart has a modern feel, caused I think by concentrating on the condition of his estate after his death, and I am sure it is no coincidence that Callart was where Allan grew up. It is more than a collection of motifs. It is also no coincidence that the influence of Sìleas na Ceapaich, mac Mhaighstir Alastair and Rob Donn comes across in three of these four poems, through choice of airs and metres.

In the specific case of elegies, the most interesting ones are those that have a lot to say about the cause of death or an unusual funeral. Cameron of Lundavra is trampled to death by a horse. Young Angus MacDonald of Achatriachatan in Glencoe is buried in Edinburgh, then his body is exhumed and brought home 'gu uaigh dhleasanach fhéin', *'to his own rightful grave'*. Col John Cameron is killed at Waterloo, and Allan paints a good picture of the ship bearing his body sailing up Loch Linnhe. It is more than a traditional elegy, as the last two stanzas contain thoughts on eternity and veiled criticism of the War Office in *Lunnainn nan cleòc*.

Glengarry himself died of an injury received when escaping from a sinking steamboat, also in Loch Linnhe.[12] In his elegy Allan seems to hint that mouth-to-mouth respiration was practised,

> Do dhà nighinn gad phògadh,
> An té bu shine le dòchas
> A' cur shéideag ad' phòraibh
>   An dùil gun d'thugadh i beò thu gu d' chàileachd.

> *Your two daughters kissing you,*
> *The elder one hopefully*
> *Putting breaths in your pores*
> *Imagining it could restore you to life.*

He says of the man who built the boat 'b' fheàrr nach beirt' e bho thoiseach le mhàthair' ('*it would have been better had he never been born*'), and points out that poets whom Glengarry paid are now in debt. Other than that it is pretty conventional stuff, though the stress laid on the heir is of some interest. The reason is obvious: Allan's cash cow is gone, that is all it ever was, and he has no great hopes of further reward from that direction.[13]

Under 'tradition' I discuss signature motifs; under 'innovation' I may mention vocabulary. A key motif in the panegyric code is the nailing down of the coffin lid, when the hero's face disappears from view;[14] in his MacDougall elegy Allan talks of it not being nailed but screwed, his word being *scru-thairnnean* (screwnails). Similarly, a hundred years earlier, violins first appeared in Gaelic verse; now, in one of his Cameron elegies, Allan mentions *spionaidean* or spinets. In the same song he uses the English word *bully*. Finally, faced with an exotic place-name, Bengal, Allan turns creative and makes it *Beinn Ghall*, literally I suppose 'Foreigners' Hill'.

The song that best challenges the concepts of tradition and innovation is Allan's elegy to his intellectual patron, Ewen MacLachlan, who died aged 49 in 1822. He begins by telling us how he met the funeral cortège coming from Aberdeen. The usual racial tension is evident. In the seventh verse he adapts the panegyric code to this novel situation in Gaelic verse, the death of an academic.

> Gur lìonmhor oighre cùramach,
> Mac iarla 's diùic fo sprochd
> Mu d' leabhraichean bhith dùinte
>   'S an oid'-ionnsachaidh 'na thost,
> 'S iad mar uain gun mhàthraichean
>   Feadh fhàslaichean is shloc
> A' caoidh 's a' bròn mun àrmann sin
>   Rinn gath a' bhàis a lot.

> *Many heirs are anxious,*
> >   *Earls' and dukes' sons worried*
> *That your books are closed*
> >   *And their tutor silenced,*
> *For they're like lambs without their mothers*
> >   *Wandering round pits and hollows*
> *Who mourn and keen that warrior*
> >   *Whom the dart of death has struck.*

The traditional motif here is 'Nature etc. grieving or damaged by loss of leadership'.[15] Allan then deploys a much less predictable one, 'Chief as navigator and reader of weather-signs'.[16]

> Bu chliù do dh'uaislibh Albainn thu
> >   Thoirt dearbhadh air gach sgeul,
> 'S bu chaileadair air aimsir thu
> >   Mar thigeadh garbh no réidh;
> Sann le d' gheur-shùil dh'aithneadh tu
> >   Mun éireadh stoirm nan speur—
> Sàr chomhairlich' neo-chearbach thu
> >   Do luchd fairg' a' chruinne-ché.

> *You were known to Scotland's noblemen*
> >   *For proving every tale,*
> *And you could foretell if the weather*
> >   *Was going to be good or bad;*
> *With your sharp eye you would know*
> >   *Before a storm rose in the skies—*
> *You were an unerring counsellor*
> >   *To the mariners of the globe.*

At first I was taken aback by this. MacLachlan's scholarly and literary interests are known to have included lexicography, medieval manuscripts, translating Homer and describing the seasons, but not forecasting the weather. Was Allan falling into the traditional Gaelic trap of confusing scholarship with wizardry? I suspect not. Meteorology was being established as a science during the two men's lifetime. John Dalton's *Meteorological Essays* appeared in 1793, and Luke Howard's 'On the Modifications of Clouds' was published in the *Philosophical Magazine* in 1803, leading in 1818–20 to his classic *The Climate of London*.[17] MacLachlan would have taken a keen interest in this; indeed, part of his task as Parochial Schoolmaster of Old Aberdeen was to teach the application of geometry and algebra to the solution of problems in natural philosophy, which will certainly have included aspects of navigation.[18] He must have discussed meteorology with Allan, who, being sightless, will have taken particular pleasure in the new nomenclature for clouds. Allan goes on:

>   Bu sgàthan soilleir fìrinneach
>   Don rìoghachd s' thu gu léir,
>   Mar speuclair glan bu chinntiche
>   No solas grinn bhon chéir
>   'S do chridhe lasadh t' inntinn dhuit
>   Mar ghathan mìn bhon ghréin ...

>   *You were a clear and truthful mirror*
>   *To this kingdom all entire,*
>   *Like the most reliable pure spectacles*
>   *Or fine light from candle-wax*
>   *With your heart illuminating your mind*
>   *Like gentle rays from the sun ...*

Then he describes some sort of academic gladiatorial contest with an unnamed Italian, and goes off into the usual thing that is said about clever people, namely the number of languages Ewen could speak. He ends with a very true statement of Ewen's legacy.

>   Do sgoileirean mar dhìlleachdain
>   Trom-inntinneach ad' dhéidh,
>   A' sealltainn air do sgrìobhainnean
>   Mar dhìleab dhaibh gu'm feum;
>   Gu bràth cha leig iad dìochuimhn' ort

'S air t' obair phrìseil fhéin
Thoirt soilleireachd don rìoghachd seo
Bho linn gu linn ad' dhéidh.

Your scholars are like orphans
　Heavy-hearted from losing you,
Looking at your writings
　As the legacy that they need;
They will never neglect you
　Or your own priceless labours
In bringing clarity to this kingdom
　From age to age now that you're gone.

So the simple answer to the question 'Where does Allan stand on the spectrum of tradition and innovation?' is – about a third of the way along.

Finally, then, what is Allan's greatest achievement? The social historian would presumably say the 'Song on the Lowland Shepherds'. As a modern work of literature, I would make a case for the 'Song to a Newly Wedded Spouse', which is incidentally the shortest of all his poems. It is searingly honest, with a complete absence of conventional pieties. But I also have a very soft spot for the poem about his book, 'Còmhradh an Ùghdair 's a Charaid mu thimcheall an Leabhair seo' ('The Author's Conversation with his Friend about this Book'), the following three stanzas of which I have cited, in translation only, in S. W. Brown and W. McDougall (eds), *The Edinburgh History of the Book in Scotland, Volume 2, Enlightenment and Expansion 1707–1800* (Edinburgh: Edinburgh University Press, 2012), pp. 178–79. These, he tells us, are the words of his friend (Ewen MacLachlan, obviously) pumping him up to get on with the slog of collecting subscriptions for the first edition.

Is fada beò thu masa ceòl leat
　Bhith ri bròn 's ri gearan air
'S a liuthad òir a chaidh 'nad phòca
　On thòisich thu as t-earrach ris;
Leabhar mór agad ga sgròbadh,

Is gòrach thu mur lean thu air,
'S gur lìonmhor fear a chuir a spòg ris
   Le dòchas gum faigh iad e ...

'S an neach a thig gu h-ealamh brisg,
   Nach dean thu chlisge gnothach ris?
Their e: 'Faigh dhomh peann is inc
   Is gabhaidh mise leabhar uait.'
Sgrìobhaidh e 'n sin ainm gu clis
   Le h-itinn nuair a gheibh e i;
Bidh fear is fear aca dol ris
   'Ga bheil a' mhisneach fhoghainteach ...

Tog á d' cheasad, 's na bi leisg,
   Na tugadh beagan sobhadh dhuit,
Siubhail greis le d' Ghàidhlig dheis
   Oir cha dean leisgeul gnothach dhuit;
Fuirich seasmhach ann ad' dhleas'nas
   'S thoir on phreas gach leabhar dhiubh
'S gum bi do chliù ga dhearbhadh
   'S nach cluinnte cearb ad' dheaghaidh ort.

You'll live long if all you harp on
   Is complaints and moans about it
When so much gold's gone in your pocket
   Since you started it in spring;
Having a big book scratched out,
   You're foolish if you don't keep going,
Since many men have put their paws in
   From the hope of receiving it ...

And with him who comes both brisk and lively,
   Won't you move fast to do business?
He'll say: 'Get me pen and ink
   And I will take a book from you.'
He'll then quickly write his name

> *With a feather when he gets it;*
> *One after another will go at it*
> *Whose confidence is heroic ...*
>
> *Stop your girning, don't be lazy,*
>   *Don't be put off by mere trifles,*
> *Travel a while with your ready Gaelic*
>   *For no excuse will bring you business;*
> *Stay firm in your task*
>   *And bring from the press each book of them*
> *So that your fame will be confirmed*
>   *With no faults heard flung after you.*

It is perhaps worth noting that the first edition contained poems by MacLachlan and others as well. But more importantly, among the 'trifles' mentioned seven lines from the end is the fact that Allan was blind. So this poem represents the triumph of the human spirit.

Notes

1. Allan's date of birth was given as 'about the year 1750' by his biographer, John Mackenzie, in *Sar-Obair nam Bard Gaelach: or, The Beauties of Gaelic Poetry* (Glasgow, 1841), p. 298. No one can gainsay a writer who had met the poet personally, albeit in old age, but I suspect that the correct date is more likely to have been after 1750 than before it.
2. For two contrasting views of Glengarry see Evan M. Barron, 'Ewen Maclachlan and Inverness Academy: The Story of a Famous Highland Controversy', *The Celtic Review*, vol. 8 (1912–13), pp. 22–48, and Norman H. MacDonald, *The Clan Ranald of Knoydart & Glengarry* (Edinburgh: author published, 1979), pp. 132–57.
3. Anja Gunderloch, 'Imagery and the Blind Poet', in *Litreachas & Eachdraidh: Rannsachadh na Gàidhlig 2*, ed. Michel Byrne, Thomas Owen Clancy and Sheila Kidd (Glasgow: Roinn na Ceiltis, Oilthigh Ghlaschu, 2006), pp. 56–82.
4. Donald MacPherson (ed.), *An Duanaire: A New Collection of Gaelic Songs and Poems, Never Before Printed* (Edinburgh, 1868), pp. 1–4 ('Bean Mhic-Raing'), pp. 85–87 ('Oran do Sgioba Toitiche'); Archibald Sinclair's *An t-Òranaiche* (Glasgow, 1879, republished by Sìol Cultural Enterprises, St Andrew's, Nova Scotia, 2004) includes the 'Òran Leannanachd' and the songs to Alexander MacRae and the *Chieftain*.
5. I exclude the impromptu verse quoted by Mackenzie as part of an anecdote (*Sar-Obair*, p. 300) and the charms ascribed to Allan by John Gregorson Campbell (Ronald Black (ed.), *The Gaelic Otherworld* (Edinburgh: Birlinn, 2005), pp. 177, 218). We need not doubt that Allan was in the habit of peddling charms, as Campbell alleges, but authorship of the longer one was claimed by an older and better poet, Duncan Ban Macintyre (1724–1812); see *The Gaelic Otherworld*, p. 482, note 749.

6. For Ewen, who has rightly received more critical attention than Ailean Dall, see for example Mackenzie, *Sar-Obair*, pp. 321–39; John Macdonald (ed.), *Ewen MacLachlan's Gaelic Verse* (Aberdeen: Aberdeen University Press, 1937, repr. 1980); Derick Thomson, *An Introduction to Gaelic Poetry* (London: Gollanz, 1974), pp. 216–17; Ronald Black, 'The Gaelic Academy: The Cultural Commitment of the Highland Society of Scotland', *Scottish Gaelic Studies*, vol. 14, part 2 (1986), pp. 1–38 (pp. 19–27).
7. Quotations in this paper are given in modernised spelling. All translations are my own.
8. Michael Newton (ed.), *Dùthchas nan Gàidheal: Selected Essays of John MacInnes* (Edinburgh: Birlinn, 2006), pp. 265–319; Ronald Black, An Lasair (Edinburgh: Birlinn, 2001), pp. 525–27.
9. The only biography known to me is in Lt John MacLennan's 'Notices of Pipers', *The Piping Times*, vol. 23, no. 8 (May, 1971), p. 30: 'MACFARLANE, JOHN. Piper to MacDonnell of Glengarry. A fine specimen of a man and an excellent player. Was the subject of verses by Allan Dall MacDougall, the bard.' Perhaps Allan's poem was MacLennan's only source.
10. Black, *An Lasair*, p. 526, motif no. 2.7.5.
11. Black, *An Lasair*, p. 527, motif no. 8.2.
12. MacDonald, *The Clan Ranald of Knoydart & Glengarry*, p. 155.
13. Allan was by no means the only poet to praise Glengarry. See the three eulogies addressed to him by a younger Lochaber poet, John Mackintosh (d 1852), in MacPherson's *An Duanaire*, pp. 157–65. They contain many of the same features as Allan's.
14. See William Matheson's review of Colm Ó Baoill (ed.), *Eachann Bacach and Other Maclean Poets*, in *Scottish Gaelic Studies*, vol 14, part 1 (1983), pp. 129–36 (p. 133).
15. Black, *An Lasair*, p. 527, motif no. 6.5.8.
16. Black, *An Lasair*, p. 526, motif no. 4.3.2.
17. Richard Hamblyn, *The Invention of Clouds: How an Amateur Meteorologist Forged the Language of the Skies* (London: Picador, 2001), pp. 118–46.
18. Black, 'Gaelic Academy', p. 20.

3. Cultural Crossings and Dilemmas in Archibald Maclaren's Playwriting

IAN BROWN AND GIOIA ANGELETTI

The playwright Archibald Maclaren (1755–1826) has, until recently, been somewhat neglected. There may be superficially understandable reasons for this. On the whole, he wrote shorter plays, often describing them as 'interludes', no doubt presented as part of a programme including a full-length play. His work was often played in Minor theatres (so called to distinguish them from 'legitimate' patent theatres). Most of his plays comprise examples of popular theatre and the so-called illegitimate genres – entertainment pieces, interludes, comic and ballad operas – or after-pieces in the legitimate playhouses. This prolific production had received very little critical attention since its first appearance and staging, until, in 1998, Barbara Bell discussed his work in her chapter on nineteenth-century theatre in Bill Findlay's magisterial *A History of Scottish Theatre*. Subsequently, Gioia Angeletti in 2010 and Ian Brown in 2011 and 2013 have discussed his work further.[1]

If the reason for his neglect does lie in the fact he wrote for popular or Minor theatre (and, as we shall see, this is not the whole picture), with an eye, above all, to providing simple entertainment, then recent scholarship has developed new perspectives on this genre. In the light, for example, of Jane Moody's *Illegitimate Theatre in London, 1770–1840* (2000)[2] and her reassessment of the ideological implications of apparently ludicrous performances, such genre hierarchisation seems no longer defensible. Indeed, as we will later demonstrate, at least some of his plays take on important issues, including those of human rights and the iniquity of slavery. This chapter argues that Maclaren's theatre deserves critical reappraisal for several reasons, some derived from two crucial, often interrelated, thematic isotopies that pervade his *opera omnia*. One is Maclaren's ability to look beyond regional and national boundaries, and to confront his audience with larger issues involving Britain within the international political arena. A second is his, as yet, widely unacknowledged contribution – though Bell, of course, does see Maclaren as a forerunner – to the later development of a 'National

Drama', the widespread and popular adaptation of, mainly, Scott's works for the nineteenth-century stage. Maclaren's plays offer a dramatic paradigm focusing on Scotland's historical, cultural and linguistic specificities, perhaps picking up cues from such earlier plays as John Home's *Douglas* (1756) and John Wilson's *Earl Douglas; or Generosity Betray'd* (1764).

Before engaging in these matters, it will help provide a context to Maclaren's work to address his career and the ways in which he was perceived soon after his death. An anonymous *Memoir*, perhaps written by a Mr Field, a collector of dramatic works, and published in Edinburgh in 1835, recognises the rapid obscurity into which he fell after his death. It also, however, suggests that in his time his plays were held in some regard. It says:

> [Maclaren] perpetrated diverse works in the shape of drama and poems to the extent of nearly one hundred, [...but] his name lives not in the memory beyond the select and aristocratic circle of dramatic antiquaries; and this must ever be a matter of surprise, as his dramas in particular possess a cleverness and an originality which we may seek for in vain in the works of more popular authors; many of them exhibit a knowledge of stage effect, and have been repeatedly performed in London and elsewhere with applause.[3]

Clearly, at least to the author of the *Memoir*, Maclaren's playwriting was clever, original and dramatically effective. This chapter considers Maclaren's life and his writing in an attempt to evaluate how these claims may be borne out in some of his surviving texts and the claims of those texts, and so his, to our serious consideration. In doing so, it discusses key texts in his oeuvre and pivotal aspects of his work (including the two macro themes outlined in the previous paragraph). These are not only relevant to continuing critical debate, but also combine to underpin what may be regarded as his important, and so far neglected, contribution to late eighteenth-century and early nineteenth-century Scottish theatre.

The little that we know of Maclaren is based on scanty and, mostly, cursory accounts. These include some passing remarks in John Genest's *Some account of the English Stage* (1832), a hasty sketch in Ralston Inglis's *The Dramatic Writers of Scotland* (1868), a few perfunctory pages in Terence Tobin's *Plays by Scots 1660–1800* (1974), and the skimpy *Memoir* of 1835 already referred to. According to the last, Maclaren was born in the Highlands in 1755. Although his exact birthplace is reported nowhere, his connection to patrons in Argyll and service in the Dunbartonshire Highlanders both tend to suggest that his roots lay in the eastern part of what is now known as Argyll and Bute. When he was born, Culloden was less than a decade in the past, its impact affecting, more or less at once, not only Highland social structures, but the region's culture, language and economics. These impacts would have implications for Maclaren, and so, in time, his work.

Maclaren clearly was a Gaelic-speaker: as will be shown, he wrote substantial dialogue in that language. He was not, however, monolingual, but also wrote fluently in Scots and in English. A dislocated Highlander throughout his life, he travelled from place to place within and outwith Britain in search of means of support. The peregrinations of his own life are translated, as it were, into his writing. This embeds the devastation and alienation inflicted on post-Culloden Highland society and manners by creating Gaelic-speaking or recognisably Highland characters who are represented as wandering in one way or another: a drover, for example, in *The Highland Drover* (1790) or a colonist in *The Negro Slaves* (1799). His Highlander is deracinated, asserting his identity not by locality, but generally by his admirable values. In both plays cited, the Highlander's role is that of conveying common sense and compassionate humanity – and, to an extent, problem-solving cunning. In the first case, this is despite the fact that his Gaelic speech is incomprehensible to all but two other characters – though, presumably, as we discuss later, not to the bulk of the probable audience. Despite this evident incomprehensibility, it is the drover, the apparently marginalised monolingual Gael, who resolves the quandary that the monolingual English-speaking characters central to the plot face, helping them to elope.

Like many men in the post-Culloden Highlands, Maclaren was recruited into the new Highland regiments. He entered the army early and served under Generals Howe and Clinton in the American War of Independence (1776–83), which broke out when he was twenty-one. According to the *Memoir*, Maclaren returned with his regiment before that War ended to engage in recruiting back in Scotland. Judging by his publication and theatrical record, it seems likely he was in the Dundee area by 1781. Even before he left the army, what appears to be his first play, *The Conjurer; or, the Scotsman in London* (1781), was performed. According to Tobin, this features regional types and a cunning Scot, was printed in Dundee and performed in Edinburgh in 1783, although it may well have earlier been played on tour in other towns, like Montrose, which formed part of a touring circuit out of Aberdeen and Edinburgh.[4]

The *Memoir* notes it was 'through the interest of Captain Walker, his officer, his farce of the 'Coup de Main' was performed by Mr Jackson's company at Edinburgh in 1783'.[5] John Jackson was, of course, manager of the Edinburgh Theatre Royal. This play employed 'the dialect comics, disguises, a letter and other devices [Maclaren] uses continually',[6] opened in Dundee and was printed in Perth in 1784. His career as a playwright appears, then, to have begun while he was a serving soldier. It is not clear what rank Maclaren reached before joining the theatre company, but the fact he re-enlisted later as a sergeant might suggest he could have achieved that rank when he left to act on the Scottish circuit. The *Memoir* describes that departure as follows:

> At the conclusion of the war [1783] he obtained his discharge and proceeded to Dundee, where the Edinburgh *corps dramatique* happened to be, and Mr McLaren was prevailed upon by Mr Sutherland, one of the performers, to accompany him to join Mr Ward's itinerant troop at Montrose, where he was allowed some merit in the performance of Scotch, Irish and French characters; but his own "Highland Drover" was the part in which he was inimitable.[7]

It appears from this that, besides being a prolific playwright, Maclaren was recognised as a proficient actor in character roles. He clearly had acting, as well as writing, talent, and no doubt that assisted him in becoming part of Henry Ward's company in Montrose, north of Dundee. Ward himself had performed in Jackson's Theatre Royal Edinburgh company. Maclaren, therefore, was linked to the major professional company of the time in Scotland and, at least when casting allowed, he acted with some of its stars like Ward and Sutherland. The fact he was performing alongside actors of such quality is not conclusive evidence he was himself a fine actor, even if only in specific roles, but it suggests that he was respected as a performer by them, not just by his memoirist.

The role in which Maclaren was 'inimitable' is – to the modern theatre-goer – striking in that all its lines are in Gaelic. In fact, two of Maclaren's plays employ Gaelic dialogue. *The Humours of Greenock Fair* (1788) makes limited use of Gaelic, which is – presumably to assist audience comprehension – almost at once translated either by repetition in English or in the response of interlocutors. In *The Highland Drover* (1790), however, which is set in the liminal 'Border' town of Carlisle, Maclaren played the monoglot Gaelic-speaking lead character Domhnul Dubh, the role in which he excelled. Domhnul, the drover of the title, speaks substantial Gaelic dialogue, untranslated in the acting text of 1790. (Confusingly, Domhnul appears in a later Maclaren play also called *The Highland Drover*, published in 1805, which is quite different in plot detail and does not employ Gaelic dialogue, though it does include Scots and some regional English dialect.) Indeed, part of the play's comedy is derived from dialogue whose comic impact depends on a bilingual audience's understanding in Gaelic what an English-speaking monoglot does not. A modern example of this was to be observed when a scene from the play was performed at Sabhal Mòr Ostaig in Skye by Ian Brown and Domhnall Uilleam Stiùbhart on Friday, 8 June 2012. On that occasion, it was evident that the Gaelic-speaking members of the audience were laughing at jokes, particularly interlingual ones, that were not available to the monoglot English-speakers present.

Domhnul speaks only Gaelic to Ramble, the lover Hartley's anglophone co-conspirator – played by Sutherland who had recruited Maclaren to the acting company – whom he interrupts attempting to assist elopement. Until the drover helps the lover succeed, many jokes depend on mutual misunderstanding between Domhnul and Ramble. When Domhnul concludes a speech '*a maddadh glas Sas'nach*' ('the grey English dog'), Ramble responds, 'What do you say? You want a glass of arsenick? […] I see we must drop our design, and in the morning send the lady a card', to which Domhnul ripostes '*Ceard! dam ort a bheil thu aig radh gur ceard mise* […]' ('Tinker! damn you, do you say that I'm a tinker […])'.[8] In the end, Domhnul shows good-hearted humanity in assisting Ramble – who, with Hartley, is clearly presented as a sincere man rather than a callous abductor – in allowing the lovers to escape together. Domhnul's Gaelic language may seem to exclude him from the discourse of the language of ostensible contemporary authority, but he is a powerful agent of benevolence and precipitates harmonious change for the better in this play. In this play at least, the Gaelic universe of discourse is one of power regained and that of English the discourse of the baffled and, without the input of the Gael, powerless.

It is evident that for this play, which, according to its first edition title page, 'was repeatedly performed at Inverness, Aberdeen, Perth, Dundee and Greenock, with universal approbation',[9] to have any impact at all requires an audience with a large preponderance of bilingual competence in Gaelic and English. For an audience to enjoy the play, for example, it would have to understand that the value-free English word 'card' might to a monoglot Gaelic-speaker sound like the insulting '*ceard*' ('tinker'). Further, that audience would have to have easy and fluent bilingualism: the joke is light and quick and has to be picked up by the ear at once to be dramatically effective. There must, for a time at least, have been such an audience in the towns for whose theatres Maclaren wrote and performed, and to which he toured such an uncompromisingly, if amusingly, bilingual script. Even allowing for a publicist's possible exaggeration, the 'universal approbation' for his repeated Scottish tours of *The Highland Drover* illustrates the likely existence of such a bilingual audience. The viability and vitality of the play's production would depend on that existence.

The venues Maclaren lists are all close to or in the Gàidhealtachd. By the end of the eighteenth century, of course, the Highland Clearances were bringing those who could not afford to emigrate abroad to live and work in the industrial and commercial towns of Scotland at the edges of that Gaelic-speaking region. It is striking, in that light, that Glasgow, even with its Highland immigrant population, is not mentioned as a venue on the touring circuit of *The Highland Drover*. There may, of course, have been an issue in bringing the play into a city with its own patent Theatre Royal. Nevertheless, the play's apparent theatrical success and, to a lesser extent, that of *The Humours of Greenock Fair*, implies that a playhouse drama, if not in Gaelic, certainly in part dependent on Gaelic-speaking audiences was at the end of the eighteenth century, at least for a time, feasible. Maclaren's work is clear evidence of a developed and diverse wider Scottish theatre culture that could include such an expression of linguistic diversity in actor and audience, hard to imagine now. The presence of such a linguistically diverse audience, at least in Aberdeen, Dundee and, particularly, Greenock, may indeed arise partly from the fact that, as important fishing-ports for the landing and marketing of catches, they attracted large fleets from Gaelic-speaking coastal districts, whose crews would supply substantial numbers of bilingual audience members.[10]

How briefly such a bilingual or trilingual theatre remained really viable may be judged, nonetheless, by the fact that, according to the *Memoir*, Maclaren rejoined the army in or around 1794 'as a sergeant in the Dumbartonshire Highlanders, and accompanied them to Guernsey, where they remained two years'.[11] *The Highland Drover* is actually the only surviving Maclaren play with substantial Gaelic dialogue, and so the reason for the move is unlikely to be linguistic marginalisation alone. It seems likely that the move arose from some issue related either to the success (or otherwise) of the theatre company or, after his eleven or so years with the company, Maclaren's professional or personal relationships within it.

In any case, he continued to write even when re-enlisted, presumably again with the support of his officers. The *Memoir* continues: 'During his sojourn there [in Guernsey], Mr Bernard, from Covent Garden Theatre, arrived in the island with a company of comedians, and engaged him to fill the situation of prompter – several of his pieces were here performed.'[12] Here, it seems his skills as an actor, playing the Scottish, Irish or French roles in which he specialised, were not called on. It becomes clear, however, that Maclaren was capable of writing edgy material. When in 1796 his regiment transferred to Ireland just before the rising of the Society of United Irishmen, he wrote *What News from Bantry Bay?* This he sent to Richard Daly at the Smock Alley Theatre in Dublin. This addressee for his work leads one to observe that his work, while often short in length, was submitted to – and at times performed in – the most prestigious theatres of his time. In fact, Daly apparently approved the piece and invited Maclaren to Dublin to discuss its production. When, however, Maclaren arrived, Daly informed him 'that he dared not bring out the farce, because it satirised the United Irishmen, who were then making secret preparations for the rebellion'.[13] In the event, after the Battle of Vinegar Hill in 1798, which concluded one phase of the United Irishmen's rebellion, Maclaren was discharged from the army. At the age of forty-three, he made his way to London.

As will become clear, his writing continued to challenge and Maclaren seems to have struggled to make a living in the London theatre. In London, however, he did manage to have some of his scripts published by subscription, appearing to have depended for success on having his plays published, like Jean Marishall (or Marshall) before him and his contemporary, Joanna Baillie. In the 1799 edition of *The Negro Slaves*, for example, he lists 123 subscribers 'for my productions in London', in which well over half have recognisably Scottish surnames or titles, including, at the head, the Duke of Roxborough [*sic*]. While Maclaren's work seems early to have sustained, as best it could, his diverse use of the languages of Scotland, including examples of dialogue in Gaelic, Scots and English, with English predominant, his London productions tended to be English-language versions, even translations, of his Scots plays. This was not, however, enough to make ends meet.

Tobin reports that he wrote the play *The Ways of London; or Honesty is the Best Policy* (1812) specifically to appeal to the sympathy of his landladies, who kept evicting him because he could not pay the rent. Clearly, not only talent pushed him to write, but pressing financial need. He himself admits this in prefaces to his plays: one instance of this is in the 'Preface' to the ballad opera *The Negro Slaves* where he writes: 'it is at the instigation of one of my worst enemies (I mean my poverty) that the world has seen this little production'.[14] This explains his repetitive appeals to his readers and audience, including the subscribers to his plays, and his quasi-obsessive need of their approbation. The financial dimension, combined with his constant *captatio benevolantiae*, cannot be overlooked, since it is linked to Maclaren's awareness of the contemporary audience's expectations, his alertness to the specific socio-political concerns of the time, and his creation of characters that he knew would meet with general applause. Hence both his Celtic nationalism, as it were, and his interest in transnational politics, however *bona fide* they may be, are also surely part of his design to produce a popular theatre.

As to the specifically national import of Maclaren's theatre, which can be seen, as proposed earlier, as foreshadowing the National Drama, several aspects are worth considering. First, he looked forward to the theatrical adaptations of Scott's works by presenting important episodes of Scotland's history on stage, albeit in the romance mode, thus turning them into acceptable subjects for representation. For example, the musical drama *Chance of War* (1801) represents the war between the King of Scots and the King of Picts, and the victory of the former. *Oliver Cromwell, or the Scotch Regalia* (1818) is set during the Cromwellian siege of Dunnottar castle where the nationally iconic Scottish regalia are preserved from capture and destruction. Walter Scott also narrates this story in *Tales of a Grandfather*, but without the dramatic licence in which Maclaren engages by his having Cromwell in Scotland at the time.

A second recurring concern in Maclaren's theatre, strongly related to his dramatisation of national history, is his representation and, arguably, exploitation of his Celtic roots and Highland background, not just in those plays with dialogue in Gaelic. Many of his plays, mostly musical dramas, evoke Highland landscape or localities, as their very titles suggest: *Bessy Bell and Mary Gray, or Love in the Highlands* (1808); *Private Theatre or the Highland Funeral* (1809); *The Highland Chiefs; or the Castle of Dunstaffnage* (1815); *Highland Robbers; or, Such Things Were* (1817); *Wallace the Brave; or, The Siege of Perth* (1819); and so forth. Although direct evidence to sustain this view is hardly traceable, it is surely not simply speculation to suggest that Maclaren was well aware of the widespread fame of Macpherson's *Ossian*. He was clearly, despite being short of money, familiar with officers with enough aesthetic bent to sponsor his writing, with theatre people and, through his subscribers, with the London-Scottish aristocracy and gentry. He would have to have been exceptionally obtuse, in a way his work does not suggest he was, not to be aware of Ossianic literary impact and influences. In this context, his depiction of a Gaelic world would certainly resonate with his audiences and readers. Thus, the significance of Maclaren's Celticism may be seen as paralleling, reflecting and adding its own dimension, to appropriate and rephrase Carla Sassi's words on writers like Macpherson, to a 'hushed diasporic identity',[15] which somehow hinges on its otherness from the dominant anglicised culture. In this way, it re-defines itself. His dramatisation of national themes, therefore, because it emerges from Gaelic culture itself, achieves a more culturally complex and nuanced National Drama even than that based on Scott's work.

In Maclaren's case, we would argue, this re-definition, this nuancing, essentially consists in a negotiation between two elements. One is a native 'diasporic' identity that he clearly intended to preserve from total deracination, in particular a Gaelic heritage that was already on the wane even in the northern regions. The other is an idea of Britishness that could assimilate, but not efface, the cultural and linguistic otherness of his native region. In some senses, in fact, in asserting and synthesising a distinctive Scottishness of such a kind, he ran counter to the (Rule) Britannia Project of which Brown has written.[16] He anticipated Walter Scott's attempts to re-establish and re-define a distinctive Scottish identity within the British state, without indulging in the Highlandism Scott encouraged. However, there is no denying the fact that this form of compromised identity was also driven by Maclaren's urgent need, not least financial, to have his works endorsed by contemporary readers and critics. This may also account for his inclusion in some dramatic pieces of versions of a more stereotyped, if free-spirited, Highlander, not so much the Rousseau-esque child of nature and *bon savage*, as the rugged and sturdy cowherd and common-sense man of the people. Yet the memorable Domhnul in *The Highland Drover* is more than a stereotype: his Gaelic is alert and lively; he is more intelligent and resourceful than the English-speaking Ramble.

Such characterisation of the post-Culloden suppressed Highlanders as free-spirited, dynamic and clever complements something we have touched on already: Maclaren's use of language, another crucial aspect of his work. This use is an important element in his expressing one of the two key themes in his dramatic works: his concern for Scottish history in general and his representation of Highland motifs and characters in particular – the latter sometimes from a humorous perspective, although that humour has a subversive, or double-edged, effect. What often triggers this humour – and perhaps provides its justification – is the use he makes of languages in counterpoint to English, whether Scots or Gaelic. Interestingly enough, comic release is not generated by the use of either *per se*, but by its co-textual interaction with mainstream English. In other words, it is the simultaneous use of both languages (Scots and English; or Gaelic and English) that gives rise to a whole series of *double entendres* and misunderstandings as we have seen in the passage cited earlier. If these varieties of language initially conflict, in the *excipit* they usually tend towards harmonisation thanks to the positive *dénouement*, usually driven by the Gaelic – or, as in the case of *The Negro Slaves* – Scots-speaker. In fact, in the published record of his plays, we generally encounter two kinds of multilingual co-texts. In one, Gaelic, though unintelligible to some of the audience, is not translated within the text as performed (like the first edition of *The Highland Drover*), though a translation is provided in the written text by the author. In the other, translation is provided intradiegetically by one of the characters (as in *The Humours of Greenock Fair*).

In this context, it is worth considering the effects and plausible meanings of this code-switching, with or without embedded translations into English. Most evidently, it brings to the fore the fallacious communicativeness between characters with different linguistic and ethnic backgrounds – English or anglicised on the one hand, Gaelic on the other. So a question arises that the text of *The Highland Drover* does not allow one to answer unequivocally: whether Maclaren, by presenting an English character totally taken aback by his Gaelic interlocutor and a Gaelic-speaking character similarly dumbfounded by the other's alien language, aimed at critiquing a modern Britain that was marginalising its Celtic heritage, or intended to highlight the limitations – even if Domhnul is the play's active hero – of a traditional Celticism impermeable to the cultural interchanges and linguistic contaminations produced by historical, culturally colonialising, processes.

However we interpret this impasse, one character, the Scottish servant Betty, can bridge the two worlds, since she speaks both languages, as well as Scots. Betty seems, therefore, to embody a solution to the fracture between the two (or three) languages and cultures. As we have noted earlier, it is significant that the play is set in Carlisle, nicknamed the Border City, because Betty is a borderland character. She inhabits the contact zone between Gaelic, Scots and English, thus becoming the mouthpiece of a counter-hegemonic discourse whereby they can coexist and interact rather than dominate one another. After all, this is perhaps a plausible message in the happy denouement of the play. Interestingly, about two decades later, in the short story 'The Two Drovers', Walter Scott would represent a tragic – rather than Maclaren's comic – version of the clash between Celtic and English cultures through the figures of a Highland and an English drover. There, the course of events is reversed from that in *The Highland Drover*: In Maclaren's play, initial confusion finds a harmonious outcome. In Scott's tale, at first the antagonists seem to manage their societal and cultural differences, but in the end these will produce a tragic outcome.

The figure of the subaltern Betty allows us to touch on what we argue is the other crucial thematic isotopy of Maclaren's theatrical *opera omnia*, in addition to its focusing on Scotland's historical, cultural and linguistic specificities. That is, his concern for issues that cross not just the Highland Line, but the national border. One such issue is the still contentious notion of the 'Scottish Empire', and, more specifically, Scotland's involvement in transatlantic slavery in the eighteenth and nineteenth centuries. Then, Jacobites – or even the very Highlanders who were evicted from their lands during the Clearances – often became settlers in the colonies or joined the British army to oppose the revolts of the colonised. In Maclaren's drama we find another Highlander figure – very different from the Highland drover – to confront and embody the paradox of Scotland's first endorsing the practice of slavery and then actively participating in its dismantling from the 1780s on.

This figure emerges in the ballad opera *The Negro Slaves*, this time a play with a transnational setting, the Jamaican plantations, but still conveying a sense of national patriotism through the central representation of a Highlander who shows sympathy towards the black slaves – hence his name McSympathy. Maclaren represents McSympathy, with his allegorical clan name, as speaking out, this time in Scots, for humane values and against the cruelty of slavery. In an exchange, after the English slave-owner Captain Racoon asks him 'And do you think I'll give up my property [his slaves] to humour your false humanity', he responds 'I wad na change my false humanity, for a' your real barbarity'.[17] The relationship between McSympathy and Quako, the protagonist black slave, immediately suggests a link between subalterns: the deracinated Highlander, possibly a Jacobite or a victim of the Clearances, and the deracinated African violently snatched out of his native country.

In the Caribbean context, however, McSympathy, despite his liberal principles, is on the coloniser's side, which complicates the apparent juxtaposition of the two characters' predicaments, so they can no longer be regarded simply as 'others' in relation to the English 'self'. In *The Infection of Thomas De Quincey*,[18] John Barrell adumbrates a paradigm that, arguably, illuminates the Highlander's position in the Caribbean. Barrell writes:

> What at first seems 'other' can be made over to the side of the self – to a subordinate position on that side – only so long as a new, and a newly absolute 'other' is constituted to fill the discursive space that had been thus evacuated'.[19]

In fact, not only is McSympathy part of the colonial establishment, he is also, as an English character mockingly nicknames him, 'the Mountain Philosopher'. He is a Highlander often speaking like a Lowlander, or a Scottish Enlightenment philosopher, who supports egalitarian and liberal ideas, but ambivalently never openly objects to British colonial occupation in the Caribbean. In this, he almost echoes Adam Smith, who argued for better management in the West Indies, but not for abolition of the slavery system. If we add to this aporia the representation in *The Negro Slaves* of savage and violent 'Indians and Squaws', McSympathy's complex position turns out to reflect Scotland's or, more generally, Britain's tension between the commercial benefits of slavery and the growing unease about its perpetuation in a supposedly 'civilised' society. So, Maclaren's Highlander in *The Negro Slaves* confutes both the stereotype of the noble savage and the Johnsonian portrait of Highlander as a savage Cherokee. He is an enlightened Highlander, but, at the same time, clearly endorses the newly acquired notion of Britishness, though not the 'Britishness' Scottish writers earlier in the eighteenth century developed within the framework of the (Rule) Britannia Project. McSympathy supports a more complex British identity when he sings in Scots about 'our ain British nation'.

If we combine what, to borrow a concept from the Caribbean critic Michael Gilkes, may be defined as the 'creative schizophrenia',[20] or the language split, in *The Highland Drover* with the final image in *The Negro Slaves* of a Britishness which welcomes racial, ethnic and cultural differences, Maclaren's theatre can first and foremost be read as one posing rather than answering crucial questions: how to preserve Scottishness and Gaeldom within the discourse of Britishness; how to define Scotland's identity within the Union; and how to cross the Highland line, to look beyond it, without erasing it from Britain's cultural geography.

Maclaren's work was, then, marked by a relatively radical social, political and intellectual agenda in a career that depended, despite the apparent popularity of some of his plays, on the patronage of, first of all, his army officers and, later, the London-Scottish elite. This patronage appears to have offered him some support, though not enough, it seems, to sustain his widow and four children when he died 'after a long and severe illness' in 1826.[21] Yet, while the anonymous memoirist talked of his name being 'not in the memory beyond the select and aristocratic circle of dramatic antiquaries', his work, as concepts of 'Britishness' are again being interrogated and Scotland's creative trilingualism increasingly celebrated, now demands the more nuanced study and deeper understanding it deserves.

Notes

1. Gioia Angeletti, 'Debating Colonialism and Black Slavery on the Scottish Stage: Archibald MacLaren's *The Negro Slaves* (1799)' in Gioia Angeletti (ed.), *Emancipation, Liberation, and Freedom: Romantic Drama and Theatre in Britain 1760–1830* (Parma: Monte Università Parma, 2010), pp. 59–86, and Ian Brown, 'Public and Private Performance: 1650–1800' in Ian Brown (ed.), *The Edinburgh Companion to Scottish Drama* (Edinburgh: Edinburgh University Press, 2011), pp. 22–40, specifically pp. 39–40. Brown follows up his interest in the relevant pages of *Scottish Theatre: Diversity, Language, Continuity* (Amsterdam: Rodopi, 2013) on which elements of this chapter draw.
2. Jane Moody, *Illegitimate Theatre in London, 1770–1840* (London, Cambridge University Press, 2000).
3. Anon., *Memoir of Archibald Maclaren, Dramatist: with a list of his works* (Edinburgh, 1835), p. 2.
4. Terence Tobin, *Plays by Scots, 1660–1800* (Iowa City: University of Iowa Press, 1974), p. 64.
5. *Memoir*, p. 2.
6. Tobin, p. 61.
7. *Memoir*, p. 2.
8. Archibald Maclaren, *The Highland Drover* (Greenock: Thos Murray, 1790), pp. 9–10.
9. Archibald Maclaren, *The Highland Drover* (Greenock: Thos Murray, 1790). Maclaren appears to have published different versions of some of his plays, often apparently as a result of either opportunistic changes in production scripts or changes arising from the demands of particular productions. In this chapter, we have followed the principle of adhering to the first available edition.
10. We are grateful to Domhnall Uilleam Stiùbhart for drawing our attention to this economic and social factor.
11. *Memoir*, pp. 2–3.
12. *Memoir*, p. 3.
13. *Memoir*, p. 3.
14. Archibald McLaren, *The Negro Slaves* (London, 1799).
15. Carla Sassi, *Imagined Scotlands: Saggi sulla letteratura scozzese* (Trieste: Edizioni Parnaso, 2002), p. 48.
16. See, for example, *Our Multiform, Our Infinite Scotland: Scottish Literature as 'Scottish', 'English' and 'World' Literature* (Glasgow: ASLS, 2012), *passim*, and *Scottish Theatre: Diversity, Language, Continuity* (Amsterdam: Rodopi, 2013), in particular, pp. 55–59, 70–73, 80–82.

17. *The Negro Slaves*, p. 7.
18. John Barrell, *The Infection of Thomas De Quincey: a psychopathology of imperialism* (New Haven: Yale University Press, 1991).
19. John Barrell, *The Infection of Thomas De Quincey*, p. 10.
20. Michael Gilkes, *Creative Schizophrenia: The Caribbean Cultural Challenge* (University of Warwick: Centre for Caribbean Studies, 1986).
21. *Memoir*, p. 4.

4. What Walter Scott Can Offer Us Today

CHRISTOPHER WHYTE

Who is included in the 'us' of my title? On the one hand, it can refer to whoever, in this second decade of the twenty-first century, chooses to take a novel or a long narrative poem by Scott down from the shelf, and read it. But I had in mind a more restricted group, comprising the men and women whose business it is to study, teach and write about Scottish Literature. For more than twenty years, until 2005, I was part of that group, before the urge to contribute directly to Scottish literature, as a poet and a novelist, got the upper hand, and led me to abandon an academic career so I could write full-time. As the 1990s wore on, I had increasingly felt that the subject was reaching an impasse. My own discovery of Scottish Literature dated back to Rome, when I was twenty-one. Reading MacDiarmid's *Lucky Poet*, recommended in the early hours of an interminable overnight party by a working-class Glaswegian who, like me, had gone to Cambridge, converted me to what might be called 'the gospel according to MacDiarmid', even if this bore a limited relation to MacDiarmid's actual assertions. In other words, I became a committed cultural nationalist. The subject itself was in a militant phase, and therefore benefited from the temporary amnesty, or indulgence, in terms of traditional scholarly criteria and standards, accorded to feminism, queer studies, and postcolonial discourse à la Frantz Fanon when each first came upon the scene.

As a teacher, I was never keen on repeating myself. Attempts to deliver the same lecture one year after another fell flat on their faces, because I personally lost interest, a fact unfailingly picked up on by the students, at which point teaching became a chore rather than a challenge. The overall problem, however, was more general and more subtle. After a phase, in the 1970s and 1980s, when the emerging discipline of Scottish studies welcomed almost indiscriminately all those capable of making a contribution, regardless of their background and provenance, things changed radically. There was now discursive and institutional space to be fought over and partitioned.

The discipline had always had unmistakably strong links to the political movement for independence. It was obvious that whoever could claim to define Scottishness, and therefore decree who was entitled to participate in the new literary formation and who not, as if issuing a species of membership card, would acquire considerable interpretive and executive power. A narrower brand of nationalist criticism came to the fore, which concentrated on issues of identity and Scottishness. The risk was that criteria would emerge which shut out as relentlessly as they boxed in. I was painfully aware that my own background, as a Catholic Glaswegian and a gay man, repeatedly led to my being excluded from formulations of what it meant to be Scottish.

To come upon a concept like 'healthy indigenous Scottishness' being seriously propagated within the discipline where I worked was worrying, as well as indicating a lamentable sagging of the prevailing intellectual standards. What was the way ahead? How to rescue the subject from the self-damaging strategies prevailing in many quarters? I came up with three answers, which I was unable to put to the test because I abandoned the profession: links to the Greek and Latin classics; the seventeenth century; and Walter Scott. Here I want to try and explain why a return to Walter Scott struck me as potentially so helpful, in the context I have described.

*

There is a passage from Canto V of *The Lady of the Lake* (first published in 1810) which has inescapable, if disconcerting, resonances for readers who grew up in the latter part of the twentieth century. In the course of a hunting expedition in the Trossachs, King James V, who is in the habit of making incognito excursions under the thinly disguised pseudonym of James Fitz-James, becomes separated from his companions, and is offered hospitality by an attractive yet mysterious young woman by the name of Ellen. In Canto IV, showing remarkable irresponsibility, James returns to the area, hoping to persuade Ellen to elope with him. She refuses, but, when the two part, he presses upon her a ring, a talisman which will allow her to trace him unfailingly when she enters his world, rather than him venturing into hers. In Canto V, James is making the return journey with the help of a guide, in actual fact the Gaelic clan leader Roderick Dhu, at that very moment intent on mounting an armed insurrection against the king. An argument breaks out between the two. James claims he cannot wait to meet his opponent face-to-face, upon which Roderick Dhu gives a shrill whistle:

> And he was answer'd from the hill;
> Wild as the scream of the curlew,
> From crag to crag the signal flew.
> Instant, through copse and heath, arose
> Bonnets and spears and bended bows;
> On right, on left, above, below,
> Sprung up at once the lurking foe;
> From shingles grey their lances start,
> The bracken bush sends forth the dart,
> The rushes and the willow wand
> Are bristling into axe and brand,
> And every tuft of broom gives life
> To plaided warrior armed for strife.
> That whistle garrisoned the glen
> At once with full five hundred men,
> As if the yawning hill to heaven
> A subterranean host had given. (V, 192–213)

We could be watching a cowboy film. The white hero has ventured into Indian territory, accompanied by a guide about whose identity, and trustworthiness, he entertains some doubts. All the guide has to do is whistle, and from behind the rocks surrounding them one hundred Indian heads pop up, two feathers perched at an angle as their headdress (corresponding to the Highlanders' bonnets), bows and arrows in their hands. What happens next is fascinating:

> Short space he stood, then waved his hand:
> Down sunk the disappearing band;
> Each warrior vanish'd where he stood,
> In broom or bracken, heath or wood;
> Sunk branded spear and bended bow,
> In osiers pale and copses low;

> It seem'd as if their mother Earth
> Had swallow'd up her warlike birth.
> The wind's last breath had toss'd in air
> Pennon, and plaid, and plumage fair;
> The next but swept a lone hill-side,
> Where heath and fern were waving wide. (V, 240–51)

The natural setting, which would appear to have generated (one could even say, regurgitated) the indigenous tribesmen, swallows them back once more. More than belonging in the landscape, they subsist half at the level of human beings, half at the level of animals or plants. They are natural, not fully, or not at all civilised, never successfully marked off from their setting. They do not inhabit the landscape, they *are* that landscape.

The Highland Clearances do not crop up as a major issue in Scott's writing, though the process was already under way at the time he died. But one could claim that, in a passage such as this, he laid the basis for the paradoxical tension between absence and presence which has since characterised representations of the Scottish Highlands and their population (or lack of it). The flora and fauna, not to mention the actual lie of the land, stand in for the human beings who are no longer there.

Writing about Walter Scott is a daunting task, not least because such extensive quotation would ideally be required. It is not that Scott is either wordy, or long-winded. But he does proceed at a leisurely pace, revelling in language and descriptive detail. In the present context, much that would benefit from patient argument will have to be put forward, due to constraints of space, in the form of barefaced assertions.

Next in *The Lady of the Lake* comes a duel that is strikingly filmic in nature (shades of *High Noon*). Dashing to seize Fitz-James's throat in his fearsomely powerful grip (unreckoning, brute force being an attribute of the 'natural'), Roderick Dhu fails to notice that he himself has already received a fatal wound. He does his best to stab the disguised monarch, but his rapidly failing strength means the blow cannot be driven home:

> Down came the blow – but in the heath;
> The erring blade found bloodless sheath.
> The struggling foe may now unclasp

> The fainting Chief's relaxing grasp;
> Unwounded from the dreadful close,
> But breathless all, Fitz-James arose. (V, 410–36)

The hypothesis (one that is receiving broader attention in the field of Scott studies beyond Scotland) is that, in his treatment of Gaelic Scotland, particularly its border areas, in relation to the rest of the country, Scott created a narrative vocabulary which was then adopted in the United States, offering an epic mode in which to represent the gradual conquest of more and more 'virgin' territory and the regrettable (if supposedly inevitable) subjugation and extirpation of its previous 'native' population. The parallels are legion. We leave at our shoulders a civilised society governed by the rule of law to enter a transitional region characterised either by absolute lawlessness, or by a very different, more primitive code of ethics. Older tribal customs prevail. The native population is uncouth and unpredictable, not infrequently savage and violent in its behaviour, yet capable of outstanding loyalty and nobility as individuals. They speak an incomprehensible language, rendering necessary the intervention of scouts, interpreters and, more generally, anomalous figures poised on the threshold between two civilisations. Sheriffs, representing a new law that aims to impose itself on the recently annexed territories, are crucial, even heroic figures. In Scott's fiction, too, the law is a heroic enterprise, even if he regularly calls its efficiency and appropriateness, where two cultures are in contact and conflict, into question.

Horses, and horsemanship, play a major role. It is worth noting that Indians do not normally mount horses in cowboy movies. Here is Fitz-James getting back onto his, at the conclusion of the duel:

> No foot Fitz-James in stirrup staid,
> No grasp upon the saddle laid,
> But wreath'd his left hand in the mane,
> And lightly bounded from the plain,
> Turn'd on the horse his armed heel,
> And stirr'd his courage with the steel.
> Bounded the fiery steed in air,
> The rider sate erect and fair,

> Then like a bolt from steel crossbow
> Forth launch'd, along the plain they go. (V, 474–83)

If we accept this debt on Hollywood's part to the fiction of Walter Scott, a series of fascinating questions ensues. It is perhaps an unjustifiable exaggeration to suggest that the United States was a society constructed on a genocide. Nonetheless, we might wonder whether the seizure of territory throughout North America on the part of immigrant white populations was a manifestation of imperialism on a par with the conquest of India, or of much of Africa. If so, can the same be said about the fate of Gaelic-speaking Scotland and its inhabitants, in the wake of the military catastrophe they underwent at Culloden? Was the relationship of England and of the Scottish lowlands to Gaelic Scotland that of an imperial power towards a colonised population? And might this be one of the fundamental concerns of Scott's fictions of Scotland?

Here the words of Fitz-James's guide, before he reveals his true identity, are very relevant:

> 'Saxon, from yonder mountain high,
> I mark'd thee send delighted eye,
> Far to the south and east, where lay,
> Extended in succession gay,
> Deep waving fields and pastures green,
> With gentle slopes and groves between:
> These fertile plains, that soften'd vale,
> Were once the birthright of the Gael;
> The stranger came with iron hand,
> And from our fathers reft the land.
> [...]
> Pent in this fortress of the North,
> Think'st thou we will not sally forth,
> To spoil the spoiler as we may,
> And from the robber rend the prey?
> Ay, by my soul! While on yon plain
> The Saxon rears one shock of grain,

While of ten thousand herds there strays
But one along yon river's maze,
The Gael, of plain and river heir,
Shall with strong hand redeem his share.' (V, 136–45, 156–65)

When I entered the field of Scottish studies, Scott was regarded with circumspection and ambivalence. To begin with, here was a writer who could not be 'discovered', but whose work had been amply studied from a different, not always narrowly 'English' perspective. At the risk of producing a caricature, I would suggest he was suspect because seen as an apologist for the union of both crown and parliament with England. He was, moreover, a bilingual writer, using both English and Scots, and there was a tendency to assume that he must perforce write badly in English, and well in Scots. Only texts dealing specifically with Scotland were taken into consideration. His apparent portrayal of Gaelic society, together with Jacobitism, as doomed to historical obsolescence, was reassuring, especially for those who had no intention of taking the trouble to acquire even a smattering of Gaelic. Then again, his fair-minded presentation of a spectrum of religious convictions and viewpoints was unacceptable for those intent on erecting a totem of unitary Scottishness, with Calvinism cast in the pivotal role. A Scottish studies powered by militant cultural nationalism was always compromised by its unwillingness to deal honestly with the enthusiastic participation of large segments of the Scottish population in the British imperial enterprise, and the benefits these segments reaped as a result. If, as I am suggesting, a sort of proto-imperialism, whose victims were inhabitants of the very same island, is among Scott's most riveting concerns, it is easy to see how troublesome his fictions could appear.

*

There are further aspects of Scott's work which can render him disquieting for us to read, even today. The next passage I want to quote comes from Chapter XXVII of *The Abbot*, a novel set at the time of Mary Queen of Scots and the Scottish Reformation first published in 1820. Again, it will be necessary to quote at considerable length. With Scott, there would seem to be no other way.

Catherine Seyton had admirable skill in gestic lore, and was sometimes called on to dance for the amusement of her royal mistress. Roland Graeme had often been a spectator of her skill, and sometimes, at the Queen's command, Catherine's partner on such occasions. He was, therefore, perfectly acquainted with Catherine's mode of dancing; and observed that his present partner, in grace, in agility, in quickness of ear, and precision of execution, exactly resembled her, save that the Scottish jig, which he now danced with her, required a more violent and rapid motion, and more rustic agility than the stately pavens, lavoltas, and courantoes, which he had seen her execute in the chamber of Queen Mary. The active duties of the dance left him little time for reflection, and none for conversation; but when their *pas de deux* was finished, amidst the acclamations of the villagers, who had seldom witnessed such an exhibition, he took an opportunity, when they yielded up the green to another couple, to use the privilege of a partner, and enter into conversation with the mysterious maiden whom he still held by the hand.

[...]

'Fair Catherine,' said the page, 'he were unworthy ever to have seen you, far less to have dwelt so long in the same service, and under the same roof with you, who could mistake your air, your gesture, your step in walking or in dancing, the turn of your neck, the symmetry of your form – none could be so dull as not to recognise you by so many proofs; but for me, I could swear even to that tress of hair that escapes from under your muffler.'

'And to the face, of course, which that muffler covers,' said the maiden, removing her veil, and in an instant endeavouring to replace it. She showed the features of Catherine; but an unusual degree of petulant impatience inflamed them, when, from some awkwardness in her management of the muffler, she was unable again to adjust it with that dexterity which was a principal accomplishment of the coquettes of the time.

'The fiend rive the rag to tatters,' said the damsel, as the veil fluttered about her shoulders, with an accent so earnest and decided, that it made the page start. He looked again at the damsel's face, but the information which his eyes received, was to the same purport as before. He assisted her to adjust the muffler, and both were for an instant silent.

It would be anachronistic to say that poor Roland is unwittingly dancing with a transvestite. His partner is Catherine Seyton's identical twin who, as we can see, derives undeniable pleasure from the deception, perhaps also from the fact of being in drag, even if running into difficulties with the technicalities of managing female attire. At this point, space makes it imperative to proceed very quickly, by assertion and hypothesis. The time has come to take Scott's fascination with cross-dressing seriously. Shakespeare can serve as an alibi here but, as with Shakespeare, we should not forget that for identical twins to be of different sexes is a biological impossibility. Shakespeare was writing for a transvestite theatre where all female attire concealed male genitals. Why is the phenomenon so crucial for Scott that he comes back to it time and again?

At times it is helpful to make a crude distinction between gender, a cultural construct, expressed through a system of signs such as clothing, and the anatomical fact of sex (not always as unambiguous as we might imagine) revealed by the genitalia these clothes conceal. It was one aspect of Scott's pact with his readership that the sexual act should never be explicitly presented, and referred to, if at all, only in the most indirect terms. For him to mention the existence of genitalia was totally out of the question. Yet a pervasive characteristic of all Scott's writing is its powerful libidinal impulses. Far from being any kind of prude, his works brim over with sexuality. Scott cannot speak of genitals. He cannot even represent the naked body. All he has left is the clothes his characters wear, which he describes at great length, in loving, lingering detail. The failure of the signifier to correspond to the signified, the moment when clothes become a lie, could not but be a focus of particular tension and excitement. Early on in *The Antiquary*, yet another of Scott's unknowing youthful protagonists knocks on the door of his friend Jonathan Oldbuck, the eponymous hero of the novel. It is opened by a woman:

> The elderly lady rustled in silks and satins, and bore upon her head a structure resembling the fashion in the Ladies' Memorandum-book for the year 1770 – a superb piece of architecture – not much less than a modern Gothic castle, of which the curls might represent the

turrets, the black pins the *chevaux de frize*, and the lappets the banners. The face, which, like that of the ancient statues of Vesta, was thus crowned with towers, was large and long, and peaked at nose and chin, and bore, in other respects, such a ludicrous resemblance to the physiognomy of Mr Jonathan Oldbuck, that Lovel, had they not appeared at once, like Sebastian and Viola in the last scene of 'Twelfth Night', might have supposed that the figure before him was his old friend masquerading in female attire. (Chapter VI)

It is wonderfully entertaining to have the narrator compare Ms Oldbuck's hairdo to a recently built architectural masterpiece of the Gothic Revival. But the first thought, or nearly, which comes into his young friend's head is that the door has been opened by none other than Jonathan Oldbuck in drag. We even have the saving reference to Shakespeare to convey a shade of literary and cultural normality upon what is a distinctly puzzling reflex on the narrator's part.

Earlier I spoke of the powerful libidinal pulses of Scott's fiction. These are pansexual in nature, rather than narrowly heterosexual or homosexual. If it is true that the cowboy film genre is deeply indebted to Scott, however, it is worth meditating on the undeniable homoerotic elements cropping up there again and again in the portrayal of a society where men are cooped up together with a minimal sprinkling of women, themselves often distinctly masculinised in nature (not infrequently, like certain of Scott's heroines, consummate horsewomen). One thinks of the Lone Ranger and his inseparable Indian sidekick Tonto, in their way prefiguring a pair such as Robin and Batman. The issue is whether or not we have the courage to read Scott directly, to look at what he is saying. These are the lines preceding the duel between Fitz-James and Roderick Dhu from which I set out:

> 'For love-lorn swain, in lady's bower,
> Ne'er panted for the appointed hour,
> As I, until before me stand
> This rebel Chieftain and his band!' (V, 192–96)

Must we maintain that the comparison is accidental? That it means nothing? Fitz-James likens his emotions to those of a man awaiting the appearance of the woman he adores in an intimate setting, where a love-tryst may very possibly ensue. After all, Fitz-James's assertion (which admittedly concerns not only Roderick Dhu, but his followers) is immediately followed by hand-to-hand grappling on the ground, in which the two males are so interlinked it is hard to distinguish the limbs of one from those of the other, culminating in the shedding of an intimate bodily fluid.

I am far from being the first person to have remarked on certain striking parallels between the plots of Scott's novel *Redgauntlet* and the *Star Wars* trilogy (the first series, directed by George Lucas between 1977 and 1983). His father Darth Vader, who has gone over to what is known as the 'dark side', traps Luke Skywalker, and attempts to persuade him to switch allegiance from the Rebels to his father's party. He refuses. At the close of the trilogy, the smuggler-turned-hero Han Solo hesitates to get together with the female protagonist Princess Leia (an intermittently masculinised warrior figure) because he has noted the strong bond between her and Luke. Only when it is revealed that Luke and Leia are in fact brother and sister can the supposed barrier separating them be removed.

Once again, we find elements related to those in Scott at the core of one of the dominant popular fictions of our time. But there is more. I have argued elsewhere that the relationship which powers the whole narrative of *Redgauntlet* is that between Alan Fairford and Darsie Latimer. The scene where the two are finally reunited has Darsie, in female clothing, fall off a horse he has difficulty in alighting from while wearing long skirts, directly into Alan's arms. It calls for open-minded, unwavering interpretation. Claims that the circumstances 'means nothing' can hardly pass muster. In a text governed by fictional conventions which set any discussion of sexuality, never mind homosexuality, out of bounds, for one of the protagonists to marry the sister of another with whom he is closely associated constitutes the strongest conceivable longer-term assertion of the bond between them. Roland Graeme is dumbfoundered by encountering the young woman he has fallen in love with alternately in male and female manifestations. The uncertainty is resolved when Catherine's impossible twin breathes his last – in Roland's arms. This reads very like a case of what Eve Kosofsky-Sedgwick might have called 'homosexual panic', where the tormenting anxiety provoked by experiencing desire for another member of the same sex, or being the object of such desire, can only be appeased by murdering, or attempting to murder, the individual in question. (In this case, one might be tempted to attribute the 'homosexual panic' not to Roland, but to his narrator).

*

If *Star Wars* can hardly fail to evoke *Redgauntlet* in the minds of those who have read Scott's novel, considerable additional pleasure can be derived by reading *The Lady of the Lake* as a reworking, a reframing, of Shakespeare's *The Tempest*. The ruler of a state stumbles unexpectedly upon the home, located on an island, of a man unjustly banished, who is accompanied in exile by his fascinating, innocent yet alluring daughter, and the fortuitous meeting eventually leads to a general reconciliation, from which Ellen's suitor, the tribal leader Roderick Dhu, is, however, excluded. If one pursues the parallel with *The Tempest*, then the figure corresponding to Roderick Dhu will have to be Caliban, an intriguing pointer, given the repeated attempts in criticism of the last decades also to interpret Shakespeare's play as dealing with the colonial enterprise, so that Caliban (i.e., Roderick Dhu) would represent the expropriated, subjugated indigenous population. Space presses, and I have to admit to going merely on a hunch in suggesting that *Redgauntlet* might profitably be read with *King Lear* in mind. If the novel's eponymous hero, who can hope to find no place in a transformed political reality, and whose rigid attachment to out-of-date schemes of thinking and ideologies condemns him to unfailing obsolescence, recalls the king, while that splendid creation of Scott's, Peter Peebles, is a miraculously appropriate and updated version of the Fool, then Darsie (crossing a gender boundary, but given what has been said above, this hardly offers cause for wonderment) would indicate Scott's refusal, his unwillingness (more than his failure) to write a Cordelia.

Again at the risk of falling into caricature, I would maintain that neither the militant cultural nationalism characterising the early phase of studies in Scottish Literature, nor the normative, identity-based rationale to which it yielded, could be comfortable with Scott's recycling, over two centuries later, of figures and patterns derived from Shakespeare. The tendency has been to concentrate on intertextual relations which are evidence of Scottishness and serve in the project of constructing it, at the expense of all others. A major author with an unmistakable debt to the iconic figure of the literary tradition from which texts and authors were being wrested, in the process of putting together a competing canon of fundamental works, must inevitably appear both troubling and inconvenient.

Scott's intertextuality, of course, goes infinitely further. He claimed to reread every year, presumably in Italian, the renaissance epics of Boiardo and Ariosto, the *Orlando innamorato* and the *Orlando furioso*. We would encounter there much that is familiar from the foregoing discussion. A female warrior mounted on horseback can knock a knight off his horse only, a few stanzas later, to stop for refreshment at a fountain, removing her helmet to reveal cascade upon cascade of long, golden hair. The setting is an unpredictable border region of impenetrable forests, where the protagonists are engaged in group or hand-to-hand combat with the representatives of a hostile, alien religion and ideology, though, as the outcome is far from being a foregone conclusion, it would be inappropriate to evoke imperialism or colonialism here. The link to Boiardo and Ariosto roots Scott's fiction in an alternative ancestry of the novel, one traced in detail by Margaret Ann Doody in her *True History of the Novel* (1996), undermining the hijacking of the European fictional tradition carried out so effectively by Ian Watt on behalf of the English Protestant establishment and the realist tradition. I cannot be the only one convinced by the argument that realism is a retroformation, a reaction against romance, a parody of its tales of the marvellous and the unexpected. After all, there is an unspoken understanding on the part of the author, the publisher, the bookseller and whoever buys a novel and reads it, that what is to be found between its covers never actually occurred. It has no correlation to reality. Otherwise, what we were reading must abandon any claim to be a novel.

*

This may be the point at which to consider the Tolkien-like aspects of Scott's fictions. Having been rescued from the treacherous Solway tides by a mysterious older man, who hoists the reckless youth up onto his own horse, Darsie Latimer is offered grudging hospitality in a grim dwelling, situated in the clearing of a glen. His rescuer and a female servant having disappeared,

> their place was supplied by an elderly woman, in a grey stuff gown, with a check apron and *toy*, obviously a menial, though neater in her

> dress than is usual in her apparent rank – an advantage which was counterbalanced by a very forbidding aspect. But the most singular part of her attire, in this very Protestant country, was a rosary, in which the smaller beads were black oak, and those indicating the *pater-noster* of silver, with a crucifix of the same metal. (Letter IV)

The reader's mind has been crowded by questions not so dissimilar to those crowding Darsie's. What is the identity of his rescuer? Who are the people residing with him? What are their political, social and religious affiliations? Catching sight of the Catholic rosary must send a *frisson* down the spine of Scott's young hero. It indicates an affiliation with the foreign, existence beyond the law, allegiance to a defeated dynasty and a discredited political system. Darsie speaks the same language as these people, but, beyond that, they have very little in common with him. One is reminded of, say, the point in Tolkien's trilogy, in the course of its second volume, where the Ents appear, tree-like giants, or giant-like trees gifted with the faculty of movement and of not only speaking their own language, but learning those of other, unrelated species. The reader is beset by questions. Do the Ents have two sexes? More perhaps? How do they reproduce? At what point do their young become capable of fending for themselves? How long can they be expected to live? The morning after, Darsie's gruff and ungracious host is showing him the road to take for a locality known as Shepherd's Bush, when what one can be pardoned for describing as yet another species makes its appearance:

> His accoutrements were in the usual unostentatious, but clean and serviceable order, which characterises these sectaries. His long surtout of dark-grey superfine cloth descended down to the middle of his leg, and was buttoned up to his chin, to defend him against the morning air. As usual, his ample beaver hung down without button or loop, and shaded a comely and placid countenance, the gravity of which appeared to contain some seasoning of humour, and had nothing in common with the pinched puritanical air affected by devotees in general. The brow was open and free from wrinkles, whether of age or hypocrisy. The eye was clear, calm and considerate, yet appeared to be disturbed by apprehension, not to say fear, as, pronouncing the usual salutation of 'I wish thee a good morrow,

> friend,' he indicated, by turning his palfrey close to one side of the path, a wish to glide past us with as little trouble as possible – just as a traveller would choose to pass a mastiff of whose peaceable intentions he is by no means confident. (Letter VI)

The man whom Scott describes with all the painstaking attention to detail of an ornithologist presenting a hitherto unknown species is the Quaker Joshua Geddes, who will in turn act as Darsie's host. This figure presents a new means of gaining one's livelihood, a new ideology, a new relationship to the prevailing political establishment, and a new understanding of morality and of the interaction between the sexes.

This feature of Scott's work is of course Bakhtinian. In the early 1980s I supervised an undergraduate thesis on Scott and Bakhtin at Rome's La Sapienza university, and learnt a great deal from the experience. Summarising radically, Bakhtin views the novel as a stage where differing social groups enter into dialogue with one another. They can be defined by their social class, their profession, their religion or their perceived ethnicity, to name but a few features. The novel's task is to allow these varying viewpoints on the world to enter into relation to one another without privileging one to the disadvantage of the rest. Scott as a novelist is instinctively multicultural. If he were writing about central Scotland today, he would lose no time in entering an Asian household, delving into human interactions which traverse the boundaries separating religious and racial communities. What sort of a description might he offer us of Pollokshields on a Saturday afternoon? And because his commitment to multiculturalism is both artistic and ethical, we could rely on him to come up with a balanced and unprejudiced account.

In the opening chapter of *The Secular Scripture*, Northrop Frye explains how he was brought back to Scott's novels by a friend's recommendation. They were discussing

> the amount of tedium in modern life caused by plane journeys and waiting in airports. He remarked that he had got through a long and exhausting trip himself with the aid of Scott. 'I love Scott,' he said. I tried the recipe. Richard was right, as he so often was: when one is traveling by jet plane it is deeply reassuring to have a stagecoach style for a traveling companion.

It's a peculiarly telling observation, as Scott himself repeatedly compares the experience of reading a novel to that of a journey, of travelling (the introduction to *The Abbot* is one instance). What is certain is that Scott makes us very aware of reading as a physical experience. It is impossible to read him in a hurry. We need to decide what chair we will sit in, how the lamp will be poised, to ensure we are in a comfortable position and can count on being undisturbed for long enough to get into his unhurried style and make some progress with the plot. I would be fascinated to hear what it feels like to read a whole Scott novel using Kindle, or an iPad. Where? In what physical stance? In what light? In an age where reading books has become only one of many possible means of accessing entertainment and information, this could be one further way in which rediscovering Scott allows us to rediscover literary culture, to experience it anew.

*

My discussion has nearly reached its close. Suddenly an objection is raised: 'But you have talked so little about Scotland!' One possible response could be: 'No, but I *have* been talking about Scottish literature.' An alternative tactic might be to tease out the assumption lying behind the question, namely, that what matters in Scottish texts is principally, if not exclusively, what they can tell us about Scotland. The boxed-in, circuitous nature of this assumption needs no underlining. At the very least, if we subscribe to it, we are liable to neglect significant aspects of the texts we select for study, to ignore considerably more than half their content and their implications. Because, if Scott's writings arguably brim over with eroticism, with libidinal pulsations, they also brim over, beyond the bounds of Scotland, in their debts to previous authors as much as in their generative capacities, where subsequent books and cultural icons are concerned. Could this perhaps be Scott's most significant contribution to Scottish studies? The greatest gift he has to offer?

Budapest, May 2014

5. James Hogg and the Highlands

SUZANNE GILBERT

James Hogg (1770–1835) engaged the Scottish Highlands in diverse and intriguing ways. His most concentrated representations of the Highlands appear in the series of letters addressed to Walter Scott, originally intended for publication as a book but later proposed as instalments in the *Scots Magazine*, reporting on journeys that he took through the Highlands and Islands in 1802, 1803, and 1804. Some of the instalments were published by the magazine in 1803 and 1804, and others appeared there in 1808 and 1809. Some only came to light in *The Scottish Review* in 1888, long after Hogg's death. Yet other portions were never published and exist only in manuscript. The jigsaw puzzle was recently put together and edited by Hans de Groot, as part of the Stirling/South Carolina Research Edition of Hogg's work, and *Highland Journeys* was published by Edinburgh University Press in 2010. The S/SC edition is the first near-to-full picture of Hogg's accounts intended for publication.[1] Hogg was writing as both an agricultural labourer and a writer with professional aspirations, and his contribution to the travel literature at the beginning of the nineteenth century reveals Highlands and Islands culture from an unusual perspective, at a time of inexorable change in the region. His Highland journeys also laid the groundwork for a preoccupation with the Highlands that deepened over the years.

Hogg's journeys

Hogg's accounts of the Highlands may be seen in relation to those of other eighteenth- and nineteenth-century British travellers encouraged northward by a perception of reduced danger following the crushing of Jacobite ambitions, General Wade's extensive road-building programme in the eighteenth century, and more and better accommodation. Their tours were driven by widely varying motives: simple curiosity, scientific or cultural observation, assessment of the agriculture and economy of the region, a search for artistic inspiration, a quest for places associated with James

Macpherson's Ossian poems. Among those from the south who had gone before were the Welsh zoologist Thomas Pennant, who toured Scotland and the Hebrides in 1769 and 1772, followed by that strange double-act of Johnson and Boswell in 1773 (Hogg was himself an admirer of Johnson). Thomas Gilpin, theorist of the picturesque, toured in 1776. Sarah Murray toured in 1796 and 1801, Thomas Garnett in 1798, John Stoddart in 1799–1800. William and Dorothy Wordsworth, joined by Samuel Taylor Colerige, made the journey in 1803, around the same time as Hogg. Lowland Scots, too, ventured north. Among the most notable, campaigner for improvement John Knox visited numerous times between 1764 and 1786 and, encouraged by the Highland Society, produced *A Tour through the Highlands of Scotland, and the Hebrides, in 1786*. Francis Jeffrey's unpublished tour in 1800, recently edited by Pamela Perkins, shows the later-formidable critic for the *Edinburgh Review* working out aesthetic principles that would later figure in his critiques of contemporary writers.[2]

Hogg travelled widely throughout the Highlands, and more times than are represented in the accounts prepared for publication. He was first in the Trossachs in 1791, at age twenty-one, not as a tourist but as a drover of sheep. In 1800 he was in the southern Highlands, exploring the possibilities of leasing a farm at the Spittal of Glenshee. He was a frequent visitor to Tayside, where he began composing his book-length poem *Queen Hynde*, published in 1824. And he claimed to have visited various parts of the Highlands every summer in later life. While surely Hogg may be considered in the broader context of domestic tourists who visited the Highlands on the cusp of the eighteenth and nineteenth centuries, his accounts make clear that he considered his travels not 'tours' but 'journeys' and that he hated 'to write about that which every body writes about' (p. 73). Indeed, he wrote in the hope that the Highland Society would eventually publish his experiences as a book, which partly explains the many observations regarding livestock husbandry and land management; the list of entries on sheep alone fill three full pages of the index in the Stirling/South Carolina edition. Though absent from Hogg's record, his (ultimately unsuccessful) attempts to secure the lease of a farm at Luskentyre on the west side of the isle of Harris figured in motivations for the 1803 and 1804 journeys.

By the turn of the nineteenth century, certain set routes for visiting the Highlands had been established, the so-called short and long tours. Thomas

SUZANNE GILBERT

Pennant, in the course of his first tour, had suggested a '*petit tour* of Scotland', which took travellers 'from Edinburgh to Taymouth via Kinross and Perth and then back to Edinburgh by way of Killin, Tyndrum, Glenorchy, Inveraray, Luss, Dumbarton, Glasgow and Stirling' (p. xxxv). An alternative 'long tour' was described by Thomas Garnett in 1801 as taking in Fort William, Fort Augustus, and Inverness. And there was the very short tour that simply involved a visit to Loch Lomond and the Falls of Clyde (not, of course, actually in the Highlands). Hogg was well aware of these conventional routes. The S/SC edition of *Highland Journeys* includes a transcription of the 1814 manuscript held by the National Library of Scotland of his suggested itinerary for an Edinburgh publisher, Robert Cadell, who was interested in taking the short tour.[3] But while Hogg visited many of the suggested sites, he also ventured more widely (as had Pennant and Johnson with Boswell), going to the Outer Hebrides in both 1803 and 1804.

Hogg also differed from the majority of travellers in his means of transportation (and, for that matter, his means full stop). Some tourists travelled by coach, either their own or a hired one; some were accompanied by servants. Hogg travelled on horseback in 1802, but his 1803 and 1804 journeys were on foot. He had to travel on a tight budget that had to cover his meals, ferries, and the occasional coach and guide. For the 1802 tour, he also had the added expense of stabling and feeding his horse. He had to pay for accommodation when he could not make use of letters of introduction provided by Scott to gentleman in the areas he planned to visit. This, of course, might be taken into account in the influence his social position had on his representation of landowners. He also had to pay someone to take care of his work at Ettrick House (p. ix).

As is common in travel writing, the reporting of events is driven by chronology, but the epistolary form (letters to Scott) highlights Hogg's skill in writing literary anecdotes, lending familiarity and charm that make his accounts entertaining in their own right. Some of the most fascinating anecdotes detail his personal experiences, for example, nearly being press-ganged into service by a king's cutter at 'Tobermurray' in the Isle of Mull ('I got an ugly fright' (pp. 147–48)); or questioning Campbell of Inveraray's insistence on dressing for dinner ('I said he was well enough dressed; it was a silly thing that they could not put on cloathes in the morning that would serve them during the day' (p. 68)). At the inn at Invershiel, he was attacked

JAMES HOGG AND THE HIGHLANDS

by bedbugs (or lice?) before having his letters of introduction stolen from his coat by a mixed crowd of Highland rabble-rousers:

> I got the best bed, but it was extremely hard, and the clothes had not the smell of roses. It was also inhabited by a number of little insects common enough in such places, and no sooner had I made a lodgement in their heriditary domains than I was attacked by a thousand strong. But what disturbed me much worse than all, I was awaked, during the night, by a whole band of highlanders, both male and female; who entered my room, and fell to drinking Whisky with great freedom. They had much the appearance of a parcel of vagabonds which they certainly were; but as the whole discourse was in Gaelic, I knew nothing of what it was concerning, but it arose by degrees as the whisky operated to an insufferable noise. [...] I bore all this uproar with patience for nearly two hours in the middle of the night, until, either by accident or design, the candle was extinguished, when every one getting up a great stir commenced, and I heard one distinctly ransacking my coat, which was hanging upon a chair at a little distance from the bed. [...] I sprung to my feet in the bed, laid hold of my thorn staff, and bellowed aloud for light. It was a good while ere this could be procured, and when it came, the company were all gone but three men [...] They were all gone before I got up next morning, and it was not until next light that I perceived I had lost a packet of six letters which I carried to as many gentlemen in Sutherland, and which prevented me effectually from making the tour of that large and little frequented county; these being rolled up in a piece of paper by themselves, and lodged in my breast pocket, some one of the gang has certainly carried off in expectation that it was something of more value. (pp. 88–89)

During a crossing to Stornoway, the vessel in which Hogg was a passenger was shaken by a whale. Having been wretchedly sick at sea, Hogg writes:

> I wished myself fairly on terra-firma again; I cared not on which side of the channel. —Early in the morning, all being quiet, I had wrapped myself in my shepherds plaid and was stretched among some cables

> on deck, busied in perusing Shakesperes monstrous tragedy of *Titus Andronicus*; and just when my feelings were wrought to the highest pitch of horror, I was alarmed by an uncommon noise as of something bursting, which I apprehended to be straight over me; when starting up with great emotion, I was almost blinded by a shower of brine; but how was I petrified with amazement, at seeing a huge monster in size like a house, sinking into the sea by the side of the vessel, something after the manner of a rope-tumbler; and so near me, that I could have struck him with a spear. (p. 118)

Alongside such personal accounts, and significant to an understanding of early-nineteenth-century travel, are Hogg's cultural observations. He remarks, for example, on the back-breaking work necessary to manufacture kelp on the isle of Harris and describes women's performance of waulking songs. He encounters difficulties in villages where only Gaelic is spoken and he 'could not get one word of English' (p. 113). He takes a critical view of construction of the Caledonian Canal, opines on the authenticity of Ossianic poetry, and notices the early effects of the Clearances.

Hogg's Highlands and cultures of landscape

A notable feature of Hogg's accounts is his engagement with the landscapes he encounters, which reveals seemingly contradictory modes in his representations of them. The first is termed by cultural geographers as landscape as a 'way of seeing', a visual phenomenon. In his depiction of the islands of Loch Maree, Hogg references the major aesthetic categories of the day: firstly, the mysterious, powerful, awe-inspiring 'sublime', as theorised by Edmund Burke, of the natural world in the Highlands; secondly, the smooth shapes and calm-inspiring presence of the 'beautiful'; and – though he doesn't use the word – the pictorial attributes of the 'picturesque' as theorised by William Gilpin:

> I was truly delighted with the view from these islands, although it consisted much more of the sublime than the beautiful. The old high house of Ardlair, faced us from a romantic little elevated plain, bounded on the north with a long ridge of perpendicular rock of a

> brown colour; and the low islands on which we stood, were finely contrasted with the precipitate shore's already mentioned on the one side, and the mountains of Sir Hector Mackenzie's forest on the other; whose pointed tops bored the firmament, and appeared of a colour, as white as the fairest marble. (1803, from Hogg's manuscript, p. 106)

He is an observer standing before a landscape and describing its attributes in terms that would have invoked for his readers the familiar aesthetic categories. The eighteenth-century and Romantic experience of the sublime involves landscape as a 'way of seeing' and interpretation – implying, according to cultural geographers, a somehow 'complete' landscape. This approach suits the Romantic dynamic of moving from describing a scene and then meditating or reflecting on it. In the following from Dorothy Wordsworth's *Recollections of a Tour Made in Scotland*, this dynamic is very clear:

> It rained [...] While we were walking forward, the road leading us over the top of a brow, we stopped suddenly at the sound of a half-articulate Gaelic hooting from the field close to us. It came from a little boy, whom we could see on the hill between us and the lake, wrapped up in a grey plaid. He was probably calling home the cattle for the night. His appearance was in the highest degree moving to the imagination: mists were on the hillsides, darkness shutting in upon the huge avenue of mountains, torrents roaring, no house in sight to which the child might belong; his dress, cry, and appearance all different from anything we had been accustomed to. It was a text, as William has since observed to me, containing in itself the whole history of the Highlander's life – his melancholy, his simplicity, his poverty, his superstition, and above all, that visionariness which results from a communion with the unworldliness of nature.[4]

Here the sublime and picturesque are completely contained – framed by the viewer's gaze, and this 'complete' landscape is literally read as a 'text'.

In Hogg, however, this approach to the landscape is not at all consistent. A recurrent pattern is the abrupt shift from this particular way of seeing – this painterly portrayal of landscape – to a different kind of visual description that evaluates landscape in terms of agricultural land management, as in the following passage that finds him looking at the towering, triangular bulk of Buchaille Etive Mhor from near the inn of Kingshouse on Rannoch Moor:

> It is one huge cone of misshapen and ragged rocks, entirely peeled bare of all soil whatever, and all scarred with horrible furrows, torn out by the winter torrents.

Immediately following this description of a sublime landscape, in language common to such experiences, comes an abrupt shift in tone:

> It is indeed a singular enough spot to have been pitched upon for a military stage and inn; where they cannot so much as find forage for a cow, but have their scanty supply of milk from a few goats, which brouze on the wide waste. There were however some very good black-faced wedder hoggs feeding in the middle of the black mount; but their colour, and condition, both bespoke them to have been wintered on a richer and lower pasture, and only to have been lately turned out to that range. (p. 77)

In its move from the sublime to the practical, Hogg's depiction reflects two divergent approaches to landscape, which can be elucidated by geographical theories. Raymond Williams famously wrote that 'the very idea of landscape implies separation and observation',[5] and cultural geographers identify the tensions between observing and inhabiting. But beyond assessing landscape in terms of a static view, *critical* geographers investigate 'styles of moving and looking, forms of land settlement and management, aesthetic ideals, exploratory discourse, scientific visual practices – as key elements within western visual cultures and within histories of travel, exploration, colonialism and imperialism'.[6] Offering an alternative view to the 'way-of-seeing' model, these geographers argue that landscapes are always 'in production; that is open to change, alteration and contestation'.[7] According to Don Mitchell, interpretive reading of a landscape falls short: it is the process of production that needs to be unmasked and understood.[8] With this in mind, the two parts of the Glencoe passage reflect Hogg as a Romantic writer gazing at and interpreting the sublime (a model of consumption) – and Hogg as an agricultural labourer encountering a landscape (in a state of 'production'). Mitchell argues further that landscape representations are exceptionally effective in erasing the social struggle that defines relations of work: 'the things that landscape tries to hide [...] are the relationships that go into its making.'[9] When the processes by which landscapes were created are hidden, seen and understood visually and aesthetically, landscapes 'work so as to make contingent sets of historical circumstances, and particular types of economic relations (for example relations between landowners and labourers), appear natural and normal'.[10] Insights from critical geographies help explain the abrupt shifts in Hogg's accounts, which offer a remarkable opportunity to see him operating on the cusp of these approaches. In reading Hogg's descriptions of landscape, the understanding of perspective is problematic; his gaze is decidedly non-aristocratic, yet influenced by his social position. The shifts in his focus and tone could be considered in terms of the ambivalences and ambiguities arising from his identity – as, on one hand, an aspiring professional writer and, on the other, a shepherd and mostly unsuccessful farmer – but also reflecting the particular circumstances of this period in his career. His rapidly shifting gaze is remarkable for its ability to take in both sides and from both perspectives. As a Romantic writer, he understands landscape aesthetically, as a 'complete construction in the eye of the beholder'. As an agricultural worker, he is also attuned to the ongoing production of landscape – for example, the effects of grazing – how it materially changes the land.

Beyond observing and reflecting on landscape or recognising its being in a state of production, Hogg's journeys demonstrate another way of thinking about landscape that draws on phenomenology. Here the stress is on 'direct, bodily contact with, and experience of, landscape', in which senses of self and landscape are together 'made and communicated, in and through lived experience'.[11] This throws light on Hogg's 'inhabiting' of the landscape in many passages of *Highland Journeys*, in which he dramatises movement within the landscape, whether by himself – as character – or by other 'characters', exemplified by the following anecdote of a scramble over the mountains, taken from Hogg's manuscript:

> Our guides [...] led us over rocks and precipieces, which on looking at I thought a goat could not have kept its feet: and had it not been

> owing to the nature of the stones, the surface of which was rough and crusty, it was impossible that we could have effected an escape; especially on such a day. I was in the greatest distress on account of the lady: the wind which was grown extremely rough, took such impression on her cloathes that I was really apprehensive that it would carry her off; and looked back several times with terror for fear that I should see her flying headlong toward the lake like a swan.
>
> It was however a scene worthy of these regions to see a lady of a most delicate form, and elegantly dressed in such a situation, climbing over the dizzy precipieces in a retrograde direction, and, after fixing one foot, hanging by both hands until she could find a small hold for the other. What would the most of your Edin,[r] ladies have done here my dear sir? (p. 106)

The guides having promised scenery which he 'should not see equalled in Scotland', Hogg ventures into the mountains of the Letterewe estate to view 'the black rock, or Craig-tullich', which he pronounced to be 'dreadful and grand beyond measure':

> It extends a whole English mile in length, along all which extent there is not a passage where a creature could pass, and it is so appropriately termed black that it appears wholly stained with ink, and its dreadful face, all of which can be seen from one view, everywhere distorted by dark slits, gaping and yawning chasms, with every feature of a most awful deformity, conveying to the attentive spectator ideas of horror which could scarcely be excelled by a glimpse of hell itself! (p. 108)

From here he writes the reader into the landscape:

> Should a merry companion choose, in order to enjoy the sight of the most profound and exquisite tumble, to give you an unmannerly push from the top of it, you might descend for nearly half a mile in the most straight line towards the centre of gravity. You might indeed happen to leave a rag of your coat on the point of one cliff, or a shoe, or your brains perhaps on another, but these are trifling circumstances.

> The worst thing attending it would be, that the pleasure arising from a view of your gracefully alighting would be entirely lost from the top, as you would appear of no greater magnitude than a forked bulrush. (p. 108)

And in yet another passage, the bodily experience of interacting with landscape produces an exhilarating destabilising of perspective:

> From a precipice near to this we had a view of a curious bason of very romantic dimensions, but in order to see it properly we were obliged to lie down full length on our breasts, and make long necks over the verge. I was afraid to trust my head, and ordered Mr Mackenzie to keep a firm hold of the tails of my coat, but before I could reach so far as to have a proper survey, I was obliged to roar out to be pulled back, my 'conscience having failed me', as I once heard a boy say in the same predicament. (p. 109)

These three modes of Hogg's engagement with landscape – as a 'way of seeing', in the process of production, and in terms of lived experience – recur in writing over the span of his career.

The shaping of Hogg's Highland perspective

Before Hogg made his first major advance into the publishing world with *The Mountain Bard* (1807), his poems had already appeared in the *Scots Magazine*, the *Edinburgh Magazine*, and the *Poetical Register*. Of these, the greatest influence on Hogg's literary career was the *Scots Magazine*, which published his first poem in 1794, followed by other poems and songs, 'letters on poetry', and Highland journeys. Significant for Hogg and other aspiring writers was the magazine's openness to a range of contributors, which helped to raise the confidence of labouring-class writers. It provided a nurturing environment for the development of new talent. The magazine's importance as a miscellany fed his vast range of interests and his multiple voices. It is clear from analysis of his journeys and early connection to the *Scots Magazine* that this relationship was to prove fundamental to his later constructions of the Highlands.

From Hogg's early impressions until his death in 1835, he wrote in a highly empathetic way about this region of Scotland, and the *Scots Magazine* certainly fuelled his interest. Topics relevant to the Highlands featured regularly in the magazine, and Hogg as an avid reader would have followed the debates. One issue playing out in the pages of the magazine and in Hogg's thinking about the Highlands was the Ossianic controversy, current at the time of Hogg's travels north. Nearly every number of the *Scots Magazine* addressed the authenticity of works attributed to the ancient bard Ossian and translated by James Macpherson from Gaelic into Anglicised, poetic prose. Leading up to the antiquarian David Laing's famous essay dismissing the authenticity of the Ossian poems, published by the Highland Society in 1805, the *Scots Magazine* ran a series of contributions insisting on their validity. After Laing's essay the magazine continued to publish arguments against his position, for example one by 'John Chisholm' in January 1802:

> I have not seen Mr Laing's Dissertation against the authenticity of Ossian's poems; but by such as have seen it, I am told it is not unanswerable. I cannot conceive how it would be otherwise; but I easily conceive that a very able genius may lose himself, when he ventures to treat a subject to which he is partly a stranger, while he may very easily dazzle others like himself, whose knowledge is inadequate to the subject, and cannot embrace every side of the question. It is a cause of very great regret, that error, at times, finds as able advocates as truth. [...] Whether MacPherson has made any changes in, or additions to any part of Ossian's poems, cannot be easily decided, till the whole original be published, which I am told is soon to take place: but that he is not the author of what I have seen of the original, I infer from the apparent impossibility of his having from himself, the expressions and ideas of the original; from the vast inferiority of the translation to the original, from his want of comprehension of the sense of the original, at times.[12]

Speaking as an authority on Gaelic, and citing specific instances in which Macpherson's translation does not quite match the intent of the original, Chisholm argues that the Ossianic material is authentic, but that Macpherson was a bad translator. Hogg's awareness of the many voices weighing in on the controversy is reflected in this response, writing from the Isle of Skye:

> It is not my intention to enter into this dispute because indeed after what I have heard from so many Creditable men of the Innumerable remains of this antient BARDS Works which continue to be practised by Mr McPherson in collecting them in every remote corner of the Mainland & Isles I deem the matter to be quite Indisputable' (p. 142, from an early transcript of Hogg's lost manuscript)

In other ways Hogg's journeys provide a snapshot of current debates surrounding the Highlands. In the *Scots Magazine* Hogg will have found arguments such as that by Thomas Telford (of Caledonian Canal fame) in his May 1803 essay 'On the Emigrations from the Highlands'. The arguments Hogg encountered here and in other periodicals certainly fed into his later story 'Emigration', published in *Chambers Edinburgh Journal* in 1833 (and reprinted in the Boston *Liberator* in 1835). In 1803, speaking as an expert on sheep, he observes:

> It is now a number of years since the system of sheep farming began to be embraced in Sky with avidity by such as farmed the most mountainous parts; it hath increased rapidly and the stocks of sheep bid fair in Time to acquire a Character equal to that which their Cattle hath long retained; Many of them are as yet a mixture of the antient breed and it will require some time to Extirpate them. But the Tacksmen spare no pains in procuring proper breeds of Hoggs and rams from the South; These thrive particularly well and the wedders rise to a superior bulk. (p. 140)

He expresses concern over the invasion of Lowland sheep-farming and observes the economic repercussions:

> The truth is, there are several low-country gentlemen getting into excellent bargains by their buying lands in that country, [...] and I cannot help having a desperate ill-will at them on that score. I cannot endure to hear of a Highland chieftain selling his patrimonial property,

> the cause of which misfortune I always attribute to the goodness of his heart, and the liberality of his sentiments; unwilling to drive off the people who have so long looked to him as their protector, yet whose system of farming cannot furnish them with the means of paying him one-fourth, and in some situations not more than a tenth of the value of his land; and as unwilling to let fall the dignity of his house, and the consequence amongst his friends, which his fathers maintained. Is not his case particularly hard, my dear sir? All things are doubled and tripled in their value, save his lands. His family – his retainers – his public burdens! These last being regulated by the old valuation, lie very hard upon him, and all must be scraped up among the poor, meagre tenants, in twos and threes of *silly* lambs, hens, and pounds of butter. (1803, from *The Scottish Review* [1888], p. 110)

Interestingly, perhaps reflecting his social position, he refrains from laying blame on Highland landlords who forced their tenants to emigrate.

During Hogg's life much changed in the Highlands. Following the Napoleonic wars, kelp ceased to be produced on Harris, which increased the level of poverty on the island. Further, Hogg's views evolved as the Clearances continued and their effects on the lives of the Highland people, particular those of his own social class, became even more evident. His views found expression in the novel *The Three Perils of Woman* (1823), written nearly twenty years after his Highland journeys – partly in answer to Walter Scott's linear, stadialist view of history in *Waverley* – and set in the aftermath of the Jacobite defeat in 1746. In a passage that traces the protagonist's harrowing journey through the devastated Highlands, following a trajectory common in Hogg's writing, landscape is filtered through human experience:

> The scene was such a mixture of the serene, the beautiful, the sublime, and the tremendous, as the wilds of Caledonia cannot equal. The broad and extensive loch of St Mari [...] lay stretched beneath her feet in burning gold; the numerous isles on its placid bosom were all covered with tall and hoary woods, whose origin seemed to have been coeval with the birth of time; the snowy sea-birds sailed the firmament above these, and, in the purple beams of the rising sun,

appeared like so many thousands of flaming meteors. Some of them swam softly on the surface of that glorious mirror, on whose illimitable downward bosom a thousand beauties and a thousand deformities were portrayed; others flew through the middle space, and aroused every slumbering echo among the rocks, with their shouts of joy; while others, again, traversed the upper stories of the air, so high, that they seemed emulous of singing their clamorous matin at the gates of the morning. The marble mountains of Applecross rose over against her, like three stupendous natural pyramids; a dense cloud covered all their intermedial columns and ravines, but their pure white tops appeared above it, like monuments hung between heaven and earth, or rather like thrones of the guardian angels of these regions, commissioned to descend thus far to judge of the wrongs of the land.

No eye could look on such a scene without conveying to the heart some exhilarating emotions; nor was it altogether lost on the jaundiced eye of our depressed and desolate wanderer. (p. 370)

The passage opens with Hogg's wide-angle lens taking in an awe-inspiring scene – described in terms of the sublime, the beautiful, and the picturesque – but by the end zooms in on the sad, human figure of Sally Niven. Like his protagonist Hogg was a Lowlander, but he sympathised with people who were oppressed in any way. It was offensive to him that in *Waverley* his friend Scott would leave out crucial events of the 1745–46 Jacobite rising, and particularly the reprisals that the Hanoverian armies, under the Duke of Cumberland, took against the rebels following Culloden. Hogg pulls no punches. Rather than being protected from the human disaster of Culloden, or diverted by its representation in buildings (the sacking of the estate of Tully Veolan in *Waverley*), the reader is led into the heart of the devastation. Davie directs Sally and Duncan to some graves: '[H]e came to the bodies of a woman and two boys, half roasted. She seemed to have been their mother, and to have been endeavouring to cover them with her own body to preserve them from the flames' (p. 366). This is followed by an even more horrifying account of a Hanoverian military leader laughing about watching his victims squirm and suffer. But Hogg refuses to let the reader turn away from these atrocities: they are meant to be raked up and exposed, not buried and ignored. Hogg's novel ends not with reconciliation, marriage, and rebuilding of the damaged castle, but with the terrible outcomes following the Jacobite defeat, the repercussions for ordinary people from both sides of the Highland line. The narrator ends with Sally Niven and her baby girl, the product of her marriage to a Jacobite,

> lying stretched together in the arms of death, pale as the snow that surrounded them, and rigid as the grave-turf on which they had made their dying bed. Is there human sorrow on record like this that winded up the devastations of the Highlands? (p. 407)

Powerfully evoking direct, bodily experience of landscape, Hogg dramatises this tragic inhabiting of – and merging with – the frozen Highland ground: a poignant indictment of the human loss resulting from this turbulent period of Scotland's history.

At one point in Hogg's 1803 journey, having been shown where, post-Culloden, the fleeing Prince Charles Edward Stuart had hidden at Loch Arkaig, he remarks, 'While traversing the scenes, where the patient sufferings of the one party, and the cruelties of the other were so affectingly displayed, I could not help being a bit of a Jacobite in my heart, and blessing myself that in those days I did not exist, or I had certainly been hanged' (p. 81, from Hogg's manuscript). Looking back from *The Three Perils of Woman*, it is clear that Hogg's Highland journeys made a profound impression on the man and writer he later became.

Notes

1. The editor drew from all the available sources of Hogg's accounts of his 1802, 1803, and 1804 journeys into the Highlands; nonetheless, the text is incomplete: there is still a gap in both the 1802 and 1803 journeys. Furthermore, as the editor observes, 'For every surviving portion of the text of *Highland Journeys* there is only one early authority: in no instance is there both a manuscript source and an early printing, and no part of the text was printed more than once during Hogg's lifetime. This means that, for each surviving portion of *Highland Journeys*, there is only one possible copy-text'. See James Hogg, *Highland Journeys*, ed. Hans de Groot, Stirling/South Carolina Research Edition of the Collected Works of James Hogg (Edinburgh: Edinburgh University Press, 2010), p. 254. All references are to this edition.
2. Pam Perkins (ed.), *Francis Jeffrey's Highland and Continental Tours* (Penrith: Humanities-Ebooks, 2009).

3. James Hogg, 'Directions to Mr Cadell for a five day's tour through the Highlands of Scotland', in *Highland Journeys*, pp. 249-49.
4. Dorothy Wordsworth, *Recollections of a Tour Made in Scotland*, ed. Carol Kyros Walker (New Haven and London: Yale University Press, 1997), p. 114.
5. Raymond Williams, *The City and the Country* (London: Chatto and Windus, 1985), p. 126.
6. John Wylie, *Landscape* (London and New York: Routledge, 2007), pp. 95-96.
7. Wylie, *Landscape*, p. 106.
8. Don Mitchell, 'Landscape and surplus value: the making of the ordinary in Brentwood, CA', *Environment and Planning D: Society and Space* 12.1 (1994), pp. 7-30 (p. 9).
9. Don Mitchell, *Cultural Geography: A Critical Introduction* (Oxford: Basil Blackwell, 2000), pp. 103-04.
10. Wylie, *Landscape*, p. 105.
11. Wylie, *Landscape*, p. 141.
12. 'John Chisholm', 'On the authenticity of Ossian's Poems', *Scots Magazine* 64 (January, 1802), pp. 39-43 (pp. 41, 43).

6. The *Noctes Ambrosianae* and the Highlands

DAVID MANDERSON

The nineteenth-century Briton often referred to himself as living in 'the age of periodicals'. Across the British Isles, journals like the *Examiner*, the *Quarterly Review*, the *Edinburgh Magazine*, *Fraser's*, *The Eclectic Review* and the *Spectator* and a host of other publications had huge readerships and influence. The journals are less studied than they once were, although academic interest in them is now maybe making a comeback.[1] Francis Jeffrey's reviews and the essays of Hazlitt, Hunt and Lamb have mostly disappeared from school and university curricula and the power of the publications they wrote for has largely been forgotten. But the ways in which these publications reported and sometimes created the news, critical debates, current affairs, entertainment and popular debates of their day is still worthy of study. Their influence on literature was direct, not just because writers and poets made a sort of living from publishing in their pages, but because of the way the journalism affected the literary work and vice versa. They were the popular media of their day – the television, radio, newspapers and social networks – providing a constant stream of information and many different kinds of creative endeavour that sat alongside literary writing, imitating it, drawing from it and in many other ways affecting it and being affected by it.

In Scotland, as ever, the field was different. *The Edinburgh Review*, a Whig-leaning publication suffused with enlightenment values and regarded more highly than any other for its critical opinions, held sway. 'This will never do', its editor Francis Jeffrey famously wrote of Wordsworth's *The Excursion*.[2] The *Edinburgh*'s pre-eminence and its Whig stance, however, were challenged when *Blackwood's Edinburgh Magazine*, which had Tory sympathies, was relaunched after a shaky start in 1818. '*Maga's*' success was assured with the controversial publication of the *Chaldee Manuscript* in its first reconstituted issue, a long poem in mock-biblical verses describing the conflict between the two magazines and their rival supporters, alongside vicious attacks on Leigh Hunt and 'The Cockney School' of London poets by the cryptically named 'Z', who was John Gibson Lockhart, one of the new magazine's leading lights. Where the *Edinburgh* wrote reviews that were regarded as the height of criticism, *Blackwood's* took a different tack. It published literary and artistic opinion and a huge amount of other material, but it thrived especially on 'personality', meaning gossip, scandal and satire.[3]

The original title of this talk was to be 'The Edinburgh Journals and the Highlands'. However, the difficulty that always surfaces whenever someone tries to work from these sources soon emerges. It's also one reason why this area of Scottish writing remains something of a neglected field. It's too big, too immense a task. The Blackwood archive alone at the National Library of Scotland in Edinburgh, described with tongue-in-cheek gallows humour as 'substantial', documents two centuries of its publishing house's affairs, everything from notebooks of accounts to files of payments to contributors. It took ten years for David Finkelstein, who has specialised in that area, to catalogue it,[4] and that is just one of the journals in question. But investigating these archives for their views on the Highlands is still a useful task because of the way these journals dominated topical affairs[5] and even shaped the minds of their readers in the early nineteenth century.

'The *Noctes Ambrosianae* and the Highlands' is a more sensible topic, not because it's easier (it is, but not by much) but because it's possible. The *Noctes* was a series of thirty-nine imaginary dialogues that ran in *Blackwood's* from 1822 to 1834. It featured real people who were semi-fictionalised as characters taking part in conversations which were wild, eccentric, exaggerated and often deliberately ludicrous, but at other times included reports on topical affairs, criticism of contemporary art and literature and political opinions or invective. Conversation itself was a fashion in early nineteenth-century Edinburgh,[6] its chattering classes chatting in accents that were modelled on London voices but mingled with Scots, increasingly the language of the lower orders safely left behind in the Old Town, but still spoken and used, if with increasing mockery, by the middle classes. It was the age of declamation. The stylishness and flourish with which you said something was more important than what you said,[7] and in the *Noctes*, which are written as dramas, the driving force was the dialogue. In these episodes, which purport to be records of conversations faithfully copied down by the journalist Gurney[8] who is hiding in a cupboard during the whole series, we can sometimes hear language as it was said rather than written, though a great deal of literary bombast goes on too.

The identities of the people the characters were based on were disguised by pseudonyms, but often these pointed to the real person. The Ettrick Shepherd, for example, could only have been James Hogg, who wore a plaid everywhere he went in Edinburgh as a proud marker of whom and what he was, while the identity of The Opium Eater needed no explanation (De Quincey's famous memoir of addiction was published in 1821). The other characters were also *Blackwood's* writers, among them John Wilson, now forgotten but in his day famous under his own name and his alter ego of Christopher North, one of the magazine's most famous creations and in real life the outrageously incompetent professor of Moral Philosophy at Edinburgh;[9] Lockhart, now also forgotten but a fine author in this own right and later Walter Scott's biographer and son-in-law; and many others including the journalist Walter Maginn (Ensign O'Doherty), David Moir ('Delta') and Robert Sym (Timothy Tickler). At first some of these identities were fluid and interchangeable, for the very good reason that *Blackwood*'s contents were so inflammatory. Lockhart and Wilson fled Edinburgh and Hogg thought it best to return to the Borders after the launch of the *Chaldee*, so thunderous was the storm of protest that broke out over Edinburgh following its publication, while William Blackwood – who'd had more than a hand in encouraging his writers to sensationalise the article – stayed at his desk sweating it out through libel suits and complaints.[10] His defence was to blame the others. It had all been his Editor's fault. He had succeeded in halting the piece only to have his Editor restore it to the edition.[11] The *Blackwood's* gang would go playing the games of anonymous authorship and Guess-the-Editor in *Maga* and the *Noctes* for many years (an example of the kind of editorial irresponsibility Hogg imitates, with devastating effect, in the first part of *The Confessions*), and they teased and swapped identities so effectively that readers were kept guessing for the entire length of the series about who exactly controlled the content of the magazine. Sometimes Wilson was to be accused of it or to claim it, sometimes Lockhart, and sometimes even, to the hilarity of the other characters, the Shepherd.[12] But the real editor of *Maga* took care never to appear in its pages.

After the *Noctes* had been running for some years the fictional characters became more famous than the people they were based on and established in the national consciousness to such an extent that people believed they were real. The real Ettrick Shepherd was assumed to have the feral vigour and wildness that was attributed to him in *Blackwood's*,[13] while 'The Scorpion', Lockhart, so-called because his criticism stung so deeply, was to carry his reputation for scything attacks with him to London where he edited the *Quarterly Review*. Wilson was soon writing openly as Christopher North beyond the *Noctes* and by the time of his death was better known by that name than his own. Hugely successful in his time, eventually touted, not least by himself, as the true successor to the mantle of Scottish literature, in a uniquely powerful position because of his status as the gatekeeper of taste in both academia and journalism, and a charlatan in both, he probably did more harm to Scottish letters than any other individual.[14] His statue, three along from the Scott Monument, is probably the least known on Princes Street.[15] He was to need as much anonymity as he could get in the years after his death.

Today we can see the *Noctes* as a sort of soap opera, one partly based on real life. It was a mixture of the high and the low, flights of high-flown prose mingled with high-spirited games and malicious gossip. It used a familiar set of characters in known settings which could change from one instalment to the next but inevitably returned to the same location, although the cast did take occasional holidays in the country, to hunting-lodges or camps.[16] But the conversations were almost always situated in the inn from which they took their name, Ambrose's Tavern, a rough, country-looking sort of place which stood on Gabriel's Lane where Registry House stands now, just round the corner from Blackwood's shop at 17 Princes Street. Later, it moved to newer premises on Picardy Place. The *Blackwood's* writers would assemble there for meetings or after a hard day's work putting that month's edition to bed (as a monthly rather than a quarterly publication, William Blackwood had committed his team to almost impossible amounts of work), and it was claimed that there was a more than a passing resemblance between the real nights at Ambrose's and their fictional counterparts.[17] In its earliest years the series was a joint effort with Lockhart and Maginn leading the way, but from 1825 it fell mostly into the hands of a single author, although others had a hand in the composition. That writer was John Wilson, who wrote whole numbers with enormous but cloudy and often violently chaotic energy, while James Hogg, despite many fall-outs with Blackwood, was sometimes still employed to 'fill out' the Shepherd's speeches. It must count as one of the most patronising tasks ever allocated to a writer, since the speeches Hogg helped flesh out were supposed to be by him although he probably had no control over their content. But Hogg's relationship with Blackwood was full of humiliation, and there were many times he was to accuse the publisher of betraying him.[18]

Maga and the *Noctes* played a teasing game with identity in more ways than one. The *Chaldee Manuscript*, which was vicious in its criticism of recognisable people, wasn't attributed to anybody, though it's now known that Wilson and Lockhart composed the greater part of it after Hogg started it.[19] The guiding hand towards sensationalism, though, was always Blackwood's. Disagreements were deliberately created and stirred up.[20] Puffs for new books published by his new company (he moved quickly into book publishing after launching *Maga*) would suddenly crop up in the *Noctes* conversations alongside stinging criticism of work written by rivals. A member of the circle, usually Hogg, would suddenly be attacked in the magazine by one of the other members, disguising himself behind a new nickname.[21] In the *Noctes* conversations and in *Maga's* critical articles everything was fair game except matters of class, which were consistently reinforced in spiteful attacks.[22] The *Blackwood's* writers and especially John Wilson, outwardly boastful but in reality deeply anxious about their own breeding, were always on edge and always unpredictable, aiming squarely at their victims' self-esteem, blending fact and fiction in a dangerous, hurtful, changeable and highly entertaining publication, one that kept the reader guessing and which sold in huge numbers throughout Britain.

The *Noctes* writers also flirted with identity in another way, their national one, partly seeking it, partly questioning it and partly making it up. *Maga* took an oppositional stance to the *Edinburgh Review* on all things. Against the *Edinburgh's* Enlightenment views it was Romantic, against the *Edinburgh's* Whig politics it was Tory, against the *Edinburgh's* controlled, balanced and rational voice it was provocative and sensual, a celebration of the appetites, especially in the *Noctes*. It was a miscellany, a cacophony of voices rather than one, containing in addition to the nights at Ambrose's a vast mixture of factual articles, reviews and 'tales' or short stories, often Gothic. In much of this content, sometimes with a subversive intent, there was a fascination with Scottish identity, its past, present and future, a search for it and sometimes a need to disinter it.[23] Inside this Tory flagship, and at odds with its grandiose imperialist declarations,[24] were quests for other, deeper things. The past, embodied by the fad for antiquarianism, was mysterious and fragmented. It had been lost and must be pieced together again, remade for a new era. Its traces might be discovered in 'found' texts that offered only partial explanations.[25] This was linked to an interest in Scots as a language, also at odds with *Maga's* official 'voice' (used mostly in its critical articles), which was pompous, belligerent and brayingly English. The magazine contained much poetry in Scots and prose fiction that centred on the uncertain and often deluded viewpoint of a character, a psychological study of madness or hallucination from a protagonist's point of view, in other words an unreliable narrator.[26] All these elements were to find their ultimate expression in Hogg's *Confessions*, ironically the greatest of Blackwoodian texts because it was written as a response to and reclamation of identity from the *Blackwood's* gang,[27] and not published by William Blackwood. This fluid interest in national identity was to disappear as the magazine grew respectable, and by the 1840s its views had set into imperialist stone. For the rest of its long life (it finally closed in 1981) it was more closely associated with empire than any other publication, eventually so synonymous with it that, it was claimed, a copy could be found in every colonial mess hall in the British Empire.[28] The fact that this quest for something Scottish which was lost and had to be retrieved from neglect directly contradicted one of *Maga's* core principles wasn't at all unusual. Contradiction was one of the magazine's characteristics.

Television writers talk today of 'the world' they create in long-running series, which is the history, customs, manners and location of wherever they set their drama, everything that adds up to the universe they want their viewers to enter. The *Noctes* writers did the same. The incidents described in the episodes are contemporary to the real world and are meant to carry on into it. They inhabit the same narrative time as topical events, openly refer to them and frequently intermingle with them.[29] This fictional world swirls with restless energy, less concerned with promoting any one view than constantly changing. It does not have one tone or voice but delights in multiple voices and contrasting accents, a dialogical dichotomy that veers between two extremes, the first a form of high English which has probably only ever been spoken in New Town Edinburgh, spoken and embodied by the elderly and infirm Christopher North, the other rich, earthy and vital, the Scots whose voice and physicality are the Shepherd's:

> (APRIL 1829)
> Scene 1 – The Snuggery. Time – Eight o'clock. The Union-Table, with Tea and Coffee Pots … Pickled Salmon &c. &c. &c. A How-towdie whirling before the fire on a large basin of mashed Potatoes.
> (Enter) NORTH *and* SHEPHERD
> SHEPHERD: This I ca' comfort, sir. Everything within oursel – nae need tae ring a bell the leeve-long night – nae openin o' cheepin', nae shuttin o' clashin doors – nae trampin o' waiters across the carpet wi creakin shoon – or stumblin, clumsy coofs, to the great spillin o' gravy – but a' things, eatable and uneatable, either hushed into a cozy calm, or –
> NORTH: Now light, James, the lamp of the Bachelor's Kitchen with Tickler's card, and in a quarter of an hour, minus five minutes, you shall scent and see such steaks!
> SHEPHERD: Only look at the towdie, sir, how she swings sae granly roun by my garters, after the fashion o' a planet … See till the fat dreep-dreepin intil the ashet o' mashed potawtoes, oilifying the crushed brown intil a mair deleicious richness o' mixed vegetable and animal matter! As she swings slowly twirlin roun', I really canna say, sir, for I dinna ken, whether baney back or fleshy breast be the maist temptin! Sappy baith!
> NORTH: Right, James – baste her – baste her – don't spare the flour
> …

Consistently, the *Noctes* uses this contrast between mannered speech and the vernacular, characters whose psychological drives and physical appetites are to the fore, and a sense of a contested past and vigorous present to make a space where their playfulness is acted out.

To finish this overview, the *Noctes* series makes a good case-study for the journals as a whole because as a partly fictional, partly real text, because they are as much journalism as literature (and blur the boundaries between them), and because they were written at great speed, we can get more of an insight into the thinking of the day than with more polished forms. The

THE *NOCTES AMBROSIANAE* AND THE HIGHLANDS

Noctes is the early nineteenth-century Edinburgh middle class at play, letting its sometimes less than dignified hair down for our entertainment. They tell us what people thought in language that reveals much of their attitudes and relationships, and reveal in the gaps between the way they see themselves and what they did more of the real state of affairs than they ever intended. Or, as Margaret Oliphant said in her admiring history of Blackwood's publishing house, the *Noctes* '... had a large, unacknowledged, perhaps uncomprehended, share in the mental training of our fathers'.[31]

*

So what, then, of the *Noctes* and The Highlands? What does this immense, topical, driven text, which seems to have had such an effect on nineteenth-century thought and arguably represents the outlook of the ruling Scottish elite, tell us about Lowland views of the Highlands?

Close scrutiny shows that references to the Highlands are sparse to say the least. Compared to, say, the Borders country they are hardly there at all. It is the area around Ettrick, Selkirk and Peebles that figures in the imagination of the writers as 'the country', the rural place where the city dwellers once lived,[32] and where their poorer relations still cling on. There is some familiarity with a few Highland place-names and supposedly Highland customs, and some awareness of Highlanders, but they are mentioned only in passing. A party of gentlemen go fishing on Loch Awe. The Shepherd, North and Bronte (North's dog) dance a gleeful Highland jig. '"You're marvellous at the Heelan' fling, sir!"' shouts the Shepherd. '"A' the caudies are Highlanders"' he drawls on another occasion, meaning the Edinburgh coach drivers.

There are few references of any substance in the *Noctes* to the Highlands as a real place. There is a description of a storm in Tomintoul, known then as now as an isolated and remote place often cut off from the rest of the world, by the Shepherd, causing North to remark that that is where the majority of the ne'er-do-well's, broken clansmen and vagabonds hide out.[33] There is an account of a whistle-stop tour from Perthshire across Rannoch Moor, then down to Inveraray and Arrochar and finally back to Glasgow by the character called Timothy Tickler. The Highland Societies, so associated with 'improvement' – which is to say the Clearances – are mentioned with approval. The General Assembly's scheme to build schools and kirks and to distribute Bibles throughout the Highlands is praised by both North and the Shepherd. Where Highlanders appear at all they are labelled with the word 'poor' in both senses of the word. Their pitiable poverty is the most striking thing about them, and often the only thing said. Two boatmen employed to row travellers across lochs are as 'lean as laths'. "'But oh! my dear North,'" Tickler shouts as this brief aside comes to an end, swiftly changing the subject, "'what grouse-soup at Dalnacardoch!'"[34]

In fact the Highlands appear in detail in only four incidents in the whole of this giant collection. The first is a report by Timothy Tickler of a hunting trip to a shooting lodge in Perthshire.[35] There, his servant attacked by an eagle, Tickler first shoots it then strips off his clothes to retrieve its corpse from the loch. Returning to the shore he pulls a giant pike from the water and kills it too, and then pots a red deer. Sending his servant for his flask of Glenlivet (there is a great deal of Glenlivet drunk in the *Noctes*), he finds his clothes have been stolen by a girl, who tries to run as he pursues her, dropping his clothes and then her own petticoat before disappearing into the forest, her long yellow hair 'streaming behind her like a banner'.

The second is where the Shepherd describes how he once wrestled with a mermaid in Skye during a visit there (the real James Hogg had travelled to the island in 1802).[36] Resting in a cave after swimming off the coast, his clothes hung up around him to dry, he hears a dream-like and seductive female voice and suddenly finds himself in the grip of a female form with a face like a boiled cod, trying to kiss and consume him. He starts chanting the Lord's Prayer until he and his seductress suddenly tumble down the rocks, and he finds himself alone in the cave again, with just the strong smell of the sea everywhere around him.

The third is the Shepherd again, this time lost in the 'moor o' Rannoch' in sweltering heat, so thirsty he fears he might die of it. He stumbles among 'the hags [...] howked out o' the black moss by demons', and is brought to the very edge of death by the heat 'o' dyin nature' before, like an explorer in the desert, stumbling over a life-saving pool.[37]

And the fourth is the Shepherd once more (the Shepherd is the most adventurous of the *Noctes* characters), this time telling one of his tall tales (he is regularly mocked by the others for his 'lees'), where, in the Cairngorms above Loch Avon, he is lowered into an eagle's nest. Two eaglets in it try to fight him off, and the parent birds attack him from the sky at the same moment. In defence he throws his jacket over the eaglets so that they fall to the river below and drown, distracting the adult birds long enough for him to escape up the same rope ladder he was lowered down on.[38]

What can we make of these isolated incidents and the fact that they are so occasional in such a lengthy document? And what do any contrasts between these passages and the rest of the *Noctes* tell us about the writer's (Wilson's) attitudes towards the Highlands?

The slaughter of wildlife is one striking thing. It doesn't just happen in the *Noctes* version of the Highlands. Other episodes of the series describe game hunting in other parts of Scotland such as the Borders. But there is perhaps a special relish here in the way the spoils are described: the killing of birds, hares, fish, deer and of course the eagle. (Later, Tickler describes how the party cooked and ate the great bird.) The size and strength of the wildlife is particular to the Highlands. The *Noctes* always exaggerate, but here the proportions are gargantuan – a twelve foot pike and the huge attacking eagle. The real *Blackwood's* writers, especially Wilson and Hogg, loved hunting and fishing and every booted sport (though Wilson and the Shepherd had entirely different attitudes to it), but in the *Noctes* it is as if the Highlands provide an especially bountiful larder for their bloodthirsty fun, one that is mythic, unnatural, beyond the boundaries of the possible. Contrast this slaughter and the feasting which follows it with the implied plight of the girl who tries to steal Tickler's clothes.

The fact that all the settings are in the wilderness is the second telling factor. There are no other people in these incidents except in the one where Tickler kills the eagle, and the local girl with the yellow hair is only glimpsed as she runs. The Highlands, where they appear in any detail, are represented as deserted, devoid of human life though full of moors and large estates where game abounds. Where human beings do congregate, as in the Tomintoul episode, it is seen as a sure sign of unrest and social chaos. When any Highlanders appear elsewhere, it is in pairs or as isolated individuals noticed only for a second, just long enough to remark on their destitution.

There is a strong flavour of the exotic and indeed the erotic in the Highlands incidents. The *Noctes* are full of appetites, mostly those of eating and drinking, but it is only in the magically Othered space of the Highlands where this kind of sensuality is unleashed. The transference of physicality is always to the Shepherd. The real James Hogg suffered greatly at the hands of his fine *Blackwood's* friends, always the butt of their jokes for his accent, background, mannerisms and high spirits, but the site of their most brutal criticism was his body.[39] Physical mockery is obviously a common element of caricature, but there were other reasons for the transference of the physical by the emerging middle class onto the lower orders, the burial of sensuality in the body of an Other. It must be immediately added that, possibly for this reason, the Shepherd is undoubtedly the best thing in the *Noctes*. The text lights up where he appears, becoming comical, physical and vigorous, and dulls when he is absent, as every later commentator on the series acknowledged.[40] When James Hogg, finally exasperated with William Blackwood's constant double-dealing over publication and payment, demanded that his imitation be removed from the series, the *Noctes* lost most of its vitality, energy and sense of fun. When Hogg and Blackwood had made up their differences and the Shepherd reappeared, he was welcomed back with shouts of celebration from the other characters.[41] In the magical Highlands and Islands, where what is not permissible in other places can happen, the erotic is explicit and involves the Shepherd. His naked wrestle with the Mermaid is clear, while Tickler's pursuit of the girl with the streaming yellow hair, who drops her petticoat as she runs, is full of resonances.

There is a strong spirit of adventure in the Highlands. That is also true of other parts of the *Noctes*, where the gentlemen often praise courage and boldness as they help themselves to another slice of beef or draught of claret, but in the Highland incidents this is coupled with a feeling of exploration, of danger, of pitting oneself against an alien environment. On Rannoch Moor the Shepherd's expedition is openly compared to an African one, while Tickler pits himself against the river and the wildlife in the Perthshire incident. The Shepherd's venture into the eagle's nest reads more like an incident from Jules Verne or H. G. Wells than anything else, a science-fiction intrusion by a wanderer into another planet.

There is the presence of the supernatural. The incident in the Skye cave might have been real or it might have been a dream – the Shepherd isn't sure. The girl in the Tickler incident might not be real, but a spirit, and the aggression of the eagles, the unlikely drought in Rannoch, and the size of the wildlife seem fantastical too. There are many descriptions in the *Noctes* of contact with the world of ghosts,[42] with the spiritual or the supernatural, usually from the Shepherd, but they are more gothic and familiar, and usually for comic effect. The strangeness of the Highlands, its difference from the normal rules of the rest of the known world, where even the rules of the fantastic are of another order, are brought out. Hogg was the only one of the group to have ever visited the Western Isles, and unlike his colleagues he travelled in the Highlands for reasons of work or to see and understand the local culture. In other words, he visited to discover, not to admire, and with the intention of becoming part of whatever he found. Wilson and his *Noctes* band travelled in the Highlands only to exploit it in imagination or in reality, without ever seeing what was really there.

And females make a rare appearance in these incidents in the *Noctes*. Women do appear as part of the rest of the text's lively life, as Edinburgh fishwives, bluestockings, servants, gentlewomen and society beauties. But in the Highland incidents two females of different sorts appear without explanation and just as suddenly vanish, materialising from an Other world, one a direct portrayal of female desire and the other with its connotations. The mermaid is naked, desirable and changeable, an obscenely shaped hybrid threatening to a man, his equal, and dangerous. The girl who flees Tickler dropping her petticoat is a clear symbol of transferred desire. And in the Rannoch Moor incident, the 'hags', meaning peat-hags, carry familiar associations with witches.

Wilderness, natives barely scratching a living from the land, the tantalising promise of forbidden desire, the dangerous, threatening female, the presence of the fantastic and the bizarre, a sense of free adventure and the tastes of the exotic. It's a familiar picture of colonialism, and one that is deeply embedded in the viewpoint of the *Noctes*. There is no Scottish writer who trumpeted the principles of empire more than Wilson. Dangerously unpredictable, physically huge, a bully capable of brutality towards both his friends and his enemies and sudden collapses into quivering fear, he was considered not quite sane by his peers,[43] or possibly addicted to laudanum.[44] Whatever the cause of his unstable 'personality', he above all the Blackwood's writers aligned *Maga* and the *Noctes* with colonialist power and the assumption of might as right. Like all imperial aggressors, his pompousness and self-importance was backed up by military threat. And there can be no doubt that this is the dominant view of the Highlands in the *Noctes*.

For anyone who feels that making this claim is pushing things on so little evidence, ultimately the most telling factor is the lack of the Highlands in the text. Except for the glimpse of the two boatmen, the girl who steals Tickler's clothes and one or two other tiny details, there is no mention of the existence of Highlanders in the Highlands, never mind an awareness of the reality of their conditions, in the whole length of this immense, popular and influential series. In fact if we could draw a mental map of Scotland as it seems to have existed in the minds of these nineteenth-century Edinburgh gentlemen, a circle Hogg was never admitted to, it would look as if mist had fallen over half of the country we call Scotland. There would be clear focus around Edinburgh and the Borders, and then the further the map extended from that centre the softer and more opaque its focus would become. At the edges of the Highlands we would still be able to make out some places such as the Dalnacardoch estate in Perthshire where Tickler kills the eagle, but as we move further west we would be able to discern only glimmers of places shining through, peaks and troughs, the mountains, the cave in Skye, legendary creatures, fabulously huge birds with human traits – no mental map to a real place, no real knowledge, no interest. And of the far north and the outer islands we see nothing at all.

The *Blackwood's* group did not just colonialise the Highlands. They colonialised far more than that. There are descriptions of tenements in Glasgow that display the same lack of care about real conditions, if more knowledge.[45] And it wasn't only the Highlands that were being cleared. The Borders were emptying of their people at the same time on the very doorstep of the Edinburgh journal-writers, and they showed no concern about that either. In fact the area of Yarrow, from St Mary's Loch to Galashiels and Selkirk, is described again and again in terms of its sublimity, overlooking the deserted nature and emptiness of the place.[46] But perhaps the greatest example of colonialism in the *Noctes* is James Hogg himself, his personality, his language, his class, his lifelong work and his ambitions appropriated by others who called themselves his friends, especially Wilson who had once been his protégé. Made into a comic buffoon, held up to ridicule to thousands of readers and ultimately better known by his double than by the many books he wrote, he was to say that sometimes he seemed no longer to know himself.[47] It was this process that he turned back on itself, and saved himself from, with the most courageous and controlled act of his life, which was the writing of *The Confessions*.

The work of the *Noctes* writers, who were in the business of appropriating Highland symbols (the kilt, the Highland fling, Glenlivet) and making new myths (the mermaid, the giant wildlife) while at the same moment destroying the area's culture and wildlife, and failing to show the real plight of Highland people and openly supporting those who cleared them, can be viewed as a window into the minds of those who stood by while the Clearances took place, or who took part in them. The *Noctes* began in the same year as George IV's visit to Edinburgh with all its paraphernalia of Highland chiefs, tartans, archers and so on carefully engineered into a pageant to display the splendour of the monarchy and Scotland's place in relation to it. Some have seen this as a piece of colonialist chicanery by Walter Scott, but it was more an attempt to forge a Scottish identity by making a bridge between Highland and Lowland, within the United Kingdom and its empire or not. Scott's attempt to create a national identity at home and abroad succeeded to such an extent that the symbols he put together lasted as a brand until today. In Hogg's case, condemned as he was to be associated with the *Blackwood's* group for reasons of class, identity was retrieved through an imaginative leap that brought about one of the most original pieces of work in Scottish literature. Wilson and Hogg were concerned with recovery of something important that was being lost, and both found it. In John Wilson's case, a writer who got everything he wanted, far beyond what he had earned, superficially brilliant and energetic though his journalism can be, the mask slips, and there, unlike Scott or Hogg, we can see in its fullest and most arrogant expression the indifference, complacency and incompetence that so brutalised the Highlands. Wilson, appointed to his post in Edinburgh through political machinations, so incapable of scholarship that he had to beg lecture notes from his friend David Blair, which he read to his students in the lecture theatres from jottings on the backs of envelopes, slapdash, inconsistent and careless in his journalism, was everything that characterised Lowland exploitation of the Highlands. Hogg skewers these attitudes and William Blackwood's greedy and scheming editing in the character of the Editor in *The Confessions*, the powerful man who seeks to explain and contain the words of the tortured Robert Wringhim without ever understanding them, always certain of his conclusions while being vague on facts, and indifferent to the implications and results of his false reasoning. His lack of interest in the real Robert Wringhim exactly echoes *Blackwood's* lack of interest in the Highlands.

If the *Noctes* did have much to do with the formation of the thoughts of powerful men, men who were to have such an influence on what came later, we can see in them some of the reasons for what was happening in the real Highlands then and later. In the world created in the *Noctes* by the new owners of empire, for all the series' huge range of topical issues and debates, there was to be no place for the real Highlands, still less for the people who lived there.

Notes

1. John Strachan (ed.), *Blackwood's Magazine: Selections from Maga's Infancy 1817–25* (London: Pickering and Chatto, 4 vols, 2006), pp. xi–xiii.
2. Francis Jeffrey, Review of Wordsworth's *The Excursion*, *Edinburgh Review* 24, November 1014, pp. 1–4.
3. Karl Miller, *Electric Shepherd* (London: Faber, 2003), p. 158.
4. David Finkelstein, *The House of Blackwood: Author-Publisher Relations in the Victorian Era* (University Park: Pennsylvania State University Press, 2005), p. vii.
5. Miller, *Electric Shepherd*, pp. 179–81.
6. Jon Mee, *Conversable Worlds: Literature, Contention, and Community* (Oxford: Oxford UP, 2011), pp. 12–13.
7. Barton Swaim, *Scottish Men of Letters and the New Public Sphere, 1802–34* (Lewisburg: Bucknell University Press, 2009), p. 168.
8. John Wilson, *Noctes Ambrosianae*, ed. J. F. Ferrier (Edinburgh and London: William Blackwood, 4 vols, 1855–6), vol. II.
9. David Daiches, *Literary Essays* (Edinburgh: Oliver & Boyd, 1966), pp. 122–31.
10. Margaret Oliphant, *William Blackwood and his Sons: Annals of a Publishing House* (Edinburgh and London: William Blackwood, 3 vols, 1897), vol. I, pp. 131–35.
11. Oliphant, *William Blackwood and his Sons*, vol. I, p. 150.
12. Miller, *Electric Shepherd*, p. 261.
13. Ian Duncan, 'Hogg's Body' in *Studies in Hogg and his World* 9, 1998, p. 2, www.english.stir.ac.uk/documents/HoggsBody.pdf (accessed 28 February 2014).
14. Andrew Nash, *Kailyard and Scottish Literature* (Amsterdam: Rodopi, 2007), p. 24.
15. Miller, *Electric Shepherd*, p. 128.
16. *Blackwood's Magazine 1817–25*, vol. 3, p. xi.
17. Miller, *Electric Shepherd*, p. 119.
18. Miller, *Electric Shepherd*, p. 192.
19. James Hogg, *Altrive Tales featuring a 'Memoir of the Author's Life'* (Edinburgh: Edinburgh University Press, 2005), p. 44–45.
20. *Blackwood's Magazine 1817–25*, vol. 5, pp. xiv–xv.

21. Miller, *Electric Shepherd*, p. 172.
22. *Blackwood's Magazine 1817-25*, vol. 5, pp. 57-61.
23. H. Segerblad, *Transcending the Gothic: The Extravagancies of Blackwood* (unpublished thesis, University of Glasgow, 2010), pp. 11-13.
24. Miller, *Electric Shepherd*, p. 166.
25. Segerblad, *Transcending the Gothic*, p. 13.
26. John Wilson, 'Extracts from Gosshen's Diary No. 1' in David Blair (ed.), *Gothic Short Stories* (Ware, Hertfordshire: Wordsworth Editions, 2002), pp. 16-20.
27. Miller, *Electric Shepherd*, pp. 224-25.
28. David Finkelstein, 'The House of Blackwood' in *Textualities*, 2005, textualities.net/david-finkelstein/the-house-of-blackwood (accessed 28 February 2014).
29. Wilson, *Noctes*, vol. III, p. 212.
30. Wilson, *Noctes*, vol. II, p. 213.
31. Miller, *Electric Shepherd*, p. 165.
32. Wilson, *Noctes*, vol. I, p. 175.
33. Wilson, *Noctes*, vol. I, p. 279.
34. Wilson, *Noctes*, vol. I, p. 51.
35. Wilson, *Noctes*, vol. I, pp. 47-49.
36. Wilson, *Noctes*, vol. II, p. 8.
37. Wilson, *Noctes*, vol. II, p. 405.
38. Wilson, *Noctes*, vol. IV, pp. 157-60.
39. Duncan, 'Hogg's Body', pp. 1-15.
40. Wilson, *Noctes*, vol. I, p. xvii.
41. Wilson, *Noctes*, vol. IV, p. 24.
42. Wilson, *Noctes*, vol. III, p. 91.
43. Miller, *Electric Shepherd*, p. 128.
44. Robert Morrison, 'Blackwood's Berserker: John Wilson and the Language of Extremity', in *Romanticism on the Net* 20 (November 2000), www.erudit.org/revue/ron/2000/v/n20/005951ar.html (accessed 28 February 2014).
45. Wilson, *Noctes*, vol. I, p. 216.
46. Wilson, *Noctes*, vol. III, p. 83.
47. Miller, *Electric Shepherd*, p. 175.

7. 'That Fairyland of Poesy': The Highlands in Early Nineteenth-Century Women's Fiction

PAM PERKINS

Crossing the Highland Line was something of a fashion in British literature at the beginning of the nineteenth century, a point emphasised by an 1814 novel called *The Saxon and the Gael* (possibly by Christian Johnstone).[1] The heroine, the daughter of a Highland earl living in Edinburgh, is thrilled and envious to hear that an acquaintance has just been on a tour of the Trossachs. '[T]he Trossachs', she cries, 'that fairyland of poesy; describe! describe!' Yet her curiosity remains unsatisfied. Her acquaintance, Miss Scott, dismisses the region as 'the horridest place ever you saw in your life' and makes clear that she has gone only because it is 'monstrous fashionable' and 'all the world has been there'.[2] She then rattles off the vocabulary of aesthetic pleasure in a manner that empties it of meaning: 'So we got into the carriages, and every one said it was enchanting! and delightful! and charming! and beautiful! and picturesque! and sublime! and some of the ladies put a number of these words together!'[3] Clearly, Johnstone (or whoever the author might have been) is having some fun here at the expense of Sir Walter Scott, *The Lady of the Lake*, and the way that the Scottish Highlands had been absorbed into a fashionable school of poetry and fiction. Yet as the novel itself demonstrates, Scott's version of the Highlands was far from the only one available to readers of his day. There were a large number of early nineteenth-century novels, mainly by women and mainly directed towards a female readership, that presented versions of Highland landscape and culture that differ strikingly from those in Scott's fiction and poetry. While in the vast majority of this work the Highlands remain a fantasy world, it was a fantasy that turns out to be quite a bit more varied in scope than the sort of paint-by-numbers sublime being satirised in the responses of the mindlessly fashionable ladies of *The Saxon and the Gael*.

Of course, it is hardly surprising that early-nineteenth century readers would see the Trossachs and the wider Highlands world through the lens of Scott's poetry and fiction. Scott is always going to overshadow any discussion of the Highlands in the literature of his era, but even though there is no question that in both his poetry and the Waverley novels Scott transformed the early nineteenth-century literary world in general, and the British perception of the Highlands in particular, there were many dozens of other novels with Highland characters and episodes published from the 1790s on. At least three of the authors of such novels – Mary Brunton, Susan Ferrier, and Christian Johnstone – have been receiving renewed critical attention over the last few years, but one result of that attention has been that the considerable differences in both plot and style between Scott and these lesser-known women contemporaries have tended to produce or reinforce a perception of a straightforward gender divide in treatments of the Highlands in the popular literature of this period. Scott, as Ina Ferris and others have influentially demonstrated, was read as a particularly 'masculine' writer, one who, in the words of Katherine Haldane Grenier, shaped the idea of the Highlands as a site for the 'development and affirmation of manliness'.[4] At the other literary extreme was what Peter Womack has called the 'woman's highlands,' which Ian Duncan describes as 'the private enclave [...] of a virtuous domesticity that repairs the faults of fashionable life'.[5]

Yet as striking as this gender divide can be in some cases, the idea that the women writers of this period did little with the Highlands other than to make them into a site of idyllic domesticity is, unsurprisingly, an oversimplification. As Duncan notes, one needs to look no further than Christian Johnstone's *Clan-Albin* (1815), which portrays the depopulated and struggling Highland villages of the Napoleonic era, to find a major and significant exception to any generalisations about women's treatments of the region (though Johnstone returns to an idyll at the end of the novel). Nor was *Clan-Albin* the only woman's novel of the time to imply that Scott's Highlands were not too masculine but simply too romantic. Even in *The Saxon and the Gael*, Lady Rosabell's enthusiasm about the Trossachs can be read as a quiet joke making precisely that point. Lady Rosabell is, after all, a Highlander herself, and even granted that she is supposed to be a native of a rather geographically vague region in the north Highlands, not the Trossachs, it remains striking that she apparently sees no connection at all between what the narrator presents as her own bleak, sterile, and economically troubled homeland and the 'fairyland of poesy' that she has discovered through her reading. Similarly, Brunton and Ferrier imply, at least in some contexts, that they see their task as providing a realistic view of the Highlands to counter romantic stereotypes, with Ferrier opening her novel *Marriage* with a satiric account of a spoilt, naïve Englishwoman whose novel-fueled fantasies of Highland life are shattered by direct, unhappy experience, and Brunton mocking the 'novel-reading misses' misled into imagining the Highlands as a landscape clad permanently in the 'verdure and sunshine of July'.[6]

Of course, Ferrier and Johnstone, at least, differ from Scott in that they are writing about the contemporary Highlands, something that Scott famously never attempted. Yet even so, the result is not simply a clear, sustainable dichotomy between past and present, or romance and realism, much less an indication of any stable distinction between 'men's' and 'women's' highlands. Instead, what emerges as one turns from Scott to his women contemporaries – and extends even beyond what is now becoming the more familiar triad of Brunton, Ferrier, and Johnstone – is a spectrum of literary tropes that range beyond the 'transhistorical idyll' that Womack has analysed to incorporate everything from satire to sentimental and vaguely historical romance.[7] The point here is not to argue that any one of the versions of the Highlands that appear in this mass of popular fiction is more accurate or realistic than another – most of it is straightforwardly fantasy – but rather to draw attention to the complex range of literary roles played by the Highlands in the culture of the time, even in obscure and often formulaic novels.

Admittedly, as Ian Duncan has pointed out – and he and Peter Garside are two of the very few critics who have paid any attention at all to these early 'Scottish' novels – many of them are anonymous or pseudonymous London productions and so are probably not Scottish at all in any literal sense.[8] Nor did they have anything approaching the literary cachet of the Waverley novels or even of the successful and generally well-reviewed work of Brunton and Ferrier. A relatively large number of these popular 'Scottish' novels appeared with the déclassé Minerva Press, best known then and now as a purveyor of disposable circulating library fiction (in 1813, a reviewer dismissed Minerva as 'that pig-stye of literature in Leadenhall-street').[9] Yet however little critical respect Minerva might have had, the point that a number of its now-forgotten authors chose to employ Highland settings is noteworthy; after all, William Lane, Minerva's proprietor, made his substantial fortune precisely through being attuned to the fashionable literary tastes of the day. Even if many of these 'Scottish' novels, whether published at Minerva Press or elsewhere, give little reason to suspect the authors of any first-hand knowledge of Scotland, the simple fact that they exist implies that, even before Scott, a mention of the Highlands on a title page would sell.

That appears to have been the case even though in a number of these books – the many quasi-medieval Gothic novels of the last years of the eighteenth century, for example – the Highland setting is strictly nominal. To take a relatively familiar work as an example, Ann Radcliffe's first novel, *The Castles of Athlin and Dunbayne* (1789), has little more to do with any historically recognisable version of Highland life or landscape than its follow-up, *A Sicilian Romance* (1790), does with the history or geography of Sicily. Radcliffe, famously, was far more interested in sentiment and mood than in historical realism, but her carefree attitude towards setting seems to have influenced her lesser-known imitators. In a slightly later 'Highland' romance – a 1799 novel called *The Rock; or Alfred and Anna: A Scottish Tale* – the author, a Mrs Barnby, breezily combines the setting of Radcliffe's first novel with major plot points of her second: Barnby's villain, like Radcliffe's evil Sicilian Marquis, fakes the death of his saintly and long-suffering wife and then not only locks her away in a subterranean dungeon, but even improves upon Radcliffe's villain by imprisoning his infant daughter as well. The grim castles and forbidding landscapes of *The Rock* might almost as well be in Sicily as the Scottish Highlands: they exist merely as threats and dangers or as occasions for characters to demonstrate their sensibility by their rhapsodic delight in spectacular landscapes.

In the cases of Barnby and Radcliffe, the Highlands are thus almost an abstraction – a sublime but more or less undifferentiated assemblage of rocks, forests, and mountains. If there are any recognisable traces of the later eighteenth-century Highlands in *The Rock,* they come in Barnby's brief frame narrative (which also borrows details from the preface of *A Sicilian Romance*), and in a rather roundabout way. The novel opens with an unnamed, modern-day narrator visiting the seat of some family friends in the North Highlands, where she is given the manuscript that contains the main plot. Yet the frame is no less crammed with romantic paraphernalia than is the central narrative of Gothic villainy. While moralising over the ruins of 'an old gothic structure', the narrator is interrupted by what she fears will be 'lawless banditti', but the intruder instead proves to be a benevolent hermit, complete with a 'long woollen gown, fastened round his waist with a leathern belt' and a 'snowy beard descending to his waist'. He conducts her to his 'humble cell,' which has apparently been 'hewed [...] by nature's chisel out of the solid stone', where she admires his 'couch, composed of swelling moss and small fibrous roots' and his 'antique worm-eaten table'.[10] The hermit himself has nothing to do with the story; he merely gives the narrator the manuscript and disappears without further explanation. Yet if he is a comically implausible figure to find wandering the eighteenth-century Highlands, his cell, so far from being out of place, evokes one of the more famous Highland tourist sites of the era, the Earl of Breadalbane's purpose-built Hermitage at Taymouth. According to a sixteen-year-old traveller who visited it in 1786, the Hermitage was 'a little Elysium,' reached by a passage 'hewn out of an astonishing rock'; she was also struck by the imaginary hermit's 'humble couch' and the humble decor of 'clay and moss'.[11] A few years later, a less impressionable observer – the future critic Francis Jeffrey, then a twenty-six-year-old struggling lawyer – was amused by the 'tolerable good taste' the putative hermit had demonstrated in choosing furniture and ornaments so well suited to 'the accommodation' of 'his visitors'.[12] Yet even if he gently mocked the place, Jeffrey still made a point of visiting it. In effect, Barnby's frame narrative turns this popular spectacle (which of course was itself a product of fashionable literary tastes) into a 'real' locale, and in the process reabsorbs, however clumsily, the emergent landscape of the tourist Highlands back into the novel.

Even when authors take some pains to evoke actual Scottish locales, rather than using Scotland as a hazily generic, tourist-friendly romance world, the Highlands can remain, in fiction of this sort, a purely fictional space. For example, an anonymous 1809 triple-decker called *The Banks of the Carron* opens with 'Donald, an Highland shepherd' leaving his 'humble cabin, on the romantic banks of the Carron' to stroll into Caithness to fetch 'some necessaries for his family'. A little later, we're told that the heroine is carried to her paternal home, the Castle of Moray, which is situated where 'the beautiful river Carron [...] divide[s] the lands of Moray and Nithsdale'.[13] While such geographic vagueness could be dismissed simply as an example of careless research or of authorial indifference, these slips or errors are significant for a couple of reasons. Most obviously, perhaps, the decision by the author of *The Banks of the Carron* to foreground Scottish geography in the title (and, in fact, to do so twice over: the subtitle is *The Towers of Lothian*) implies the attractions of at least a gloss of realism, and in doing so, it points to yet another way that the tourist versions of Scotland were drawn into this fiction. Even if one assumes that the main readers of *The Banks of the Carron* were the sort of half-educated young Englishwomen satirised in contemporary attacks on the novel and novel-readers and that they remained cheerfully hazy in their ideas about Scottish geography, the implicit assumption remains that the mention of the River Carron in the title would be an attraction. The most obvious reason for that to be the case is the fact that, like the Breadalbane Hermitage, Carron and its iron works had a relatively major place in contemporary tourist discourse. If not as conventionally romantic as the Hermitage, they still were still sought out as an exemplar of a certain type of sublimity. An anonymous traveller in 1789 went to see them because they were 'so justly celebrated all over Europe' and found them so overwhelming that, as he wrote, '[t]o attempt a Description would be ridiculous.' A year earlier, an Englishwoman named Elizabeth Diggle had compared the town and its ironworks to 'the infernal regions,' but nevertheless made a point of visiting and describing at length this 'whole town of smoke & fire.'[14] Obviously, the pseudo-medievalism of *The Banks of the Carron* is very far removed from the industrial sublime that attracted these late-eighteenth-century tourists, but the glamour of the compellingly unfamiliar that brought Carron into the era's tourist discourse might still explain its presumed literary appeal.

The idea that tourism and travel narratives influenced the novel should hardly be surprising; Scottish travels were a burgeoning genre in the last decades of the eighteenth century, so much so that, as early as 1776, Edward Topham opened his volume of letters from Edinburgh with the demure observation that since the Highlands had been the subject of so many recent works that he dared to publish on Scotland only because he *wasn't* talking about them.[15] Yet the concepts of place in this fiction evoke not just the late eighteenth-century Highland tour but also imagined travels to much more distant locales. Most notably, perhaps, the careless geography of *The Banks of the Carron* aligns it – and other books of its sort – with a range of other fiction of the day in which more remote areas of the world are compressed into a tidily compact package of sublimity. A New Jersey estate in the 1796 novel *Berkeley Hall*, for example, somehow contrives to be enclosed on one side by the Bay of New York and on the other by a range of 'rugged mountains' that 'ascend [...] to the clouds', while characters in *All's Right at Last* (1774) live in a version of Canada in which it is possible to make a leisurely day trip from Trois Rivières to Niagara Falls.[16] Even if one might have hoped that early nineteenth-century British readers would have been more familiar with Scotland than with Quebec or New Jersey and thus able to register incongruities more readily, the sort of creative geography found in *The Banks of the Carron* implicitly absorbs the Highlands into the sort of imperial fantasy exemplified in these earlier novels. In effect, the use of actual Scottish place names paradoxically reinforces the sense of the Scottish Highlands as a not-quite-real place, hovering at the exotic edges of the British literary world.

The result might not be a story that has much to teach the reader about Scottish history or geography, but the practice does point towards another function that this literary version of the Highlands served in the fiction of the time. Precisely because Highland locales were associated with an exoticised world that was culturally as well as geographically distanced from modern England, they rapidly became a form of literary shorthand that authors could use to explore ideas about links between character and culture. In particular, the fictional Highlands became a means of presenting concepts of 'proper' femininity, as sweet Highland heroines are both marked out from and threatened by the mainstream society of their day. Whether that threat takes the form of a predatory London roué, as in Elizabeth Helme's 1794 *Duncan and Peggy*, or of the brutal medieval courtiers who threaten the innocent heroines of *Glencarron* (1811), a frothy take on fourteenth-century political intrigue by a Miss Wigley, the dynamic is the same. A somewhat more elaborate example of the heroine who is shown as being both desirable and vulnerable because of her association with the Highlands occurs in *The Wood Nymph*, an 1806 novel by a Mrs Isaacs, which opens with the heroine Jessica, 'a pupil of nature', being raised by her recluse father in a cottage at the foot of Ben Lomond.[17] Admittedly, there is nothing that marks Jessica's childhood home out as specifically Scottish other than the name, and there is no sense that Isaacs is interested in the cultural specifics of early nineteenth-century life in the southwestern Highlands. On the contrary, the mountainous landscape that she describes is more or less indistinguishable from the mountains of the Savoy, where the heroine finds herself late in the novel, and its geography is shaped entirely by the demands of the plot. (While Ben Lomond was already a major tourist site by the turn of the nineteenth century, Isaacs presents it as a place 'where seldom the traces of human feet [...] were discernable').[18] Yet, even so, character and setting converge as Isaacs uses Jessica's absorption into this dramatically isolated landscape to signal to the reader that she possesses not just the nineteenth-century literary essentials of beauty, youth, and virtue, but also that she is (and will remain) culturally separate from the London world that she enters later in the novel. For Isaacs, 'Highland' identity is a matter of costume and picturesque tableaux; we are told that in her rambles, Jessica habitually wears 'a short habit of grey cloth [...] a Tartan plaid across her shoulder, and a bonnet of the same [...] decorated with a green falling feather'.[19] Significantly, this is the costume that she is wearing both when the hero first sees her as she is posed picturesquely on a cliff edge, attempting to rescue a kid 'frolicking among the tufted declivities of the mountain',[20] and later, when she has moved into fashionable society and they meet again at a masquerade. The novel invites us (and the hero) to read this costume as a both a revelation and a guarantee of Jessica's true character, untouched and untainted by the accoutrements of a dissipated London life.

The point here is not that Isaacs's version of life in the shadow of Ben Lomond is a fantasy – that's too obvious to need saying. The more interesting issue is that Isaacs uses that fantasy to establish Jessica (who of course turns out to be an aristocratic English heiress) simultaneously as an exotic outsider and as a model of conventional, if idealised, English femininity. In one respect, this is simply an example of what Duncan identifies as a tendency to turn the Highlands into a site of feminised 'redemptive premodernity',[21] but Isaacs complicates matters slightly by making her fantasy version of Ben Lomond not just the site and source of Jessica's virtues but also, and perhaps slightly paradoxically, a signal of her heroine's fitness for her English estate and rank. This use of an idealised or fantasy version of the Highlands to signal 'proper' English femininity is, in fact, a device that is found in a surprising number of the sentimental romances of the time, in which a nominally 'Highland' heroine is used as a standard against which English moral decay can be measured and assessed. In effect, these novels function as late and somewhat sentimental cousins of the 'oriental spy' fables of the eighteenth century, in which innocent outsiders more or less inadvertently reveal the failings of western European society. Of course, Isaac's Jessica doesn't approach the moral complexity of Montesquieu's Usbek and Rica, Johnson's Rasselas, or even – to take an example closer to Isaac's time – Elizabeth Hamilton's Hindoo Rajah; Isaacs, after all, was writing sentimental romance, not social satire. Even so, the use of an exotic outsider both as a measure of where a culture is going wrong and as an embodiment of its supposedly lost or vanishing virtues links these two otherwise very different genres and suggests the degree to which, in the popular literature of the day, the Highlands become not just an exotic fantasy world but also a way of representing an idealised and supposedly lost England.

Of course, this was not the only way in which the Highlands were imaginatively entangled in the wider English world, as one can see by turning from *The Wood Nymph* to a superficially similar book: *Precipitance: A Highland Tale*, an 1823 novel 'by a Lady'. Like *The Wood Nymph*, *Precipitance* features a Highland heroine who moves to London and into fashionable English life, although in at least some respects *Precipitance* differs sharply from its forerunner in offering a much more realistic version of Highland life. (It might be significant that *Precipitance* is one of the relatively few anonymous 'Highland' novels of this period to have been published in Edinburgh.) For one thing, Elizabeth Fraser, the heroine of the later novel, is the daughter of a respectable Highland clergyman, rather than, like Jessica, an orphan with a mysterious past. The fictional west Highland parish of Glenerrach in which she grows up is also far more geographically precise than is Isaacs's version of Ben Lomond. While both Jessica and Elizabeth marry English tourists visiting the Highlands, Isaacs turns the meeting of her hero and heroine into a series of picturesque tableaux set amid generically crumbling castles and dizzying mountain vistas. In contrast, the travelling hero of *Precipitance* meets Elizabeth in considerably more prosaic circumstances: while on a walking tour along the Caledonian Canal, he takes refuge from a storm in her father's parsonage. This attempt to evoke a more or less historically and geographically specific version of the Highlands makes the conclusion of the novel all the more striking. Jessica, the fantasy embodiment of Highland virtue, moves easily into English society, while the otherwise more realistic Elizabeth is killed by being transplanted from her native Highlands to London. The doctor attending her as she lies dying of consumption explains to her brother that the problem is partly physical – 'Few constitutions could stand the change from the salubrious bracing air of the Highlands to the heated atmosphere of London' – but he also makes clear that the contrast between the 'bracing' Highlands and the enervating 'heat' of London is at least as much a matter of the moral as of the physical climate.[22] Its relative realism notwithstanding, *Precipitance* thus creates a version of the virtuous Highland woman who is not just culturally but also, to some degree, physically distinct from her English counterparts, quite literally unable to breathe the same air as they do. Even as the novel establishes Elizabeth Fraser as an embodiment of ideal womanhood, that is, it also establishes her as being fundamentally different in kind from contemporary Englishwomen.

Granted, the idea that dissipation could kill was typical of the sentimental novel of the day. The heroine whose moral strength is inversely proportional to her physical delicacy is almost omnipresent in the genre, and in her protracted deathbed scene, which occupies much of the second volume, Elizabeth aligns herself with any number of tragic sentimental heroines, from Samuel Richardson's Clarissa onwards. By focusing so closely on the role played by the Highlands in Elizabeth's physical decay and (eventual) spiritual redemption, however, the author of *Precipitance* implies not that the Highlands are a straightforward refuge from modern corruption but rather that they are a dangerously rarified environment that unfits women for life in a less morally sheltered climate. Not all writers presented the Highlands in such headily exalted terms, of course; there is also a large body of this early nineteenth-century women's fiction that is much closer in tone and style to the conventionally 'masculine' Highlands of Scott and the Waverley novels than to works such as *Precipitance* or *The Wood Nymph*. Even if it is the case that some elements of fantasy continue to seep into fiction that actively resists a more or less mystical, sentimental vision of a 'feminine' Highlands, the result is not inevitably the sort of jarring discordance between the historically and geographically realistic Highlands in which *Precipitance's* Elizabeth begins her story and the idealised spiritual haven in which she ends it. In at least some of these works, one can also find writers offering intriguing, even challenging, explorations of how and whether such different ways of looking at or living in the Highlands can be reconciled, and, in the process, raising implicit or explicit questions about the impact of imaginatively transforming the region into a spiritualised retreat from modernity.

One of the most striking examples of this sort of treatment of the Highlands occurs in *The Highland Castle and the Lowland Cottage*, an 1819 novel by a woman who wrote under the pseudonym Rosalia St Clair. In this book, the Highlands are anything but the site of a redemptive idyll or the marker of idealised femininity, as the first half of the novel traces the breakdown of the marriage of an Edinburgh heiress and a Highland baronet, who clings to the trappings of traditional clan life in his grim, decaying estate on the northern Argyll coast. In some ways, this opening episode of the novel reads like a much less comic – and more melodramatic – version of Susan Ferrier's satiric account of Highland life in *Marriage,* published the year before. Yet it is as useful to read St Clair in the context of her forgotten Minerva Press counterparts as it is to measure her against a better-known writer such as Ferrier, as doing so highlights the flexibility of even the standard Highland clichés used in the sentimental novel of the day. Like Isaacs, for example, St Clair includes an important episode set in the vicinity of Ben Lomond, as Marion, the Edinburgh heiress, heads north after her wedding. St Clair is more carefully detailed than Isaacs in her treatment of landscape and setting; her lengthy description of Ben Lomond would in fact fit comfortably enough into any of the many contemporaneous Scottish travelogues:

> From the spot where she stood, waiting the approach of the boat, [Marion's] eye caught an extensive reach of the loch, only broken and interrupted by jutting rocks and picturesque promontories. Through the transparent azure of its waters were distinguished the various-coloured pebbles which form its bottom [...] Amid this enchanting display of grand and varied scenery, not the least captivating to her imagination were the isles with which the loch is studded. Some of them exhibited only open green pastures, dotted here and there with patches of tall trees; but the elevated hills on others, clothed with wood to their very summits, seemingly formed a delightful shade, impervious to the rays of a meridian sun.[23]

Rather than simply dropping the names of or alluding to fashionable tourist sites, as do novelists such as Isaacs and Barnby, St Clair turns her heroine into a tourist, and, through her, creates a form of proxy tourism for her readers. In stopping the narrative for a leisurely description of the landscape, she presents the Highlands as an elaborate aesthetic spectacle, rewarding thoughtful and attentive observation, rather than merely as an idealised backdrop for feminine virtue.

Granted, on some levels Marion recalls a more stereotypically romantic heroine such as *The Wood Nymph's* Jessica as she demonstrates both her good taste and her virtuous femininity in her delight in the scenery on and around Ben Lomond. Yet St Clair differs from Isaacs in making clear both that the setting is not the source of those virtues and that Marion's response to the landscape is more complex than it might initially appear. For one thing, the episode carefully juxtaposes Marion's responses to Ben Lomond with those of her husband, Sir Simon Frazer, whose very different way of loving his country highlights not just their fundamental incompatibility as a couple but also what St Clair implies is the impossibility of assigning any single literary meaning to the Highland landscape. Sir Simon is 'a staunch Highlander', we're told, but the narrator explains that this deep patriotism arises not from pride in the 'romantic' Highland past nor because of any 'kindly and tender associations' with the landscape, but rather 'because [Sir Simon] could lord it over a wretched and ignorant herd of clansmen and vassals' and because he is an ardent sportsman.[24] Marion, in contrast, like Jessica – or perhaps even more like Lady Rosabell in *The Saxon and the Gael* – sees the Highlands as a land of poetry and magic, finding in the landscape of Ben Lomond a 'charm' that 'wholly withdraw[s] her from herself' and her unhappy marriage.[25] This contrast between the Highlands as site of sport and aristocratic display and as a source of enchantment and aesthetic delight is underscored just a little later in the novel, as Marion listens to her husband enthusiastically discussing Ben Lomond and its environs with a friend:

> [L]ady Frazer heard, with a sigh, the delightful region she had traversed, the grand and sublime scenery of which was worthy the pencil of a Salvator Rosa, only spoken of as affording a haunt to

> the roebuck, the ptarmigan, and osprey, which, even in the wild forests and lofty summits of Ben Lomond, are not safe from the pursuit of the hunter.[26]

In effect, what St Clair is doing here is bringing together stereotypically 'masculine' and 'feminine' versions of the Highlands and, by encouraging the reader to share Marion's perspective, she creates a moral and aesthetic hierarchy in which it is made very clear that Marion's response to the region is 'better' than her husband's, despite her being an outsider.

Just in case the reader misses this point, St Clair includes several subplots that reinforce the central message that Sir Simon's attitude towards his homeland is unsatisfactory. In one, Sir Simon's aunt, who values nothing but clan and country, eventually redirects her loyalties from her nephew to her 'Saxon' niece by marriage; she is won over in part by Marion's sweetly virtuous femininity, but the novel also makes clear that the aunt rightly suspects that Sir Simon's pride in his role as clan chieftain is strictly selfish. A more complex example of this moral hierarchy features in a subplot about one of Sir Simon's distant and impoverished cousins, a former soldier who marries an Englishwoman. Unlike Sir Simon, however, this cousin ensures his marital happiness in part by allowing his wife to remodel his ancestral home in accordance with her aestheticised concept of what a Highland retreat should be. Using what St Clair presents as a combination of good sense and refined good taste, Emily Frazer transforms her husband's 'damp, cheerless' house on the banks of Loch Fyne into a place that 'would not have been disgraced in comparison with the *cottage ornée* of the south';[27] the result is a domestic idyll that both contrasts with Sir Simon's 'traditional' Highland household and that evokes the feminine Highlands discussed by Peter Womack and most famously exemplified in the Mrs Douglas plot in Susan Ferrier's *Marriage*.

Yet even if the novel is clear in attacking the version of Highland culture embodied by Sir Simon and in preferring Emily Frazer's idyllic, quasi-English cottage life to Sir Simon's hollow Highland pomp, the novel is not an unequivocal celebration of the 'women's Highlands'. For one thing, the simple fact that the Frazers' house becomes a version of an English *cottage ornée* emphasises the degree to which, under Emily's management, it turns into a place that is in, but not truly of, the Highland landscape in which it is set. That point is reinforced by the more subtle implication that the cottage exists to frame the landscape as an aesthetic object, rather than being part of that landscape itself, an idea first suggested when Emily first looks, with 'delighted enthusiasm', out of what becomes the library window:

> The mountains [...] extended their broad and lofty masses along the opposite shore of Loch Fyne, opening so as to afford a view across the water into the gloomy but picturesque vale of Kinglass. The stillness and desolation of this solitary glen were strikingly in opposition to the picture of cheerful, active industry that fell more immediately under [Emily's] view. The sunbeams danced gaily on the bosom of the loch, which was covered with fishing craft of every description, whose white and sometimes well-patched sails fluttered in the breeze, as they scudded backwards and forwards into the little creeks and bays which vary the outline of this noble water.
>
> Farther to the right, the curling smoke which arose from a well-sheltered valley marked the site of an unobtrusive village, concealed among the surrounding copsewood [...][28]

Like Marion on Ben Lomond, Emily is positioned here as an aesthetic tourist. The main difference is that in this case, the spectacle incorporates and absorbs signs of a working culture – the smoke, the boats with their 'well-patched' sails. This aestheticising of rural labour was conventional in the art of the time, as John Barrell and others have pointed out, but given the emphasis earlier in the volume on Sir Simon's mistreatment of his impoverished tenants, the passage is jarring to a degree that not only undercuts Emily's privileged observer's perspective but even invites a more nuanced reading of Marion's earlier travels on Ben Lomond. However much, in other words, the novel encourages identification with Marion and her aesthetic engagement with the landscape, it still leaves readers with some rather uncomfortable questions, as we see that neither Emily nor Marion is any less inclined than Sir Simon to treat the Highlands as a form of pleasure ground. The women's pleasures might be more refined, as well as less violent, than his, but whether treated as artistic spectacle or as a game park, the Highlands are implicitly reduced to a static landscape and stripped of both history and living culture.

The point that this version of the 'women's Highlands' is part of a fantasy world is reinforced even in the name of Emily Frazer's *cottage ornée*: Fairy Cottage. As the name implies, Emily is in effect living in a 'fairyland of poesy', rather than in the economically and socially troubled culture that St Clair describes earlier in the novel. Through this subplot, St Clair thus underscores the fantasy elements of this vision of the Highlands as a feminised retreat into 'redemptive premodernity', even as she strongly criticises Sir Simon's masculine world. While this is not an issue that St Clair pursues in the second half of her novel, as she turns back from the Highland castle to the Lowland cottage and shifts her focus from an unhappy marriage to a romantic farrago of angelic foundlings, star-crossed lovers, and stolen wills, the point remains that her novel shows how standard literary clichés about the Highlands could be deployed to raise complicated and challenging questions even within the boundaries of circulating-library fiction.

That said, my aim in this paper isn't to make a case that Mrs Isaacs or Rosalia St Clair or any of these authors of early nineteenth-century popular fiction about the Highlands is an unjustly neglected writer. Some of them are more interesting than others, but these aren't lost masterpieces. What I do want to suggest is that, taken as a group, these novels demonstrate not just how pervasive the Highlands were as a subject in early nineteenth-century fiction, but also how varied the literary impact of a Highland episode could be. If, as Duncan and others have established, it is impossible to divide up representations of the Highlands in early nineteenth-century literature into Scott and everybody else, it is just as impossible to draw a clear dividing line between masculine and feminine Highlands, or realist and fantasy Highlands. Reading this fiction might not teach us much about actual Highland history or geography, but it does show how important even fantasy versions of the Highlands could be in shaping the popular literary culture of the day.

Notes

1. Peter Garside has recently found an early nineteenth-century attribution of the novel to 'a Mrs. Johnson'. See Garside, Peter, with Sharon Ragaz, Anthony Mandal, and Jacqueline Belanger, 'The English Novel, 1800–1829 & 1830–1836: Update 6', *Romantic Textualities: Literature and Print Culture 1780–1840*, 19 (winter 2009 www.romtext.cf.ac.uk//reports/engnov6.pdf [accessed 27 May 2012], pp. 70–77 (pp. 72–73).
2. [?Christian Johnstone] *The Saxon and the Gael*, 4 vols (Edinburgh: T. Dick, 1814), vol. 2, p. 170.
3. *The Saxon and the Gael*, vol. 2, pp. 170–71.
4. Katherine Haldane Grenier, *Tourism and Identity in Scotland, 1770–1914: Creating Caledonia* (Aldershot: Ashgate, 2005), p. 108.
5. Peter Womack, *Improvement and Romance: Constructing the Myth of the Highlands* (London: Macmillan, 1989), p. 139; Ian Duncan, *Scott's Shadow: The Novel in Romantic Edinburgh* (Princeton: Princeton University Press, 2007), p. 79.
6. Mary Brunton, *Emmeline; with Some Other Pieces* (Edinburgh: Manners and Miller, 1819; repr. London: Thoemmes Press, 1992), p. lxxvii.
7. Womack, p. 175.
8. Duncan, p. 316, n. 75.
9. Review of *Trecothick Bower* by Regina Maria Roche, *The Critical Review*, vol. 5, s. 4 (Jan 1814), pp. 99–101 (p. 99).
10. Mrs Barnby, *The Rock; or, Alfred and Anna: A Scottish Tale*, 2 vols (London: Crosby and Letterman, 1799), vol. 1, pp. 4–11.
11. Eliza Fletcher, *Journal of a Scottish Tour*, Edinburgh: National Library of Scotland, ACC. 12017, p. 45.
12. Francis Jeffrey, *Highland and Continental Tours*, ed. Pam Perkins (Penrith: Humanities eBooks, 2009), p. 84.
13. Anon., *The Banks of the Carron; or, The Towers of Lothian: A Scottish Legend*, 4 vols (London: J. Hughes, 1809), vol. 1, pp. 1, 48.
14. Anon., 'A Tour in Scotland', Edinburgh, National Library of Scotland, MS 1080, f. 14; Elizabeth Diggle, *Journal of a Tour from London to the Highlands of Scotland*, in Alastair J. Durie (ed.), *Travels in Scotland 1788–1881* (Woodbridge, Sussex: Boydell Press, 2012), pp. 18–40 (p. 32).
15. Edward Topham, *Letters from Edinburgh written in the Years 1774 and 1775*, 2 vols (London: J. Dodsley, 1776), vol. 1, p. vi.
16. Anon., *Berkeley Hall; or, The Pupil of Experience: A Novel*, 3 vols (London: J. Tindal, 1796), vol. 1, p. 63 (emphasis in original); Anon., *All's Right at Last; or, the History of Miss West*, 2 vols (London: F. & J. Noble, 1774), vol. 1, p. 223.
17. Mrs Isaacs, *The Wood Nymph*, 3 vols (London: Minerva Press, 1806), vol. 1, p. 23.
18. *The Wood Nymph*, vol. 1, p. 1.
19. *The Wood Nymph*, vol. 1, p. 5.
20. *The Wood Nymph*, vol. 1, p. 24.
21. Duncan, p. 79.
22. [A Lady], *Precipitance: A Highland Tale*, 2 vols (Edinburgh: Bell & Bradfute, 1823), vol. 2, p. 82.
23. Rosalia St Clair, *The Highland Castle and the Lowland Cottage*, 4 vols (London: Minerva Press, 1820), vol. 1, pp. 52–54.

24. *The Highland Castle and the Lowland Cottage*, vol. 1, p. 52.
25. *The Highland Castle and the Lowland Cottage*, vol. 1, p. 50.
26. *The Highland Castle and the Lowland Cottage*, vol. 1, pp. 57-58.
27. *The Highland Castle and the Lowland Cottage*, vol. 1, pp. 111-12.
28. *The Highland Castle and the Lowland Cottage*, vol. 1, pp. 113-14.

Bibliography

Anon., *All's Right at Last; or, the History of Miss West*, 2 vols (London: F. & J. Noble, 1774).
Anon., *The Banks of the Carron; or, The Towers of Lothian: A Scottish Legend*, 4 vols (London: J. Hughes, 1809).
Anon., *Berkeley Hall; or, The Pupil of Experience: A Novel*, 3 vols (London: J. Tindal, 1796).
Anon., 'A Tour in Scotland' (Edinburgh, National Library of Scotland, MS 1080).
Barnby, Mrs, *The Rock; or, Alfred and Anna: A Scottish Tale*, 2 vols (London: Crosby and Letterman, 1799).
Brunton, Mary, *Emmeline; with Some Other Pieces* (Edinburgh: Manners and Miller 1819; repr. London: Thoemmes Press, 1992).
Duncan, Ian, *Scott's Shadow: The Novel in Romantic Edinburgh* (Princeton: Princeton University Press, 2007).
Durie, Alastair, *Travels in Scotland 1788-1881* (Woodbridge, Sussex: Boydell Press, 2012).
Ferris, Ina, *The Achievement of Literary Authority: Gender, History, and the Waverley Novels* (Ithaca: Cornell University Press, 1991).
Fletcher, Eliza, *Journal of a Scottish Tour*, Edinburgh: National Library of Scotland, ACC. 12017.
Garside, Peter, with Sharon Ragaz, Anthony Mandal, and Jacqueline Belanger, 'The English Novel, 1800-1829 & 1830-1836: Update 6', *Romantic Textualities: Literature and Print Culture 1780-1840*, 19 (winter 2009) www.romtext.cf.ac.uk//reports/engnov6.pdf, pp. 70-77.
Grenier, Katherine Haldane, *Tourism and Identity in Scotland, 1770-1914: Creating Caledonia* (Aldershot: Ashgate, 2005).
Helme, Elizabeth, *Duncan and Peggy: A Scottish Tale*, 2 vols (London: J. Bell, 1794).
Isaacs, Mrs, *The Wood Nymph*, 3 vols (London: Minerva Press, 1806).
Jeffrey, Francis, *Highland and Continental Tours*, ed. Pam Perkins (Penrith: Humanities eBooks, 2009).
[?Johnstone, Christian], *The Saxon and the Gael*, 4 vols (Edinburgh: T. Dick, 1814).
[A Lady], *Precipitance: A Highland Tale*, 2 vols (Edinburgh: Bell & Bradfute, 1823).
Roche, Regina Maria, review of *Trecothick Bower*, *The Critical Review*, vol. 5, s 4 (Jan 1814), pp. 99-101.
St Clair, Rosalia, *The Highland Castle and the Lowland Cottage*, 4 vols (London: Minerva Press, 1820).
Edward Topham, *Letters from Edinburgh written in the Years 1774 and 1775*, 2 vols (London: J. Dodsley, 1776).
Wigley, Miss, *Glencarron: A Scottish Tale*, 3 vols (London: Henry Colburn, 1811).
Womack, Peter, *Improvement and Romance: Constructing the Myth of the Highlands* (London: MacMillan, 1989).

8. The Unknown William Livingston (Four Songs)

CHRISTOPHER WHYTE

The Islay poet William Livingston (1808–1870) or, to give him his Gaelic name, Uilleam MacDhunlèibhe, is perhaps best known for a series of poems dealing with significant battles in Scottish history, from Calgacus fighting against the Romans to the Wars of Independence and the 1598 Battle of Gruinart Bay in Islay, which are characterised in certain passages by a disconcertingly bloodthirsty macho heroism. It is indicative of the contradictions of the Scotland of his times that he should also have a piece celebrating the feats of Highland soldiers at the Battle of the Alma in the Crimea in 1854. The background to these strikingly original poems, in places limpid and resonant in their diction, elsewhere so confused and muddled as to make one wonder about errors in transcription (and Livingston's editor, Robert Blair, does confuse what may be termed 'stage directions' with the actual text of a poem) is complex, and requires careful and persistent teasing out. One almost certain influence is the fake Gaelic literature of the late eighteenth and early nineteenth centuries, to which Derick Thomson has devoted an essay.[1] Among the more intriguing aspects of Scottish (and European) cultural history is the image of reverend ministers in more than one Highland manse concocting (a better word might be forging) a spurious Gaelic text to correspond to Macpherson's prose versions of the works of Ossian, which could then be published face-to-face with a Latin translation (making the material accessible to a cultivated European audience) as irrefutable proof that the heroic age in Gaelic Scotland had produced a literature of its own which was second to none.

In his prose writings, Livingston showed himself to be a passionate, if, for us, not entirely convincing, defender of the authenticity of this literature. He edited in 1852 a repeat publication of Donald MacNicol of Lismore's refutation of Dr Johnson's humiliating aspersions on the history and culture of the Scots. Livingston was largely an autodidact, in a way that curiously anticipates MacDiarmid, an aspiring intellectual lacking in formal education who made it the hard way. He learned Latin so as to tackle the ancient chronicles, and picked up enough Greek and Hebrew to read the scriptures without the aid of a dictionary, before turning to Welsh and French. While he may enjoy our full sympathy in taking up cudgels against Dr Johnson, it is rather harder to give him credence when, on the basis of scattered placenames, he attempts to construct a watertight case for Ossian having lived his life in Scotland rather than Ireland, or indignantly rejects the allegation that the Gaelic speakers of Scotland were Irish in origin.

At a distance of a century and a half, the Ossianic controversy can appear a storm in the proverbial teacup, confined in terms of geographical and historical relevance. If, however, the frame of reference is extended, like adjusting the focus of a lens so it takes in a wider panorama, then the European resonances of the principal issues at stake become undeniable. In the early 1830s the Finn Elias Lönnrot (1802–1884) decided that the orally transmitted poems he had been collecting since 1828 could be fitted together to form a larger entity of epic proportions. Lönnrot merged different versions of a single poem, trimming and in places supplying connecting material of his own for what would first appear in 1835–36 as the *Kalevala*. Further expeditions, financed in part by the Finnish Literary Society (reminiscent of the subscription raised by Hugh Blair and others so that James Macpherson could visit the Inner and Outer Hebrides in search of Gaelic manuscript materials) led to further editorial work which resulted in an expanded version of the poem, published in 1849. In Estonia, Friedrich Reinhold Kreutzwald (1803–1882) reconstructed a national epic on the basis of orally transmitted tales, completing a first version in 1853, published in sequels from 1857 to 1861 with a facing German translation. In both cases, a process which, in Scotland, ran aground, the supposed national epic being neither recovered nor reconstructed, reached a successful conclusion. The degree of editorial intervention in both the Finnish and the Estonian epics continues to be a matter of discussion among scholars today. In the Czech lands, starting from 1816, Josef Linda (1789–1834) and Václav Hanka (1791–1861) discovered a series of manuscripts, one of which was published in thirteen languages with the title *Polyglotta* in 1852, detailing the glorious deeds of ancient heroes in a manner compared with Homer and Aeschylus, which purported to place Czech culture on a par with German. That they were forgeries was not generally accepted until the 1880s.

THE UNKNOWN WILLIAM LIVINGSTON (FOUR SONGS)

The confused mess of ancient or not so ancient manuscripts, variant materials orally collected, and sheer forgeries, constituting the background to Livingston's battle poems and to much of his prose, rendered still more complex by the overwhelming presence of a competing language, more developed and more powerful than that of the materials itself, is not an idiosyncracy, but the expression of cultural dynamics active on the European continent as a whole.

Derick Thomson, in a relatively brief discussion of the battle poems from his *Introduction to Gaelic Poetry*, is dissatisfied by 'a vagueness of plot' which makes it 'difficult to keep the thread of the action in mind'. He finds the poems 'full of anachronisms, many of them deliberate', which fail to 'carry much conviction'.[2] In a more extended treatment, Sorley MacLean is disconcerted by

> the irritating formlessness of Livingston's heroic poetry. Not that anything in Livingston approaches real epic. I am afraid that Livingston suggests, at several removes, Walter Scott rather than Homer or the Ultonian Hero Ballads.

He considers 'the most impressive', 'Na Lochlannaich an Ìle' ('The Vikings in Islay') to be

> a formless semi-epical fragment, in which the verse varies from strong adequacy to utter wordy formlessness, lit up occasionally by a striking image.[3]

Yet a convincing case can be made for the battle poems in terms of their evident ambition, if not their actual execution. 'Na Lochlannaich' is endowed with a filmic quality, switching abruptly, as it does, between heroes, as we exchange one perspective for another. A penchant for dramatic presentation makes stretches of verse a close equivalent of theatrical dialogue. The narrator is dispensed with and we are able to listen in to the protagonists themselves. Here, as in the longer 'Blàr Shunadail' ('The Battle of Sunadale'), Livingston experiments with large-scale structures characteristic of extended written rather than oral narratives, designed, that is, for reading more than listening. In 'Blàr Shunadail', the reader accompanies a reconnaissance expedition sent out by Vikings from the Isle of Man, planning an invasion of Kintyre. The interaction between 'goodies' and 'baddies' is entertaining, at times distinctly humorous. This, combined with Livingston's readiness to step across cultural boundaries and humanise the aliens, suggests he had access to, and imported, narrative modes far beyond the scope of the oral tales and ballads available to him in Gaelic. After a concise introduction skilfully setting the mood, 'Cath Monadh Braca' ('The Battle of Mons Graupius') consists of a dawn soliloquy by Calgacus, a figure tormented by self-doubt and gloomy premonitions, distinctly reminiscent of the stage dramas Livingston could well have attended in Glasgow. Next comes a vision, after which the treatment of the battle itself can come over as distinctly perfunctory. Uneven in quality, at times slapdash in execution, Livingston's battle poems nevertheless benefit from repeated and careful consideration. Their most successful moments are impressive indeed.

*

Livingston was a bilingual writer, producing prose in English and verse in Gaelic. In literary terms, the prose is far inferior to the poetry. His wife Margaret, a native of Comrie in Perthshire, is said to have observed of his incomplete *History of Scotland*, issued in five parts by William Gilchrist in 1856, then failing due to lack of subscribers, that 'Nae doot it has merits if yin had the sense tae tak' it oot o't'. For Donald Meek, Livingston's verse

> is like another world, compared with the explosions of wild indignation which mar his non-poetic composition. By contrast, it shows much greater control.[4]

One reason for the evident difference in quality is that prose and poetry belong to overlapping periods of Livingston's maturity, with the prose coming first, to be progressively superseded by his activity as a poet. Blair writes that 'most of the pieces we have, were the product of his mature years, and that it is questionable whether he composed anything expect the few verses to his dog, until comparatively late in life'.[5] Nigel MacNeill highlights

> the long time he was a wooer of the muses before he arrived at the intensity of poetical composition which distinguished his later poetry

THE UNKNOWN WILLIAM LIVINGSTON (FOUR SONGS)

A' Cheòlraidh
Rinn thu gearan air mo luasgan
's gun d' iomain mi deas is tuath thu.
Nàire dhuts' a chuir uait mi,
gus an do liath thu 'toirt fuath dhomh!
Nam biodh tu dìleas nad òige
nuair a thairg mi 'n tùs do phòsadh
sheasainn do chùis anns gach dòlais
's bhearrainn feusagan luchd-fòirneart.

You complained about me being giddy,
that I drove you north and south.
Shame on you for rejecting me,
treating me with spite till you turned grey!
If you'd been faithful in your youth
the first time I proposed marrying you
I'd have stood up for you when things got tough
and clipped the beards of your oppressors.

What angers the Muse is having been kept at bay for so long, until Livingston's hair has started turning grey. She regrets not having been able to offer him her services as a species of female bodyguard, championing him in the face of opponents and detractors. The poet himself, however, is not interested in raking up old arguments. He wants to get down to work:

A' Bhàrd
Mas sean cuimhneachan as ceòl duit,
chan eil mi 'g iarraidh do chòmhradh
no t' fhuran an cuideachd, no 'n còmhdhail.
Cha tèid mise fad' an tòir ort.
A dhrollach leisg, tog ded dhroch mhein,
na cas fiacail 's na druid rosg rium.
'S fad' o chualas mun bheul thostach,
gur seirbh' a mhùig na teang' a bhrosgail.
'S iomadh bliadhn' o nach d' fhuair mi
òran, iorram, rann no duan bhuait.

CHRISTOPHER WHYTE

> Èirich gu grad 's bitheadh buaidh leat,
> labhair a-mach mar bu dual duit!
> Thoir mac-tall' à creagan cruaidh
> a' spreigeadh le Gàidhlig an cluasan
> nan òigear ...

> *If raking up the past is your music,*
> *I've no wish to converse with you,*
> *or greet you in company, or an assembly.*
> *I won't go far to seek you.*
> *You lazy trollop, enough of your scowling,*
> *stop grinding your teeth and frowning at me.*
> *We've heard long since about keeping silent,*
> *that snivelling's more bitter than a stirring tongue.*
> *Many years have gone by since I got*
> *a song, a rowing tune, a verse or a ditty from you.*
> *Up with you quickly and show your best,*
> *hold forth the way your nature teaches!*
> *Set the echo ringing from hard rocks,*
> *make them resonate with Gaelic, in the ears*
> *of young folk ...*

Livingston vividly evokes the twisted face, grinding teeth and frowning brow of his old friend. He sees his poetry as aimed at a young audience, compares its sound to the echoes evoked from the Highland landscape with which he identifies, and admits the shameful nature of a talent lying unused. In the end the two make peace, reaching a negotiated agreement. For all the humour, and the hint at an end to domestic violence on the wife's part, it is clear Livingston is making a commitment to poetry he sees as valid for the remainder of his life:

> **A' Cheòlraidh**
> Gheibh thu do thoil, ach bi gleusta!
> Suidh a-nall 's nì sinn rèite.
> Glacaidh sinn làmhan a chèile
> 's gu là bhàis cha toir mi beum duit.

THE UNKNOWN WILLIAM LIVINGSTON (FOUR SONGS)

You'll get your way, but be at the ready!
Sit down and we'll make peace.
We'll clasp each other's hands
and you'll receive no blow from me till the day you die.

*

Arthur MacLachlan originated from Kilbride Parish in Argyll, specifically from the Island of Luing. He became a successful businessman in Glasgow in the wine and spirits trade, marrying his wife Catherine there in 1825, and was also a leading figure in the city's Gaelic community. His sons included a doctor, who practised in the English Midlands, and John (1826–1893), from 1849 to 1853 parish priest of the newly opened Catholic Church in Inverness. When in 1878 Pope Leo XIII restored for the third time the Catholic diocese of Galloway (comprising Dumfries, Kirkcudbright, Wigtown and four-fifths of Ayrshire), John MacLachlan was appointed the first bishop. He numbered the 3rd Marquess of Bute among his flock. A 'Luinneag do Art MacLachlainn' by Iain Cameron survives in the library of Mountstuart House near Rothesay. Livingston's song is conventional enough in its praise. He lists the sorts of men who should be pleased to be associated with MacLachlan, and recalls the part he took in the celebrations commemorating Duncan Bàn MacIntyre, the poet of Ben Doran. It is interesting to have Livingston recommend young Gaels recently arrived in the metropolis to look to MacLachlan for support and advice. The reference to a network of immigrants from Gaelic Scotland capable of sustaining and directing newcomers to the city can hardly be rhetorical in nature:

> Fhir òig, a thig à tìr nan àrd-bheann,
> air t' aineòil, 's tu gun nì gun chàirdean,
> ma tha thu saor do mhì-mheas tàireil,
> gheibh thu bàigh o Art MacLachainn.

> *Young man, arriving from the land of high mountains,*
> *astray, with no possessions, or friends,*
> *if you are void of shameful disrespect,*
> *you'll get support from Art MacLachlan.*

The assistance offered will naturally be selective in nature, dependent on the character and upbringing of the individual in question. At this stage, the song's addressee being a Catholic is not a problematic issue, even if he was to supply, through his offspring, new blood for expanding church structures in Scotland which were soon to find themselves catering overwhelmingly to the massive population of immigrants arriving from Ireland.

Livingston is generally defined by his Islay origins, yet he is quintessentially a Glasgow poet, living an urban existence and making only occasional sallies to the scenes of his childhood and early maturity. The definitive move to Glasgow occurred in 1850, or early 1851. The 1861 census records him as living with his wife in Govan parish, without children, in a tenement at 68 Dale Street. Both were aged fifty-three, and they possessed only one room having a window (perhaps their only room). Twenty-nine homes are listed at the address, where 153 people resided, twenty-two of whom were school-age children. Robert Blair recalls visiting them there in a 'little garret', and 'finding himself and his wife busily engaged in translating a French history of the Druids' (most likely Simone Pelloutier's *Histoire des Celtes et particulièrement des Gaulois et des Germains*, published posthumously in two volumes in Paris, in 1740 and 1750). This is also the setting for 'Òran do Dhòmhnaill MacDhiarmid', which is included in Livingston's first collection, the 1858 *Duain Ghaelic* published by William Gilchrist, where the genealogy mentioned in the song also features. Blair explains that a young Islayman had written to Livingston requesting this genealogy which, as compiled by the poet, 'passed through no fewer than one hundred and nine Kings of Ireland, before it comes down to the great-grandfather of Diarmad O'Duibhne, the Ossianic hero who slew the boar, whose head forms so prominent a figure in the coat of arms of the Sìol Dhiarmaid!'

Livingston's song is oddly reminiscent of certain verse epistles by Burns, for the peculiarly intimate picture it offers of the poet in action. Curiously, he self-presents not as a poet, but as an antiquarian. It is a song about reading and transcribing, inhabiting, as it were, a middle ground between the aural and the written (though there is no reason to think it ever entered oral tradition). Livingston shows the same fondness for dramatisation evident in several of the battle poems, with a use of direct speech which,

THE UNKNOWN WILLIAM LIVINGSTON (FOUR SONGS)

interestingly, does not include the poet himself. The postman is the first to speak, commenting on the unusually lively state of Livingston's postbox:

>	An ann an seo tha Mac Dhunlèibhe?
>	Chan eil latha tha mi 'g èirigh
>	gun litir o fhear no o thè dha.
>	'S iongantach leam fhèin na tha diubh.
>
>	Tha cuid diubh à Manainn 's à Èirinn,
>	cuid à Sasann 's à Dùn Èidinn
>	le gearradh-àrm gach fir 's a sheula –
>	's bithidh aon o Dhubh-shlèibh dha màireach.
>
>	*Is this where Livingston abides?*
>	*Never a day I get out of my bed*
>	*but there's a letter for him from a man or a woman.*
>	*I can't get over how many there are.*
>
>	*Some come from the Isle of Man, and from Ireland,*
>	*some from England and Edinburgh*
>	*with each man's coat of arms and his seal –*
>	*he'll get one from the dark side tomorrow.*

The last line is difficult to interpret. It might be a reference to a real person or location. But it seems more probable, given the poet's precarious state of health (the stanza immediately preceding these says he was "am chreòlain chrùbach, / uair air leaba 's uair air ùrlar' ('a huddling invalid, / alternating the bed and the floor')) that the postman is hinting at a summons from the other world. Now the poet's wife intervenes, encouraging him to throw his lethargy aside and get down to work:

>	Ged tha thu leasganach, crùbach,
>	chunnaic mis' thu dàna, lùghmhor.
>	Tha mi mar a bha o thùs duit,
>	's is làidir ar cùra nach fàilnich.

CHRISTOPHER WHYTE

> Tòisich gabh an dàil an Fhrangaich
> 's mar leughas tu, eadar-theangaich.
> Cha chost an duais-sgrìobhaidh *planc* dhuit –
> fòghnaidh dhomhsa rann mar chàch bhuait.
>
> Gabhaidh mise Wyntoun fòghlaimt',
> chì sinn an dèan iad còrdadh ...
>
> *You may be bent and crippled,*
> *but I've seen you bold and full of energy.*
> *I feel the same way about you I always did*
> *and we have a strong, unfailing guardian.*
>
> *Consult the Frenchman to begin with;*
> *translate as you're reading.*
> *You won't have to pay a penny for your secretary –*
> *I'll be contented with a verse, same as the rest.*
>
> *I'll take the learned Wyntoun,*
> *and we'll see how they match ...*

She is of course talking about the chronicle of Andrew of Wyntoun (*c*. 1350–*c*. 1423), and the allusion to collating different texts and accounts is worthy of note. Livingston's wife is aware of the value of the secretarial assistance she offers him, and of the price it might fetch on a professional market. Most engrossing of all, however, are the last four stanzas of the poem, in which Livingston describes the preparation of the tools needed for writing with an almost fetishistic satisfaction and delight:

> Dh'fhosgail i bòstan glaiste
> sam bheil seòrsachan an tasgaidh.
> Fhuair i it' a' gheòidh ghlais ann
> 's chaidh i air thapadh mar b' àbhaist.
>
> Thug i 'n t-seirceag sgaiteach, lìobhaidh
> à truaill bhig nan òrachd rìomhach

THE UNKNOWN WILLIAM LIVINGSTON (FOUR SONGS)

a bha còig linntean aig a sinnsear
an gleann tiorail fad on t-sàile.

Gheàrr i gu sgeineil seòlta
an it' o bàrr ma leth òirlich
le sgoltadh cho caol ri ròineig,
guibein glan bu bhòidhch' a thàirr'neadh.

She opened the lock on the little coffer
where the treasures are stored away.
There she got a grey goose feather
and set to work in her usual fashion.

She took the sharp little polished darling
from its gold-embellished sheath,
passed down for five centuries through her family
in a dry glen far from the sea.

With a neat and skilful incision
about half an inch from the feather's tip,
as fine and as thin as a hair,
she devised the neatest little beak that was ever fashioned.

It would be inaccurate to speak of Gaelic tradition as having been at any time in its history exclusively oral. But Livingston, as the Ossianic controversy demonstrates, lived at a period which was incapable of coming up with an adequate theoretical framework for the specific mechanics of oral transmission. The fragmentary nature of oral 'texts', and the presence of variants, were too often interpreted as symptoms of debasement, of the progressive contamination of a unified original. The anxieties arising from this perception necessarily coloured the struggle to prove the value and validity of traditions in languages other than those which were politically and culturally more empowered. At the same time, Livingston's own poetry marks a significant stage in the passage of modern Gaelic poetry from oral to predominantly written modes. His battle poems are written to be read, or at the very least read out. What makes them so distinctive and innovative in Gaelic literature is their setting in motion complex narrative structures, characteristic of written texts, which are foreign to oral tradition (and which Livingston himself has difficulties in managing over longer stretches). A song such as this is peculiarly resonant for a culture poised problematically between the two. The quill which Livingston's wife sharpens becomes a 'guibein glan', the neat little beak of a bird (and it originates with a bird) preparing for song, for utterance. But the concluding stanza is given over to Livingston's delight in the qualities of his wife's shapely, elegant written hand:

> Na cruthanan maiseach, neònach,
> ri taobh a' chèil' an deagh òrdugh,
> 'nan sreathan snasmhor, dìreach, dòigheil,
> m' èibhneas sònraicht' an làmh ud.

> *The marvellously shaped characters*
> *in good order side by side,*
> *forming elegant, unwavering, well-arranged lines;*
> *that hand gives me especial pleasure.*

Just as the quill is related to the body from which it came, so Margaret Livingston's writing is referred to quite simply as a 'hand' (whether this be an English calque, or not, makes little difference). Yet, if we remember today the genealogy concocted for the antiquarian's Islay correspondent, this is paradoxically because he turned the request into a song.

Livingston comes back to the issue of his return to poetic composition in a song addressed to the Irish historian Eugene O'Curry (1794–1862). Extrapolating a poet's biography from his or her poems is a perilous task. Yet it is clear that this return was a crucial element in the 'fabula' Livingston constructed of his own poetic career, and the twenty or more years mentioned here would bridge rather neatly the time between his arrival in Comrie and his settling in Glasgow:

> A dhuin'-uasal fhòghlaimt' mhùirnich,
> ged bha mo cheòlraidh san smùraich
> còrr is fichead bliadhna, dhùisg i
> nuair chual' i ainm an fhir chliùtich.

THE UNKNOWN WILLIAM LIVINGSTON (FOUR SONGS)

You well-studied, good-humoured gentleman,
though my Muse had been buried in ashes
for more than twenty years, she awakened
on hearing the famous man's name.

Here is a parallel, and complementary, account to the one prefacing 'Blàr Dhàil Rìgh' which, as there, establishes a fundamental connection between the historian or antiquarian's activity and the poet's. Born in Doonaha in County Clare, O'Curry in 1824 moved to Limerick, where he worked as a labourer then got a job in the lunatic asylum, all the while engrossed in the study of Irish manuscripts. In 1835 he joined the staff of the Ordnance Survey in Dublin, and after its dispersal worked for the Royal Irish Academy and for Trinity College, restoring, deciphering and transcribing Irish manuscripts. In 1849 and 1855 he made important discoveries among those of the British Museum, which has a catalogue of Irish manuscripts written in O'Curry's hand. In 1854 he was appointed Professor of Archaeology and Irish history in the newly founded Catholic university at Dublin. Donald Meek informs us that Livingston's uncle John worked as a teacher of mathematics and languages in Dublin. The poet's father studied there for a while, and was a competent Latin scholar, interested in poetry. The family connection to Dublin may have predisposed Livingston to overlook the difference in religious allegiance between the Gaels of Ireland and the majority of those in Scotland, emphasising instead the points common to the cultural struggle being carried out in both realms. The song to O'Curry even smooths over the differences between the two languages, presenting them as, in their shared antiquity, substantially the same:

> Cànain aosda chlanna Mìlidh
> a bh' anns an t-saoghal riamh 's nach dìobair;
> cha chuir gàmhlas nàmhaid sìos i
> 's i nis an làmhan a fear dìdein.

> Cànain àigh nam buadhan òirdheirc
> a b' fharsaing' cliù air feadh na h-Eòrpa,
> bithidh i fhathast mar a thòisich
> os ceann gach cainnt na h-iuchair eòlais.

> *Venerable language of the Milesians,*
> *in the world from the start, never to die out;*
> *its enemy's malice will not bring it down*
> *now it is in the hands of its saviour.*
>
> *Delightful language, illustrious in virtues,*
> *whose fame spread widest throughout Europe,*
> *it will yet be as it was to begin with,*
> *a key of knowledge superior to all other speech.*

It is not difficult to make out the elements in O'Curry's biography which must have inspired a feeling of kinship in Livingston: the humble origins, the antiquarian ambitions and the years of selfless endeavour. Livingston's scholarly achievements sadly remained at an amateurish level, meaning he could never hope for the academic recognition O'Curry finally obtained. But note that the recovered status Livingston joyfully predicts for Gaelic and Irish is that of a key to learning, a tool for, means of access to, knowledge of the highest kinds.

*

The greatest of all Livingston's songs, 'Fios thun a' Bhàird', has encountered universal admiration. So it can hardly be spoken of as unknown. Sorley MacLean considered it 'perhaps the finest poem of the century ... throughout the poem the description of nature has a fine gravity, and clearness of line, which, with the sonourous plangency of the description of human desolation, make it a perfect poem'.[7] High praise indeed! If Donald Meek pushes praise of Livingston's craftsmanship just a little too far, his enthusiasm is easily shared:

> Livingston could sometimes (but not always!) be precise to an astonishing degree, as if he were working with a bardic ruler, set square, proportional dividers, and compasses. He was aware of structural requirements, even planning a poem so meticulously that it hinged on, or changed gear powerfully at, a clear mid-point.[8]

Derick Thomson also notes how 'half way through the poem – literally and exactly half way through it – there is a sudden reversal of mood, which we must conclude was anticipated and planned'.⁹ The hypothesis here is that, if not the degree, then the kind of planning evident in 'Fios thun a' Bhàird' is characteristic of a written text, or more precisely, of one committed to writing before entering oral tradition (if, indeed, this were ever destined to happen). It is worth pausing to consider certain surprising aspects of the poem. Blair tells us its composition was prompted by Blair's mother's gift of a piece of homemade Islay cloth, to which was attached the note: 'Fios thun a' Bhàird Ilich, o bhean Dhonnchaidh' ('a piece of news for the Islay poet, from Duncan's wife'). Livingston took this as the title for his song, which therefore represents the message he 'ought to have' received. The poet is not the originator, but the addressee of the text. As elsewhere, Livingston prefers to hand the matter of a poem over to voices other than his own (the parallel would be with the abdication of the narrator in the battle poems, in favour of dramatic presentation). Communication travels from Islay to Glasgow, the latter being the poet's place of residence.

The poem (or song) has fourteen stanzas, and the change which occurs in the middle of stanza 7 has the effect of a carefully prepared ambush on the reader. Until that point, everything is calm, unruffled, lulling the reader into a false sense of security:

>Na caochain fhìor-uisg' luath
>a' tighinn a-nuas o chùl nam màm,
>bho lochain ghlan gun ruadhan
>air na cruachan fad' on tràigh,
>far an òl am fiadh a phailteas,
>'s bòidheach ealtan lach gan snàmh ...

>*Rivulets of pure, swift water*
>*descending from the back of gently curved mountains,*
>*from a small, clear loch whose surface is unsullied*
>*on the hills far from the shore,*
>*where the deer can drink their fill,*
>*and fine-looking flocks of ducks swim ...*

The use of the present tense and of verbal nouns (roughly equivalent to the continuous forms in English – 'is coming', 'are swimming'), more generally, the absence of verbs, comes over as the very opposite of a narrative, which must be characterised by events, intervention, change and reaction:

> Tha Bogha Mòr an t-sàile
> mar a bha le reachd biothbhuan,
> a' mòrachd maise nàdair
> 's a' cheann-àrd ri tuinn a' chuain,
> a rìombal geal seachd mìle,
> gainmhean sìobt' o bheul an lain ...
>
> *Bowmore next to the sea*
> *as if by an eternal decree*
> *magnifies the splendour of nature,*
> *its promontory against the ocean breakers,*
> *its pale circle stretching seven miles,*
> *sand swept from the mouth of the full tide ...*

The mention of a 'reachd biothbhuan' is deceptive, as is hinted in 'mar a bha', words repeated when the turn-around in the poem is heralded halfway through the following stanza:

> Nuair a thuiteas sgàil na h-oidhche,
> mar gum b' ann a' caoidh na bha ...
>
> *When night's shadow falls,*
> *as if mourning what once was ...*

Stanza 8 has two lines of an absolutely lapidary quality, the second beginning with a verb in the simple past which indicates a single action, irreversible and pitiless, with an emphatic alliteration between 'chuir' and 'chaor':

> Tha ÌLE 'n diugh gun daoine.
> Chuir a' chaor a bailtean fàs ...
>
> *There are no people on Islay today.*
> *The sheep have emptied out its townships ...*

The simple past verbs which follow have an abrupt, catastrophic quality ('chuir gamhlas Gall air fuadach', 'sgap mì-rùn iad thar fairge', 'dh'fhalbh 's cha till na Gàidheil') ('*the venom of Lowlanders has dispersed*', '*ill-will chased them over the horizon*', '*the Gaels have gone and will not return*'). These elements are blindingly obvious yet perhaps all the more effective given the dignified simplicity of the means being employed. The parallelism which characterised the first half of the poem recurs in its second half, but with concessive 'ged', then with the negative particle 'cha, chan' ('cha chluinnear', 'chan fhaicear', 'chan fhaigh': '*will not be heard/seen/found*'). Most devastating of all is this summing up from the middle of the last stanza but one, overwhelmingly powerful thanks to the verb's three subjects and the jolting zeugma they involve: 'Bhuadhaich eucoir, Gaill is cìs' ('*injustice, the Lowlanders and extortion have triumphed*'). The contented animals engaged in a self-regenerating natural cycle of the poem's earlier sections are replaced by ''n nathair breac 'na lùban / air na h-ùrlair far an d' fhàs / Na fir mhòr a chunnaic mise' ('*a speckled serpent curled in loops / on the floors where there grew up / the big men that I saw*'). Note how the message-bearing part of the stanza spills over here into the regular refrain. The concluding lines exhibit an alternation of seemingly positive observations with the bitter reality which can be taken as summing up and epitomising the poem's two halves:

> Tha 'n Learga ghlacach ghrianach
> 's fuidheall cianail air a taobh;
> tha 'n gleann 'na fhiathair uaine
> aig luchd fuath gun tuath, gun bhàrr ...
>
> *The Learga, exposed to the sun, filled with hollows,*
> *has a forlorn remnant on its side;*
> *the glen is a green sward*
> *at the mercy of those whom we detest, who neither sow*
>   *nor reap ...*

All in all, it seems that in order to fully comprehend this poem, we need to have it on the page in front of us. In its printed form, the text has a quality of all being there at the same time, of co-presence, allowing our eyes to dart back and forth, checking what we remember and establishing comparisons, which is fundamentally different from the unidirectional, ribbon-like perception prompted by an oral delivery. (And yet, and yet… The constant repetition of one and the same tune, when the poem is sung, could give an underlying impression of sameness, of returning to or remaining in one place, against which the tragic alteration in the poem's second part must stand out all the more tellingly. It may be impossible, and unnecessary, to pin certain texts of Livingston's down on one side or the other of a putative oral/written, heard/read divide.)

*

Anyone investigating the intellectual roots of Livingston's poetry very quickly comes to regret the absence of a thoroughgoing treatment of Scottish historiography. The patriotic historians writing in the later seventeenth century, and around the time of the Union of Parliaments, were living presences to him, but are largely forgotten today. The gap is a glaring one, given that the history of a nation is also the story of its historymakers, in the sense of those who struggled to shape a narrative from its past. A study of the kind desired would not measure the resulting accounts against 'what actually happened', but would instead respectfully assess the aims which the writers were pursuing, the tools available to them, and the ideologies powering their efforts.

The broader background against which Livingston's poetry emerged serves to illuminate our understanding of it, while at the same time being illuminated by the poetry, and by his predicament. His battle poems can be seen as one more expression of the tensions behind the Ossianic controversy, an attempt to provide Gaelic Scotland with the heroic, historical poetry that could supply a founding myth, in terms of both nation and language, such as Lönnrot successfully supplied in Finland, and Kreutzmann in Estonia. That the Czech chronicles eventually proved to be forgeries did not render them any less effective, in the shorter term, in offering a battery of figures and events, for use in a campaign of national and linguistic self-affirmation.

Why were such attempts doomed to failure in Scotland? Empire, and the Enlightenment, are likely to play an important role in any answer we come up with. It would be necessary to contemplate the more unsavoury aspects of the Enlightenment; to face the implications of its repeated claims to universality; to accept that, if indeed it constituted the intellectual powerhouse of the French Revolution, by doing so it paved the way for one of the greatest spontaneous outbursts of civilian violence in modern history. We would have to consider the arrogant monolingualism of the French revolutionary legislature, evaluating the relationship then current between English and French, languages of culture, and the emerging, hitherto downtrodden languages of Europe. From the point of view of English, or of French, these languages were not only unneeded but incomprehensible, subsisting in the utter darkness of unintelligibility. We would consider why certain of those languages, such as Czech, or Slovak, or Lithuanian, succeeded in bodying forth a modern literature and becoming the official idioms of civil states, while Gaelic, Breton and Basque have so far failed, or are still struggling, to do so. We would need to decide why the interface between Gaelic and English became so clogged up. What sort of an image could, or can, a language such as English hope to offer of the contents of a language it is ruthlessly engaged in extirpating?

Were we to think poetically for a moment, rather than rationally, taking Gaelic and English for animate entities, endowed with sensations, feelings and memories, what then must have occurred in the relationship between them, each time, in a schoolroom, a child was shamed, or physically beaten, for speaking Gaelic rather than English? How ephemeral were those repeated injustices, those violences? Did they leave a trace? And if so, of what nature? To what extent, in discussing Livingston's poetry through English, embedding the Gaelic quotations in a foreign text as jewels might be mounted in a casing, their inner darkness impenetrable to all but a few eyes, are we perpetrating once more, and thereby perpetuating, that violence?

The gift to us of Livingston's poetry lies not just in the artefacts he handed on, muddled and imperfect as these sometimes are, but in the questions we are prompted to formulate as we attempt to read him fairly and competently. The challenges he poses are not merely aesthetic in nature, but historical and intellectual too, no less urgent than his repeated demands for justice.

Budapest, May 2014

Notes

1. D. S. Thomson, 'Bogus Gaelic Literature c.1750–c.1820', *Transactions of the Gaelic Society of Glasgow* 5 (1958).
2. Derick Thomson, *An Introduction to Gaelic Poetry* (London: Victor Gollancz, 1977), p. 234.
3. Somhairle Mac Gill-eain, 'The poetry of William Livingston' in *Ris a' Bhruthaich: Criticism and Prose Writings*, ed. William Gillies (Stornoway: Acair, 1985), pp. 136, 134.
4. Donald E. Meek, 'The World of William Livingston' in J. Derrick McClure, John M. Kirk and Margaret Storrie (eds), *A Land That Lies Westwards: Language and Culture in Islay and Argyll* (Edinburgh: John Donald 2009), p. 158.
5. See the 'Memoir' in *Duain agus Òrain le Uilleam MacDhunleibhe am Bard Ìleach* (Glasgow: Archibald Sinclair, 1882). All poems are quoted from the edition undertaken by Robert Blair, on the prompting of Colin Hay of Ardbeg. Both were personal acquaintances of the poet. Spelling has been normalised according to current usage. Punctuation is supplied by the writer of this essay and is to be regarded as provisional. Blair's text repeatedly allows for differing interpretations in this respect.
6. Nigel MacNeill, *The Literature of the Highlanders* (Stirling: Eneas MacKay, first published 1892, second edition 1929), pp. 460–61.
7. Somhairle Mac Gill-eain, 'The poetry of William Livingston', pp. 148–49.
8. Donald E. Meek, 'The World of William Livingston', p. 158.
9. Derick Thomson, *An Introduction to Gaelic Poetry*, p. 236.

9. Gaelic Periodicals in the Lowlands: Negotiating Change

SHEILA M. KIDD

The nascent Gaelic periodical press which emerged in the period between 1829 and 1850 is of fundamental importance in demonstrating the effect which changing demographics were to have on the production of Gaelic literature. Increasing levels of Gaelic literacy, technological advances in both print production and in transportation and, not least, concentrations of Gaelic-speakers in the urban Lowlands were to provide an environment in which a number of attempts were made at publishing Gaelic periodicals. Charles Withers' important analysis of the movement of Highlanders to urban Lowland centres in the course of the eighteenth and nineteenth centuries has drawn extensively on official records such as census data and focused on cultural institutions including churches and Highland societies.[1] Offering a counter-balance to this is the work of scholars such as Kenneth MacDonald and Michel Byrne who have placed Gaelic literature at the centre of their work on Glasgow Gaels in the nineteenth century, with Byrne drawing primarily on verse and MacDonald using both prose and verse.[2] Consideration of the periodical press, its writers and its content, can bring a further dimension to the debate, demonstrating some of the ways in which Gaelic culture, and particularly Gaelic literature, adapted and responded to this new social milieu. This paper outlines some of the ways in which the early Gaelic periodical press in particular emerged in, and was influenced by, this new and changing environment, attempting to reconcile its Lowland base and its readership dispersed in the Lowlands, Highlands and beyond. The focus will be primarily, although not exclusively, on the first periodical founded and edited by the Rev. Dr Norman MacLeod, *An Teachdaire Gae'lach*, which was published in Glasgow between 1829 and 1831.

The Rev. Dr Norman MacLeod (1783–1862), a native of Morvern, known to Gaels by the sobriquet *Caraid nan Gàidheal* ('Friend of the Gaels') and minister of Campsie and latterly of Ingram Street Church in Glasgow (later St Columba's Gaelic Church), was instrumental in establishing the Gaelic periodical press. When he established the first of his two periodicals, *An

Teachdaire Gae'lach, in May 1829, this represented the first sustained attempt at producing a Gaelic journal, and twenty-four issues would appear in print before publication ceased in 1831, due primarily to MacLeod's ill-health.[3] This did, however, provide the impetus for a further seven Gaelic periodicals which would be published in Scotland by 1850, including MacLeod's second publication, *Cuairtear nan Gleann* (1840-43).[4] That periodicals were very much a product of the Highland diaspora is reflected not only in these publications which were all produced in the Lowlands, but also in the appearance of Gaelic periodicals overseas in the shape of *Cuairtear nan Coillte* in Kingston, Canada, in 1840; *An Cuairtear Og Gaidhealach* in Antigonish, Nova Scotia, in 1851; *An Teachdaire Gaidhealach* published for ten months in Hobart, Tasmania, in 1857; and, most successfully, *Mac-Talla* between 1892 and 1904 in Sydney, Nova Scotia.

The Gaelic periodical press in the nineteenth century, and indeed beyond, was nonetheless very much a product of the Lowlands, and more specifically of Glasgow, with all periodicals before 1850 published in the city or, in the case of two periodicals, with publication shared between a Glasgow and an Edinburgh firm. None of these publications enjoyed a particularly long run, the average being seventeen issues and the longest, MacLeod's *Cuairtear nan Gleann,* running for forty issues. Nonetheless, even after a hiatus of over twenty years in Gaelic periodical publishing in Scotland between 1850 and the mid-1870s, Glasgow retained its position as a centre for the production of Gaelic and Highland-oriented periodicals, albeit rivalled by Inverness. The short-lived *Highland Pioneer* with its subtitle 'A Monthly Journal, Devoted to the Consideration and Advancement of Matters Relating to the Welfare of Highlanders at Home and Abroad' was published in Glasgow in 1875, and *The Highland Echo/Guth nan Gaidheal* during 1877 and 1878, although the medium of the former was entirely English and of the latter primarily English. The Canadian-born Gaelic-language publication *An Gaidheal* and its English supplement (1871-77) became Glasgow-based in 1872 when its editor, Angus Nicolson, was appointed Dominion Emigration Agent for the North of Scotland.[5]

Just as London became a centre for Welsh periodical publishing in the very early nineteenth century due to its expatriate Welsh population, so too the emergence of Glasgow as a centre for Gaelic periodical production is not entirely surprising when demographics are considered. By the mid-1830s

GAELIC PERIODICALS IN THE LOWLANDS: NEGOTIATING CHANGE

Glasgow was home to a sizeable Highland population of around 25,000, according to a census overseen by Norman MacLeod, and of these 16,115 were recorded as being 'capable of receiving instruction solely through the Gaelic language'.[6] By 1841, and in the wake of the famine years of the late 1830s, MacLeod estimated Glasgow's Highland population to be approaching 30,000.[7] This, combined with ease of access to printing presses and to an expanding transport network linking Glasgow with the Highlands and Islands, left the city well-placed to flourish as a centre of Gaelic publishing, and more specifically of periodical publishing in the course of the nineteenth century. Another equally crucial factor was the existence of a small group of literary-minded Gaels in the city. Henry Whyte (1852–1913), himself a Glasgow Gael and Gaelic writer and poet, wrote of the coterie of Highland writers who frequented the hosiery shop of Lachlan MacLean, a native of Coll and founder and editor of *An Teachdaire Ùr Gàidhealach*, in the later 1830s and early 1840s:

> Dr MacLeod [Norman MacLeod] found in Mr MacLean a man after his own heart, so full of Celtic enthusiasm, and so anxious to spend and be spent in the service of his fellow-Highlanders, and his shop at 23 Argyle Street became a Celtic *rendezvous*, where such literary Highlanders as Dr. MacLeod, John MacKenzie, of the 'Beauties of Gaelic Poetry', and Evan MacColl, the Lochfyne bard, met and exchanged views'.[8]

The impetus for establishing *An Teachdaire Gae'lach* was primarily educational. It was intended to provide suitable reading material for a Highland population becoming increasingly literate in Gaelic through the efforts of the Gaelic School Societies from 1811, and the General Assembly of the Church of Scotland schools from 1825, and thus, as MacLeod himself stated, 'knowing that when they are taught to read, if they do not get good books they will get bad ones', there was a vacuum to be filled.[9] The journal's impact was, however, far wider than its original aim and it was in fact paradigm-changing in many ways, providing an unprecedented opportunity for aspiring Gaelic writers to experiment with genre, style and register in Gaelic, by creating new book-selling and purchasing patterns and, most significantly of all, it stimulated the writing of original, secular Gaelic prose, of which there had been an almost complete dearth before 1829.

Catering for an audience in the Highlands, Lowlands and further afield, as MacLeod acknowledges in his very first editorial in *An Teachdaire Gae'lach*, periodicals provided a new opportunity for communication among an increasingly disparate Gaelic-speaking population, whether ''s na bailtean margaidh, agus air feadh mhachraichean na'n Gall, [...] fo ghréin loisgich nan Innsean, no fo dhubhar choiltean fàsail America'(*'in the market towns and throughout the Lowlands [...] under the burning sun of the Indies or under the darkness of the desolate American forests'*).[10] By 1840, when he penned the introductory editorial to *Cuairtear nan Gleann*, MacLeod offers a more personal perspective on the diaspora, reflecting upon his own transplantation from the Highlands to the Lowlands, an experience to which many of his readers would have been able to relate personally and one with which he seems wholly at ease, albeit not without a hint of nostalgia:

> Gur h-ann sna glinn a fhuair mi m' àrach, am measg ghleann agus bheannta na Gàidhealtachd a chuir mi seachad a' chuid a b' fhaide 's a' chuid gu mór bu chridheala chunnaic no chì mi do m' aimsir san t-saoghal so. Tha greis fhada nis o'n a dh' fhàg mi tir m' òige; tha mo thuineachadh sa' bhaile-mhór; 's è 's fasgaiche do'n aois, agus 'se a chabhsair leacach a's freagaraiche do m' cheuma goirid na garbh-lachd agus farsuinneachd nam beann.

> *It was in the glens I was raised, among the glens and mountains of the Highlands was where I spent the longest and most enjoyable part of my life I have experienced or will experience. It is a long time now since I left the land of my youth; I now live in the city; it better shelters old age and its slabbed pavement is better suited to my short steps than the rough ground and expanse of the mountains.*[11]

MacLeod's bicultural perspective is one which is echoed throughout the pages of the nineteenth-century Gaelic periodical press. Arguably one of the key functions of the periodicals which stemmed from this diasporic context was that of negotiating change. MacLeod's two periodicals were very much representative of the bicultural world in which they were produced, containing writings by both Highland and Lowland Gaels for Highland and Lowland Gaels alike, and indeed by and for Gaels abroad too. This included secular and spiritual writings, mostly original, some translated from English; and the subject matter ranged from traditional tales to accounts of modern technology.

The 'còmhradh' (*conversation*) was a genre popularised by MacLeod's periodicals and in the first one, published in the very first issue of *An Teachdaire Gae'lach*, some of the dualities of the period are evident. In the 'còmhradh' between Eoghann Brocair (a fox-hunter) and Lachlann nan Ceistean (the catechist), Eoghann represents the secular, the oral and the past on the one hand and Lachlann the spiritual, the literary and the future (including Glasgow) on the other. The conversation turns to the periodical itself as Eoghann asks Lachlann, the 'còmhradh's' voice of authority, about it:

> Eoghann: Cò e am fleasgach ùr so [*An Teachdaire*]? Agus cò às a tha esan a' teachd oirn [*sic*]?
> Lachlann: A' Glaschu.
> Eoghann: Ciod e nach d'thig a' Glaschu!
> [...]
> Lachlann: ... Anns a cheud àite, ma ta, tha iad a' gealltuinn mòran do eachdruidh na Gaeltachd sna linntibh a chaidh seachad. A' bheil sin a' còrdadh riut?
> Eoghann: Tha gu math; ach c'àit am faigh iad e? Na'n cuireadh iad fios air Iain-dubh-mac-Iain-'ic-Ailein, gheibheadh iad barrachd uaithe den t-seorsa sin, na tha ac' air a' Ghalldachd.

> *Eoghann: Who is this youth [An Teachdaire], and where does he come to us from?*
> *Lachlann: From Glasgow.*
> *Eoghann: What doesn't come from Glasgow!*
> *[...]*
> *Lachlann: ... In the first place, then, they are promising much Highland history from centuries gone by. Does that suit you?*
> *Eoghann: Yes indeed; but where they will get it? If they were to get in touch with Iain-dubh-mac-Iain-'ic-Ailein they would get more of that sort of thing from him than they have in the Lowlands.*[12]

Eoghann's suspicions of the Glasgow periodical are, however, quickly allayed and he becomes a subscriber, and a place is thereby negotiated for this Lowland periodical in the Gaelic literary landscape.

Glasgow remains a constant presence in the pages of MacLeod's periodicals, whether in the form of news, information about markets and employment, or as a backdrop to 'còmhraidhean', or to the few tales which appear. Events in Glasgow on occasion provide the inspiration for a piece of writing although this may not always be immediately apparent to a modern reader. One such example is a pair of dialogues by Norman MacLeod between Eachann Tirisdeach (*Eachann from Tiree*) and Cuairtear nan Gleann (*The Traveller of the Glens*), published in the journal in October and December 1840, dialogues which discuss the eruption of Mount Vesuvius and destruction of Pompeii and Herculaneum leading on to a more general discussion of volcanoes. Glasgow may seem an unlikely inspiration for a text on volcanoes, but when the text is considered within its contemporary context the reason for this particular choice of subject becomes apparent. The first of these 'còmhraidhean' begins with Eachann recounting what he had witnessed in Glasgow, the eruption of a model of Mount Vesuvius in the city. This was in fact a real, rather than a fictional, event which was part of a grand spectacle held in Cranston Hill Zoological Gardens between July and October 1840 and attracting large fee-paying crowds. In advance of its opening the *Glasgow Herald* advises readers that:

> The effect is so truly grand and sublime, bordering so nearly on reality, as to defy description, and which to appreciate and fully comprehend must be seen during the Eruption; the different Stages of this eventful occurrence are ingeniously displayed, finishing with a terrific rush of molten lava down the mountain, burying the ill-fated city in one common ruin; the whole of the dreadful conflagration is beautifully reflected on the lake and distant mountains.[13]

In the 'còmhradh' Eachann describes witnessing this spectacle, situating it within a West Highland frame of reference for readers, with Pompeii and Herculaneum's coastal location compared with that of Oban and Tobermory:

> Eachann: ... lochan mara àillidh air an robh iomadh bìrlinn chaol, rìomhach, a' snàmh. Chuala mi ainm an lochain seo, ach dhìochuimhnich mi e.
> Cuairtear: Bàgh Naples – caladh cho àillidh thèarainte 's a tha air uachdar an t-saoghail.
> Eachann: Bha baile mòr taobh eile a' chaoil seo, an cois na tràghad, cosmhail ris an Òban no Tobar Mhoire, nuair tha duine a' seòladh a-staigh do na h-àiteachan sin, ach gun robh na sràidean 's na taighean rìoghail air chumadh ro-neònach, eu-coslach ri aon taigh a chunnaic mi riamh.

> Eachann: ... *a lovely sea loch on which many beautiful, narrow galleys were floating. I heard the name of this loch, but I have forgotten it.*
> Cuairtear: *The Bay of Naples – as beautiful and safe a harbour as exists on the face of the earth.*
> Eachann: *There was a town on the other side of this strait, beside the shore, similar to Oban or Tobermory when one sails in to these places, but for the fact that the streets and regal houses were in a very strange style, unlike any house I have ever seen.*[14]

Similarly Glasgow-influenced is a text from 1830, 'Bàta nan Speur' (*'The Sky Boat'*), which is primarily informative, detailing the invention of the hot-air balloon almost fifty years earlier. Based on the evidence of the text itself this clearly found its inspiration in an ascent by balloon made by a Mr Green in Glasgow at the end of May 1830 and which the writer uses as a springboard for discussing the development of the hot-air balloon along with more general evangelising about the benefits of contemporary technological innovations, particularly in transport.[15] Transport in the shape of the steamship and the railway was a common topic in the pages of MacLeod's periodicals, as has been discussed by Donald E. Meek in his analysis of a number of MacLeod's writings on transport, serving to underline the role of the periodicals in introducing and explaining these innovations to a Gaelic-speaking audience, many of whom would not necessarily have seen either steamship or train.[16]

One of the dominant themes of nineteenth-century Gaelic verse is that of 'caochladh' (*change/decay*) in the face of immense and rapid social change, with much verse infused with a nostalgic view of a pre-clearance idyll. This theme is not, however, limited to Gaelic verse and in the pages of the periodicals nowhere is it more evident than in the 'còmhraidhean' which appeared in these early journals, although the way in which this theme is handled by writers differs from the poetic approach. MacLeod's early dialogues are pervaded by a sense of nostalgia through characters' observations on changing social relationships, such as the lack of patronage for poets and musicians, and on the effect of improved communications between Highlands and Lowlands on language, culture, food and the economy. In general the authority figures who are present in most dialogues tend to be forward-looking individuals who embrace the future and, in contrast with the poetic voice, challenge the nostalgic impulse, whereas the more 'humble' Gaels tend to look to the past. We see Fionnladh Pìobaire (*Finlay the Piper*) – his mere name marking him out as a representative of the traditional rather than the new – lamenting the way in which books are replacing songs and tales in one of MacLeod's earliest 'còmhraidhean', with the journal itself standing accused of usurping oral tradition:

> Cha chruinnich a nis cuideachd nach d'thoirear làmh air leabhar, is coma c'àite; ma's ann ri tìre no cruadhachadh san àthaidh, m'as ann a' bleith sa mhuileann, m'a sann an déigh na cabhruich air a' bhlàr-mhòine, m'as ann air oìche choinnle, no oìche collainn, cha'n fhaicear fearas-chuideachd ach leughadh. Cha chluinnear sgeulachd na duanag. Cha teichd na bha dheth so 'nar measg roimhe so, ach chuir an Teachdaire Gaelach cinn daoine gu tur air aimhreidh. Tubaist air fein agus air a theachdaireachd, mhill e mo cheird. Cha chuirear ni's faide fios air Fionnlath pìobaire, no air Callum fidhleir, no air Donnacha nan aoirean, no bodach nan dàn, an duine truagh.

> *Folk don't gather now without a book being picked up, regardless of where they are; whether drying or parching in the kiln; grinding at the mill, after taking sowens out at the peats, on Candlemas or Hogmanay, there's no pastime but reading. Stories and wee songs aren't to be heard. We used to have no shortage of them among us before,*

> but the *Teachdaire Gae'lach* has set folk's heads completely wrong. May an accident befall him and his message, he damaged my craft. Finlay the piper, Calum the fiddler, Duncan the satirist, and the old songster, the poor man, are no longer in demand.[17]

So too in another Fionnladh declares that he will not teach his son to play the bagpipes as 'tha là na pìobaireachd seachad' (*'the days of piping have passed'*).[18] The steamship, while on the one hand a sign of progress for the Highlands, is also portrayed as an eroder of traditional ways, taking away Highland produce to be sold in Lowland markets while bringing in poor Lowland substitutes such as tea and sugar, useless Lowland fashions in clothes and, not least of all, English. In one 'còmhradh' the code switching in the language of Mòr Òg (*Young Marion*), who has just returned from the Lowlands, reflects contemporary language usage as she intersperses her Gaelic with English words – 'Tha e coltach nach feumadh daoine aodach *decent* sam bith a chur orra san dùthaich so' and 'O *Uncle!* Is *droll* an duine sibh: bithidh sibh daonnan ri *fun*, 's ri magadh' (*'It seems that folk don't need to wear decent clothes in this country' ... 'O Uncle! You're a droll man: you're always into fun and mocking'*).[19] This is much to the chagrin of her uncle who cannot abide this mixing of the two languages.

The 'còmhradh' as a genre allows for a duality of perspective and, while MacLeod may be seen here to be attempting to explore and relieve some of the anxieties which he perceived to be felt commonly among his readers in this age of change, they may also be seen as indicative of a degree of unease in his own mind as he weighs up the benefits and costs of change. While in his essays on technological advancements he borders on the evangelical with his exposition of, and enthusiasm for, the steamship and the railway, his 'còmhraidhean' speak more to the process of adjustment involved in accommodating these changes, adjustment for him as much as for his readers.

Where fictional journeys to, and settlement in, the Lowlands are dealt with by writers, Glasgow on occasions takes on something of a liminal quality, as Donald Meek has suggested of the steamship, with individuals experiencing a transition, a rite of passage, which reflected that being experienced on a wider scale by thousands of Gaels.[20] The most obvious example of this is Fionnladh Pìobaire, who discusses with his wife the prospect of him going to the Lowlands to seek employment at harvest time; this is then followed in subsequent issues of *An Teachdaire Gae'lach* by letters which he sends home to his wife in which he chronicles his experiences, detailing his journey by steamship and his impressions of Glasgow. Unlike thousands of Gaels Fionnladh returns home, his sojourn having been seasonal rather than permanent. Attempts at fiction, which it must be acknowledged are few and far between, tend to involve a journey to the Lowlands with Glasgow as a place of sorrow and personal tribulation but also of triumph over adversity, often with a moral underpinning. 'Sgeul mu Mhàiri nighean Eoghainn bhàin; air aithris leatha fein' begins with the eviction of the subject and her family, their settling in Glasgow and her husband and sons finding work in a cotton mill. One son dies from a fever, her husband recovers from the same fever but is left too weak to work and the family fall into the depths of poverty. Despite pressure being put on the son to take part in a strike in the cotton mill, he refuses – a not too subtle message to readers – and instead enlists in the army, thereby securing the family's future. In 'Trioblaidean na h-Òige' by an anonymous Glasgow writer a young man is sent to live with his uncle and aunt in Paisley. They abuse him but he is saved by his master, a weaver who more or less adopts him, and his tale again becomes a more positive one with the Lowlands as the locus for this transformation to a new life.[21]

Another example of a Glasgow-based contributor whose location and experiences in the city are reflected in his choice of subject-matter is Dr Robert MacGregor. MacGregor (1809–55), a native of Ardchattan, was a physician at Glasgow Royal Infirmary who contributed to *An Teachdaire Ùr Gàidhealach*, *Cuairtear nan Gleann* and *Fear-Tathaich nam Beann*. The first of his contributions is 'Tigh-Eiridinn Rìoghail Ghlascho' (*'Glasgow Royal Infirmary'*) in which he details both the history and contemporary details of the hospital. Readers are told that in the five months to May 1835 there had been seventy-two patients with smallpox in the hospital, of whom eighteen had died, most of them from the islands, and he uses this to remind Gaelic-speaking parents to ensure that their children are vaccinated 'agus nach bi uiread a' dh-aodannan bòidheach nan caileagan Gàidhealach air am breacadh leis a' ghalar ghràineil so' (*'so that there will not be so many Highland girls' lovely faces marked by this horrible disease'*).[22] He also highlights the importance of their native language to Highlanders in the infirmary, describing the boost which it gives Gaelic-speaking patients to hear their language spoken to them in an alien Lowland hospital environment: ''s minic a chunnaic mi leis a so, an inntinn lag agus ìosal a' togail gu grad agus an urra a' faighinn faochaidh, seadh, nach robh e comasach dha fhaotainn bho chungaidh-leighis sam bith' (*'it's often I saw thus, the weak, depressed mind, lifting suddenly and the person gaining relief, indeed, that he could not get from any medicine'*).[23]

That is not so say that the periodicals suggest that Glasgow and the Lowlands offered an entirely trouble-free future. Fionnladh Pìobaire's experiences, related in one of the letters sent home to his wife, detail how he was arrested when the police suspected that the box containing his pipes held the body of a child. Norman MacLeod's depiction of the prison cell in which Fionnladh and his friend Para found themselves reveals the darker side of life in the city with 'daoine nan sìneadh an dall na daoraich thall agus a bhos, a' call fola, is mallachadh 'nam beul ... duine marbh 'na shìneadh air an ùrlar' (*'men stretched out blind drunk here and there, bleeding, and cursing ... a corpse lying on the floor'*).[24]

In the same issue of *An Teachdaire Gae'lach* as the story of Màiri Nighean Eoghainn Bhàin appeared, there is a page-long text which recounts the murder of a Lamont from Mull on the steamer between Tarbert and Glasgow when his drink is fatally drugged by a couple intent on robbing him. This is immediately followed by an account of another Gael who was deceived by a woman in Glasgow, lost all his money and was almost murdered. Readers are told 'biodh na nithe sin nan sanus do mhuinntir na Gae'ltachd iad a bhi furachair, faicilleach, m'an chuideachd a thadhalas iad' (*'let those things be a warning to the people of the Highlands to be wary and cautious about the company they keep'*).[25] The warning is not against going to the Lowlands but rather about the importance of exercising caution while there.

Issues relating to identity and to Gaelic linguistic and cultural continuity in the urban Lowlands appear occasionally, as when Fionnladh Pìobaire tells his wife back in the Highlands, ''Smòr an cothrom a th'aig na Gaedhil anns a Bhaile mhòr so, thigeadh iad o'n ear no o'n iar gheibh iad Gaelic an dùthcha fein ann an eagluisibh a bhaile' (*'Great is the opportunity afforded to Gaels in this city, whether they come from the west or the east, they will find the Gaelic of their own country in the city's churches'*).[26] Similarly, Lachlan MacLean prefaces his account of a New Year shinty match in Glasgow with the explanation 'Chuir mi so chugaibh, a Theachdaire, a' leigeadh fhaicinn d'ar càirdibh ann an tìr nam beann nach do dhì-chuimhnich sinn gu h-uile iad fathast' (*'I've sent you this, Teachdaire, to let our friends in the land of the mountains see that we haven't forgotten them all yet'*).[27] This of course also served to demonstrate to prospective migrants that familiar Highland traditions were alive and well in the Lowlands, just as periodical writing promoting emigration to Canada would do ten years later in the early 1840s.[28]

For MacLean, who established *An Teachdaire Ùr Gàidhealach*, which appeared during 1835–36, midway between MacLeod's two journals, publishing a periodical served a purpose beyond mere education and in fact presented a means of raising the status of Gaelic. MacLean, whose *Adhamh agus Eubh; no, Craobh-sheanachais nan Gàel* was subsequently published in 1837, a work in which he traced Gaelic back to the Garden of Eden, announced in his first editorial:

> Tha sinne agus iomadh caraid teas-chridheach, a' cur romhainn nach sguir sinn d' ar saothair gus am bi EOLAS SGRIOBHAIDH AGUS LEUGHAIDH NA GAILIG CHO CUMANT' AIR GAIDHEALTACHD 'S A THA EOLAS NA BEURLA AIR GALLDACHD, no gus an tog sinn i CO ARD RI AONA CHANAIN EILE SAN ROINN-EORPA.[29]

> *We, and many warm-hearted friends, have settled that we will not stop our efforts until the* ABILITY TO READ AND WRITE IN GAELIC IS AS COMMON IN THE HIGHLANDS AS KNOWLEDGE OF ENGLISH IS IN THE LOWLANDS, *or until we raise it* AS HIGH AS ANY OTHER LANGUAGE IN EUROPE.

The influence of English journals on the Gaelic periodical press merits detailed study, however, their existence, and success, clearly served as an example to Gaels as is evident when the Rev. Alexander MacGregor attempted to shame more Gaelic speakers into subscribing to *Cuairtear nan Gleann*:

> Tha na Goill a' cumail suas fichead no dhà do na pàipeiribh luideagach, leathann, libideach, Gallta, aca féin ; agus is duilich, agus is truagh an nì e, mar cum na Gàidheil gu léir suas aon Chuairteir cuimir,

ceanalta, agus eireachdail, chum eòlas a chraobh-sgaoileadh air am feadh, ann an cainnt bhrìghmhor an dùcha féin!

The Lowlanders support a score or two of their own shabby, worthless broadsheets; and it is a poor, sorry matter if all the Gaels cannot maintain one neat, fine, handsome, Cuairtear [Traveller] to spread knowledge among them in the expressive language of their own country![30]

Given the short lifespan of all the journals, cultural benchmarking strategies such as this clearly had very little effect in attracting more subscribers, a problem which was to dog all nineteenth-century Gaelic periodicals.

While these early journals undoubtedly fulfilled their primary purpose in extending the range of suitable reading material available in Gaelic, their role was wider than that as they provided readers with an intrinsically Glasgow-centric view of the world. Not only did they emerge from an emigrant context but the periodicals may well have played their own role in encouraging, or at least facilitating, the movement of Highlanders to the Lowlands, familiarising readers and listeners with the Lowlands, and reinforcing what they may have heard from friends and relatives, and thereby allowing readers to enter imaginatively into the migrant experience with Fionnladh Pìobaire and other characters. *Cuairtear nan Gleann* was set up in 1840, in the inter-famine period, with the explicit purpose of informing Gaelic speakers about emigrant destinations beyond Britain, but in actual fact it was simply following in the footsteps of *An Teachdaire Gae'lach* in which emigration to the Lowlands was implicitly, and at times explicitly, supported and indeed expected. The comment from MacLeod himself when giving evidence to the parliamentary committee on emigration in 1841 observed that 'those taught in our schools in the Highlands are more disposed to come to Glasgow than those who are not taught'.[31]

This implicit encouragement of migration is evident in MacLeod's periodicals. In an 1830 letter from one 'Eoghan Òg' – a pen-name used by Lachlan MacLean – the author of the letter to the journal purports to be seeking advice, having met a girl in the Lowlands whom he wants to marry and then return to the Highlands with her. The editor replies:

> Ach ciod a tha 'gad thoirt air t-ais a rithist do'n Ghaeltachd? Fuirich far a' bheil thu Eoghain [Glaschu], agus oidheirpich le dichioll agus stuamachd èiridh gu meas agus miagh sa bhaile mhor. Cuimhnich ged a tha cuid de nithe saor sa Ghaeltachd, gu bheil an t-airgiod gann da reir sin.
>
> *But what's taking you back to the Highlands? Stay where you are, Eoghan [Glasgow], and try with diligence and sobriety to rise to a position of esteem and respect in the city. Remember that, although some things are cheap in the Highlands, money is scarce despite that.*[32]

The message is clear; financial security lay outwith the Highlands, a message which would feature even more prominently in later journals.

*

These early periodicals, originally conceived as an extension of the education system, not only linked disparate Gaelic-speaking communities within Scotland and beyond, but with their urban Lowland publication base and a significant number of the contributors, not to mention editors, located in Glasgow, they provided a new lens through which the changing world was placed before, and interpreted for, Highland readers. Their role was clearly a broad one and, in addition to their educational and literary role, they also served a social function, particularly in preparing readers for life beyond the Highlands and reinforcing Glasgow's place in the Gaelic mind as an emigrant destination with an already established Gaelic community. The pro-migration message espoused by the most prominent literary characters in the journals cannot but have had an impact on the journals' audience who would have heard Fionnladh Pìobaire saying of his children's future 'Ciod is urrainn doibh a dheanamh san dùthaich bhochd so le fuireach innte?' (*'What can they achieve in this poor country by staying in it?'*).[33]

Notes

1. Charles W. J. Withers, *Urban Highlanders. Highland-Lowland Migration and Urban Gaelic Culture 1700–1900* (East Linton: Tuckwell Press, 1998).
2. Kenneth D. MacDonald, 'Glasgow and Gaelic Writing', *Transactions of the Gaelic Society of Inverness* 57 (1990–92), pp. 395–428; Michel Byrne, '"Chan e chleachd bhith an cabhsair chlach": Am Bàrd Gàidhlig 's am Baile Mòr bhon 17mh Linn chun an 20mh' in Sheila M. Kidd (ed.), *Glasgow: Baile Mòr nan Gàidheal/City of the Gaels* (Glasgow: University of Glasgow Celtic Department, 2007), pp. 55–88.
3. The first known Gaelic periodical was *An Rosroine* which ran for four issues in 1803 and of which there are no known extant copies. For a more detailed discussion of the emergence of the Gaelic periodical press see Sheila M. Kidd, 'Early Gaelic Periodicals: Knowledge Transfer and Impact', in Colm Ó Baoill and Nancy McGuire (eds), *Rannsachadh na Gàidhlig 6* (Aberdeen: University of Aberdeen, 2013), pp. 177–206.
4. *An Rosroine* (1803); *An Teachdaire Gae'lach* (1829–31); *An Teachdaire Ùr Gaidhealach* (1835–36); *Cuairtear nan Gleann* (1840–43); *Teachdaire nan Gaidheal* (1844–45); *Caraid nan Gael* (1844); *A' Bheithir Bheuma* (1845); *An Fhianuis* (1845–50); *Fear-Tathaich nam Beann* (1848–50).
5. In the 1870s and 1880s Inverness was a flourishing centre of newspaper and periodical publishing. Although none of these was produced entirely in Gaelic, newspapers such as *The Highlander*, *The Scottish Highlander* and *The Northern Chronicle* contained a regular Gaelic column and periodicals included *The Celtic Magazine*. Note that from 1875 *An Gaidheal* began to be published simultaneously in Glasgow and Edinburgh.
6. See Huw Walters, 'The Welsh Language and the Periodical Press', in Geraint H. Jenkins (ed.), *The Welsh Language and its Social Domains 1801–1911* (Cardiff: University of Wales Press, 1999), pp. 349–78; John N. MacLeod (ed.), *Memorials of the Rev. Norman MacLeod (Senr) DD* (Edinburgh, 1898), p. 115.
7. *Parliamentary Papers 1841 VI. First Report from the Select Committee on Emigration, Scotland; together with the Minutes of Evidence and Appendix*, p. 115.
8. 'Fionn' [Henry Whyte], 'Lachlan MacLean, Coll', *The Celtic Monthly* 6:3 (1894), 109–10 (110). See also MacDonald, 'Glasgow and Gaelic Writing', pp. 399–402.
9. *Parliamentary Papers 1841 VI*, p. 81.
10. *An Teachdaire Gae'lach* 1 (1829), p. 2.
11. *Cuairtear nan Gleann* 1 (1840), p. 1.
12. *An Teachdaire Gae'lach* 1 (1829), p. 5.
13. *Glasgow Herald*, 10 July 1840.
14. *Cuairtear nan Gleann* 9 (1840), p. 174.
15. *An Teachdaire Gae'lach* 14 (1830), p. 39.
16. Donald E. Meek, 'Early Steamship Travel from the Other Side: An 1829 Gaelic Account of the Maid of Morvern', *Review of Scottish Culture* 20 (2008), pp. 57–79; Donald E. Meek, 'Sitirich an Eich Iarainn ("The Neighing of the Iron Horse"): Gaelic Perspectives on Steam Power, Railways and Ship-building in the Nineteenth Century', in Wilson McLeod, Abigail Burnyeat, Domhnall Uilleam Stiùbhart, Thomas Owen Clancy and Roibeard Ó Maolalaigh (eds), *Bile ós Chrannaibh. A Festschrift for William Gillies* (Ceann Drochaid: Clann Tuirc, 2010), pp. 271–92.
17. *An Teachdaire Gae'lach* 3 (1829), pp. 54–57 (p. 55).
18. *An Teachdaire Gae'lach* 17 (1830), p. 112.

19. *An Teachdaire Gae'lach* 21 (1831), p. 197.
20. Donald E. Meek, 'Early Steamship Travel from the Other Side', p. 60.
21. *An Teachdaire Ùr Gàidhealach* 7 (June 1836), pp. 173–76.
22. *An Teachdaire Ùr Gàidhealach* 7 (June 1836), p. 166.
23. *An Teachdaire Ùr Gàidhealach* 7 (June 1836), p. 166.
24. *An Teachdaire Gae'lach* 6 (1829), p. 132.
25. *An Teachdaire Gae'lach* 5 (1829), pp. 118–19.
26. *An Teachdaire Gae'lach* 8 (1829), p. 132.
27. *An Teachdaire Gae'lach* 21 (1831), pp. 211–12.
28. Sheila M. Kidd, '"Caraid nan Gàidheal" and "Friend of Emigration": Gaelic Emigration Literature of the 1840s', *Scottish Historical Review*, Vol. 81: 1 (2002), pp. 52–69.
29. *An Teachdaire Ùr Gaidhealach* 1 (1835), p. 2. The capital letters are MacLean's own emphasis.
30. *Cuairtear nan Gleann* 29 (1842), p. 120.
31. *Parliamentary Papers 1841 VI*, p. 119.
32. *An Teachdaire Gae'lach* 9 (1830), p. 203.
33. *An Teachdaire Gae'lach* 16 (1830), p. 112.

10. Màiri Mhòr – Victim of Circumstance or Self-Made Celebrity?

MARK WRINGE

If there is a theme which runs consistently through the songs of Màiri Mhòr MacPherson (1821–1898), it is vindication: personal vindication, vindication of the Gaels, and vindication of the Gaelic language. The start of her poetic career can be identified with unusual precision: it began in April 1872, ignited by a humiliating court case to which she frequently refers in her work: "'S e na dh'fhuiling mi de thàmailt, / a thug mo bhàrdachd beò' (Meek 1998, p. 110: *'What gave birth to my poetry was the terrible shame I suffered'*).

The case brought before the Police Court in Inverness transformed her from someone who, at the age of 51, was 'entirely unconscious of possessing any poetic gift' (Mac-Bheathain 1891, pp. xii–xiii) to someone who would become the most famous Gaelic poet of the modern age before Sorley MacLean. It is common to think of Màiri Mhòr in terms of this context of personal miscarriage of justice, and all too easy to think of her as a hapless victim: the lower-class monoglot Gaelic-speaking widow with children, being tried in an English-language court by middle-class, privileged and educated prosecutors. This was the kind of image portrayed in John McGrath's play 'Mairi Mhor the Woman from Skye' (toured by the 7:84 theatre company in 1987), and even more so in the subsequent TV adaptation of that play (BBC, 1993). And yet, in any published photograph of Màiri (five portraits were included in her 1891 collection of poems and songs), one sees not a downtrodden, broken woman but a self-assured celebrity. There is undoubtedly a righteous anger behind a great deal of her poetry, and anguish in the initial early works, but there is something quite remarkable in this transformation from victimised woman of the underclass to celebrity of Gaelic soirees, Land League meetings and the Highland election trail. In popular tradition, certainly in Skye, the stories of Màiri Mhòr tend to give the impression of a confident woman who knew she could presume on others. Humorous anecdotes I have heard are told with pride, counterbalanced by a sting in the tail that cautions against thinking too much of oneself – telling, for example, how she might visit widely and enjoy hospitality, but sometimes overstay her welcome; or how she seeks a 'lift' by boat from Portree to Braes, but the poor oarsman has to make a superhuman effort when she settles in the stern and raises her umbrella, catching the breeze like a drag-anchor; or the often recounted story of the late Col Jock MacDonald being allowed as a small boy to hide under her skirts – but finding his refuge none too fragrant. She could tell the same kind of stories against herself. In 'A' Chlach agus Màiri' (*'Clachnacuddin and Màiri'*, Mac-Bheathain 1891, p. 62; Meek 1998, p. 186), she is travelling with Alexander Mackenzie, Charles Fraser-Mackintosh and others. At Strome Ferry Mackenzie tells her 'Fuirich thusa muigh, a Mhàiri … Bheir thu àite triùir a-mach!' (*Wait for the boat to come back, Màiri / you'll take up room for three!*) and continues:

> Ma thig thusa staigh don bhàta
> Bidh sinn uile 'n cunnart bàthaidh;
> Feumaidh mise beagan dàil
>   Gum faighear fàth air m' iompachadh.

> *If you get into the boat*
> *We'll all be in danger of drowning;*
> *I need more time*
>   *Before I find a reason to convert.*

Another in the party avers that it is dangerous to sail with 'màraisgich gun iompachadh' (*unconverted hefties*), that Màiri is seventeen stone and Mackenzie something similar.

There seems no danger of hubris here. Margaret Bennett recalls that Màiri was something of a political yardstick for the Skye bard Iain MacNeacail ('An Sgiobair', 1903–1999), to be (favourably) compared to contemporary politicians on the national stage. Sorley MacLean, in Part 3 of *An Cuilithionn*, identifies with her in contrast to the unreachable art of Hugh MacDiarmid or Alasdair Mac Mhaighstir Alasdair (Whyte & Dymock 2011, pp. 372–73). In *Dàin do Eimhir* XIX Maclean references Màiri to claim the same instigation as a poet 'rinn thu bàrd dhiom le dòrainn' (*you made a poet of me through sorrow*), as Christopher Whyte points out (Whyte 2002, p. 213). In his own essay on Màiri Mhòr, MacLean is clear that her 'sorrow' is a catalyst, not characteristic: 'of all Gaelic poets not even Alexander MacDonald had more vitality and joie de vivre than Màiri Mhòr' (Gillies 1985, p. 253).

Tracking the process of her emergence as a self-assured, public figure involves some joining of dots and speculation, for hard facts and precise details of her life are not abundant. Even in her own lifetime, the biographical sketch drawn by Alexander MacBain (Mac-Bheathain 1891, pp. xi–xiv) contains some conflicting information. To begin at the end, the place of her death in what is now a hotel facing the harbour in Portree has recently been marked by a plaque. She is buried in Inverness, her imposing headstone funded by her friend, the lawyer and by then former MP Charles Fraser-Mackintosh. According to the inscription she was eighty when she died in 1898, but this goes against MacBain's claim, now generally accepted, that she was born in March 1821 (Mac-Bheathain 1891, p. xi). Her birthplace is disputed. Although she was certainly brought up in the family home in Skeabost as MacBain says, local tradition in Uig is insistent that it was there, as her mother's native district, that she was born. Whichever is the case, she might just as easily have been born in Glasgow or Canada. Indeed all of her brothers and sisters save one were born in Glasgow, where her parents, John MacDonald (Iain Bàn) and Flora Macinnes, had temporarily settled after withdrawing from an unreliable emigration scheme and returning to Skye (Mac-Bheathain 1891, p. xi).

The 320-page collection of Màiri's poems and songs, published in 1892 in Inverness, contains ninety poems, MacBain's biographical introduction and five photos. All printing and binding costs for the book were covered by Lachlan MacDonald of Skeabost, who had also given her the cottage Bothan Ceann na Coille (now called Woodend) rent-free when she returned to Skye in 1882 (Mac-Bheathain 1891, p. xiv). In his introduction, MacBain remarks that 'she rivals [Donnchadh Bàn Macintyre] to some extent in educational disadvantages', and that 'though she can read her own poetry in print she cannot write it' (p. xiii). Noting that the eight to nine thousand lines of poetry were taken down from memory by John Whyte (brother of the better-remembered 'Fionn' or Henry Whyte), he adds that 'she has at least half as much of her own, and twice as much ... of floating, unpublished [traditional] poetry, mainly that of Skye and the Western Isles' (p. xiv).

At the same time, Màiri's very ordinariness is part and parcel of what makes her so extraordinary, as she is representative of the experience of so many Gaelic speakers and Highland women of her time. She could have been born the child of emigrants in Canada. She migrated from Skye to Inverness in the mid-1840s, and soon married a cobbler/shoemaker, Isaac MacPherson (Meek 1998, pp. 21–22). We know very little of her for almost the following twenty-five years. We know that she and her husband were living in the Maggot area of Inverness (a name now, unsurprisingly, dropped from usage, denoting an area on the east bank of the river, in the vicinity of the modern Friar's Bridge), and it seems she attended the nearby Gaelic chapel in what is now Leakey's bookshop. We also know that the social mix in mid-nineteenth-century Inverness was an interesting one – a town of two languages, according to the New Statistical Account of 1835, where 'many of [the rising generation] are wholly ignorant of Gaelic', but 'some of the poorer classes' speak the language 'exclusively' (Withers 1984, p. 314). It would have been perfectly possible for a person like Màiri to function in Inverness as a Gaelic monoglot, if indeed she was a monoglot at that time. Her husband would probably have had at least some English, but he wouldn't have needed a high level of fluency to be able to run his business successfully.

When Isaac died in 1871, with probably two children still not of working age, Màiri had to find employment. By spring 1872 she was working as what we would nowadays call a care assistant in a house at 8, Ness Bank, just yards along from Ness Bank Church, the residence of a Captain Turner and his young wife Harriet, who had contracted typhoid. Màiri nursed the sick Mrs Turner until her rapid death, but was then accused of stealing clothing from her mistress's wardrobe while the very funeral was in progress directly across the river at the Cathedral. As the relevant court papers have been lost, the only report of the case known to survive is a very brief outraged snippet in the *Inverness Courier* of 11 April 1872, castigating the accused (Meek 1998, p. 23). We know, however, that in spite of being sentenced for forty days she did not serve her full term, through some intervention. Màiri's own indignant account of the court and sentence is given in a number of songs, particularly 'Luchd na Beurla' (*The Speakers of English*), where she answers back to the Prison Governor with a clear conscience. Meek quotes from William MacKenzie's *Old Skye Tales* (Meek 1998, pp. 24–25), where the author describes hearing how another servant, having formed a grudge against Màiri, planted the 'stolen' clothing among her possessions. Màiri had important friends in Inverness, including the lawyer-politician Charles Fraser-Mackintosh, the shopkeeper/writer/editor Alexander MacKenzie (Clach na Cùdainn) of *Highland Clearances* fame, and radical campaigner John Murdoch (who would establish his *Highlander* newspaper the following year). Did new information allow them to intervene? How did someone in her position come to have such distinguished allies? MacBain's assertion, noted above, that she held in her memory thousands of lines of unpublished traditional poetry – that is, song – may be a clue. It seems reasonable to assume that she was already well known as a tradition-bearer and performer before she was moved to compose songs of her own. Inverness was not very large. Its population was under 15,000 in 1871, a large proportion of whom spoke Gaelic and English or Gaelic only. Furthermore, the songs relating to Inverness name or allude to a number of officials and worthies of the town, and she clearly expects her audience to know who she means. The voice of the early songs is aggrieved, but confident. Her comment on religious affairs and individual ministers in 'Clò na Cùbaid' (*The Pulpit Cloth*, Meek 1998, pp. 68–70) is forthright and independent-minded. One senses an unusually strong, even charismatic, personality with exactly the kind of qualities and perspectives that Mackenzie, Murdoch and Fraser-Mackintosh sought to encourage in their fellow Gaels.

A few months after the court case Màiri moved to Glasgow and there trained for a diploma in nursing/midwifery at Glasgow Royal Infirmary. Allan Macinnes tells us in another contribution that, according to one John McLaren, Gaels in Glasgow could learn to speak English after six months' residence (see page 18 of Professor Macinnes's paper in this volume), but one suspects that a hospital training in basic obstetrics would have demanded a more advanced level of fluency, and one can speculate that she had already achieved a degree of bilingualism before she left Inverness. Indeed, the notion that she had little English may rest on a particular interpretation of the refrain 'Tha mi sgìth de luchd na Beurla' ('*I'm tired of English speakers*', Meek 1998, p. 60) and similar lines which are fitted to the construct of the crushed, helpless widow. I would suggest it is more fitting and useful to recognise this line as a forthright comment on social stratification. It is not self-pitying. In a Highland town like Inverness, 'Luchd na Beurla' are the stratum who run the place, the men of privilege and power.

She lived around Glasgow and Greenock for ten years, and in 1882 returned to Skeabost, by now an established celebrity among Gaels. Her rise to fame seems to have been rapid: clearly her work was in tune with popular sentiment. In the transformation from the underclass widow in distress to the prestigiously connected celebrity, her association with the land struggle of the 1870s and '80s is central. Of all the poets of the later nineteenth century, it is Màiri Mhòr who is seen to be the voice of the land struggle, and the 'Bernera Riots' of April to June 1874 probably played a crucial role in establishing her voice. That *cause célèbre* was the first case where crofters successfully resisted threats of eviction in regard to grazing rights, by confronting the actual landowner (Sir James Matheson) face-to-face, and ultimately bringing about the conviction for assault of the sheriff officer and the sacking of the estate's all-powerful chamberlain, i.e. factor (Meek 1995, pp. 88–89). It was a turning point in the campaign for land rights, a landmark case which Màiri Mhòr immortalised in several songs and which seems to have been central to her rise in fame. One such song, 'Ceatharnaich Bheàrnaraigh' (*'The Heroes of Berneray'*), describes the procession to doorstep Matheson at the castle in Stornoway, and salutes the crofters and their success in court, with allusion to her own trial:

> A dhaoine còire Bheàrnaraigh,
> Gun òlar ur deoch-slàinte leam,
> 'S ged b' ann a dh'fhìon na Spàinte
>   Gum pàigh sinn i gun sòradh ...
>
> Sheas fear a-mach sa champa dhibh
> 'S a bhoineid ghorm na làimh aige,
> 'S le Beurla chruaidh gun mheang
>   Gun d' rinn e cainnt ris mar bu chòir dha ...
>
> *Good people of Bernera,*
> *I'll drink your health,*
> *We'll not stint the payment*
>   *Even for Spanish wine ...*

MÀIRI MHÒR – VICTIM OF CIRCUMSTANCE OR …?

> *One of your camp stepped forward*
> *His blue bonnet in his hand,*
> *And with hard, faultless English*
> *He spoke to him* [Matheson] *the way he should …*
> (Nic-a-Phearsain 1892, pp. 272–74)

Màiri's association with the Bernera crofters is touched upon in a letter from her in November 1876, sent from an address in Bridge of Weir to a '[caraid] ionmhainn' (*'dear friend'*), Dr Ruairidh Ross from Lewis, then in Strathpeffer, and whose wife belonged to Bernera (see appendix). The letter came to light only a few years ago (Meek 2008). The letter is apparently written and signed by Màiri herself. It could of course have been transcribed from dictation by an amanuensis, but the tone of the letter suggests otherwise, and although the hand is assured, there are occasional quirks of spelling which seem to add authenticity. Màiri was of the generation most likely to have learned to read Gaelic, or at least the Gaelic scriptures, in the various Gaelic charity schools operating in the first half of the century, a literacy drive that was at its very peak around 1830 when Màiri would have been a potential attendant. Professor Donald Meek, the foremost Màiri Mhòr scholar and editor of the letter, is inclined to accept that it was written by the poet herself (Meek 2008 and personal communication). At the very least we have insufficient reason to insist it was *not* written by her, and we should be prepared to question MacBain's claims that she could read her own poetry but 'cannot write it' (Mac-Beathain 1891, p. xiii). It is neither surprising nor remarkable that Màiri's natural preference would be to compose and retain her repertoire orally. But that in itself does not preclude the possibility of her enjoying functional literacy in Gaelic. Indeed the letter appears to suggest she had previously sent Dr Ross a song for comment.

In her letter, Màiri references her own song on the Berneray heroes: 'Cuimhnich mi do dhaoine coire Bhearnar[aigh]' (*'Remember me to the good people of Bernera'*). Mention in the same letter of 'airgead-cinn' (*a reward, or price on her head*) recalls another song of the same period, 'Airgead-Cinn Alasdair Bhàin' (*'Alasdair Bàn's Reward'*), which she seems to have composed in response to a request by one Alasdair Bàn printed in the *Highlander* in January 1875 for something from her, and which indicates her celebrity status:

> Nuair ràinig mi doras an talla,
> 'S a dh'fhairich mi caithream nam pìob,
> 'S a chuala mi Gàidhlig ga labhairt,
> Toirt crathadh dhen làmhan dhomh fhìn,
> 'Cuin thàinig thu Ghlaschu, Mhàiri?
> Gur fhada o dh'fhàg thu Port Rìgh;
> 'S math a b' aithne dhut m' athair 's mo mhàthair,
> Nuair a bha sinn a' tàmh anns na glinn.'
>
> Cha mhòr gun d' tharraing mi m' anail
> Nuair chruinnich na Gàidheil mum cheann,
> A dh'fhaighneachd dhiom 'Ciamar a tha thu,
> No a bheil thu nad shlàint' aig an àm?
> Nach tusa bha dèanamh nan òran
> Chuir onair cho mòr air ar clann,
> Thug a leithid a stialladh don Bhàillidh,
> 'S do churaidhean Bheàrnaraigh taing?'
>
> *When I reached the door to the hall*
> *And heard the sound of the pipes,*
> *I heard Gaelic being spoken*
> *As people shook hands with me:*
> *'When did you come to Glasgow, Màiri?*
> *It's so long since you left Portree;*
> *You knew my father and mother well*
> *When we were living in the glens.'*
>
> *I had scarcely drawn breath*
> *When the Gaels pressed around me*
> *To ask 'How are you,*
> *Are you well?*
> *Aren't you the one who composed the songs*
> *that have brought such honour to our kin,*

MÀIRI MHÒR – VICTIM OF CIRCUMSTANCE OR …?

> *the one who tore strips off Baillie Simpson* [the judge at her own trial]
> *and who thanked the Bernera Heroes?'*
> (Meek 1998, p. 100; translation by present author)

She seems particularly pleased here with the success of her 'Ceatharnaich Bheàrnaraigh'. The gathering she refers to was one held in February, 1875, by the Glasgow Highland Association, addressed by John Murdoch and apparently attended by 1600 people (Meek 1998, p. 103), so clearly by that date, even if her billing was as a support to Murdoch, she was already a celebrity. Her humiliating trial was a mere three years before. It would take more than just word of mouth or purely oral transmission of her early songs to make her a legend so quickly, and we can be sure that publication in Murdoch's paper *The Highlander* (1873–1881) greatly enhanced her impact and celebrity.

Such publication did not end when Murdoch's *Highlander* folded. Its successor, the similarly titled *Scottish Highlander* (1885–1898), edited in Inverness by Alexander Mackenzie, has an intriguing piece headed 'Òran Cumha an Ibhirich' in the issue of January 6, 1887 (also printed as a broadsheet), purportedly by 'Màiri nan Dàn à Bràigh Thròtairnis', a less than opaque disguise for Màiri Mhòr nan Òran. Here she is bolder and more vituperative than in the earlier songs as she imagines Sheriff Ivory, the *bête noire* of the Skye crofters, with a noose tightened round his neck, stuffed naked into a bog-hole, then hauled out while old women dance for joy at his demise ('Òran Cumha an Ìbhirich', Meek 1995, pp. 167–69; translation pp. 267–68, 'Elegy-song on Ivory').

The term 'agitprop' was yet to be invented, but such it was, with publishing and oral transmission in vital symbiosis to create the public persona of Màiri Mhòr. We should bear in mind that the widely held opinion that Gaelic poetry was all oral is erroneous: it has never been entirely oral, and ever since Alasdair Mac Mhaighstir Alasdair's publication of his work in 1751 (*Ais-eiridh na Sean Chánoin Albannaich*, 'The Resurrection of the Ancient Scottish Language') books have been of great significance to Gaelic poetry. MacDonald's groundbreaking publication established a convention very quickly adopted by any Gaelic poet worth their salt. This did not preclude oral transmission – on the contrary, the two media worked in tandem. For spiritual poetry the printed medium is primary, as demonstrated by the forty-plus reprints and editions of hymns of Dùghall Bochanan (1716–1768), or the bootleg edition of the works of Pàdraig Grannd (1783–1867). For secular poetry it also became an established norm, whether initiated by the poet or not: Donnchadh Bàn's editions were arranged by a third party, Rob Donn only achieved publication posthumously, while Duncan Campbell from Cowal published in a very irregular orthography in Cork in 1798 for a captive market of Highland soldiers.

The appearance of Màiri Mhòr's work in print, not necessarily at her own behest and regardless of her personal level of literacy, is very much part of an established norm by the late nineteenth century, part of the means by which people became familiar with her songs and maintained that familiarity. Màiri Mhòr was undoubtedly an extraordinary exponent of the oral tradition, with her prodigious memory her preferred means of storage, but the printed book and printed broadside texts were important in establishing her legendary status.

There is now significant evidence, in the letter to Dr Ross, that she was literate in Gaelic. Literacy is not the only aspect of Màiri we might re-assess. A considered reading of her compositions shows a woman who feels vindicated – self-aware, and comfortable with her celebrity. Her political loyalties are of course informed by her friends, notably Mackenzie, Murdoch and Fraser-Mackintosh, and she is galvanised by her trial and imprisonment to make the connection between the personal and the political, the individual injustice and wider social justice. Although she has always been recognised as a campaigner, at a time when the practice of politics was only beginning to open up to *men* of her social class, perhaps it would be appropriate to consider more carefully the level of her independent political awareness, and whether she was more than the medium with the gift for popularising the message of others.

(I am indebted to Professor Donald E. Meek for his generous support in the preparation of this article – MW)

Appendix: Letter from Màiri Mhòr MacPherson to Dr Ruairidh Ross, 29 November 1876

Lead Cottage
Barr's Garden
Bridge of Weir

Nov. 29 1876

Charaid ionmhuinn,

Fhuair mi do litir no mar 's fearr a dhfhaodar a radh fhuair do litir mi – agus tha mi gu mor nad chomain airson a chrioch cholionta a chuir thu air na dhearb mi riut, agus tha mi nise creidsinn gum faodte earbsa asad. Tha mi duilich bhi agam ri innse dhuit gu 'm bheil m. piobaire dha 'n robh sinn cuir n ordugh chungaidhean leighis nuair ma dheireadh a choinnich sinn, a nise air triall do shaoghal eile – Ged tha fada 's nach fhaca mi Domhull Domhnullach do charaide tha thu faicinn gun do ghnathaich mi uiread do shaorsa agus gun do chuir mi a bheannach thugad anns na ruinn a tha mi cuir gad ionnsuidh maille ris 'n litir so – Chuala mi gun robh Padruig Ross a' cur airgead cinn asam n Glaschu ged nach dfhuair e mi – bha e san Eilean Sgiathanach nuair a sgriobh e gu a luchd eolais mu 'm thimchealsa. Tha fada on uair sin agus chaneil fhios agamsa nise caite m bheil e gu sgriobhadh da ionnsuidh. Bhithinn fada na do chomain nam b urrainn thu chuir gam ionnsuidh ainm n aite anns am bheil e air aoidheachd air chor s gum burrain mi sgriobhadh thuige. Chaneil fios agam air moran naigheachdan aig n am. Cuimhnich mi do dhaoine coire Bhearnara agus ma bhios galair sam bith nam measg fiach gun cleachd thu do dhurach leighis ach m bi iad air n cuimhnadh gu sliochd a ghleidheadh nan aite agus n Duthaich a ghleidheadh don cloinn.

Tha dochas agam nach bi e doirbh dhuit mo litir a leughadh ged a tha a Ghaelic air fas gann sna bailtean mora tha againn fhathast dhith na chumas air chuimhne gnàths ar ducha agus nòs ar cainnte.

Slan leat agus le neach sam bith a dhfhoinichdeas air mo shon.

Bi cinnteach gur mise do bhana charaid dhìleas

Mairi Nic a' Phersoin

Dear Friend,

I got your letter or it might be better to say your letter found me – and I am obliged to you for the polished finish you put on what I entrusted to you, and I think of you now as one who can be relied upon. I am sorry to have to tell you that the piper for whom we arranged medicines when we last met has now passed away – Although I haven't seen your friend Donald MacDonald in a long time you will see that I have been presumptuous enough to send you his good wishes in the verses I am sending to you with this letter – I heard Peter Ross had offered a reward for tracking me down in Glasgow although he didn't find me – he was in Skye when he wrote to his acquaintances about me. That was long since and I don't know now where he is in order to write to him. I would be much obliged if you could send me the name of the place he is visiting so that I could write to him. I don't have much news just now. Remember me to the good people of Bernera and if there is any sickness amongst them please administer to them with your medical knowledge in order that they may be saved to maintain their lineage in their own place, and preserve their country for their children.

I hope you won't find my letter difficult to read – although Gaelic has grown scarce in the cities we still have enough of it to uphold the memory of the custom of our homeland and the character of our speech.

Greetings to you and to anyone who asks after me.

Be sure that I am your faithful friend

Mary MacPherson

Bibliography

Gillies, William (ed.), *Somhairle Mac Gill-eain/Sorley MacLean: Ris a' Bhruthaich/ Criticism and Prose Writings* (Stornoway: Acair, 1985).

Mac-Bheathain, Alastair, 'Life of Mrs Mary MacPherson, the Skye poetess', in Mairi Nic-a-Phearsoin, *Dàin agus Òrain Ghàidhlig* (Inbhirnis, 1891).

Meek, Donald E. (ed.), *Màiri Mhòr nan Òran: Taghadh de a h-Òrain* (Edinburgh: Scottish Gaelic Texts Society, 1998).

Meek, Donald E. (ed.), *Tuath is Tighearna: Tenants and Landlords* (Edinburgh: Scottish Academic Press, 1995).

Meek, Donald E., 'Litir bho Mhàiri Mhòr nan Òran', *Gath* 9 (2008), pp. 35–42.

Whyte, Christopher (ed.), *Somhairle MacGill-Eain/Sorley MacLean: Dàin do Eimhir* (Glasgow: Association for Scottish Literary Studies, 2002).

Whyte, Christopher and Emma Dymock (eds), *Caoir Gheal Leumraich/White Leaping Flame: Sorley MacLean: Collected Poems* (Edinburgh: Polygon, 2011).

Withers, Charles W. J., *Gaelic in Scotland, 1698–1981: The Geographical History of a Language* (Edinburgh: John Donald, 1984).

11. Niall MacLeòid, Bard of Skye and Edinburgh

MEG BATEMAN

This paper looks at the effect that crossing the Highland line had on the work of Niall MacLeòid. He was born in Glendale in Skye in 1843 and at the age of twenty-two he moved to Edinburgh where he remained till his death in 1913. A rare opportunity for examining the influence of life in the Lowlands on his work is afforded by his father and brother also being poets, who remained culturally attached to Skye. It was my fellow post-graduate student at Aberdeen University in the 1980s, Anne Loughran, who first suggested making this comparison between Dòmhnall, who was born in the eighteenth century, and his sons, Niall, the Edinburgh tea-merchant, and Iain, the sailor, whom some would rate more highly than his famous brother.[1] Changes in poetic taste are clear in the work of the three poets in the same family, spread over two generations and three centuries, with their different lifestyles, urban, rural and maritime. It will be seen that the requirement to produce songs for the Gaelic diaspora in Lowland cities made for a different sort of song from those produced to entertain and edify a Highland community.

I know of no other Gaelic poet who has suffered such a dramatic fall in reputation as Niall MacLeòid. Nowadays many consider him facile and superficial.[2] Derick Thomson and Dòmhnall Meek have compared him unfavourably with Màiri Mhòr, criticising him for a softness of focus and lack of political engagement with the Clearances and Land Wars. While Màiri Mhòr shared a platform with politicians such as Charles Fraser-Mackintosh, Niall spoke in generalities from a distance. While Màiri Mhòr's poetry is passionate and gutsy, Niall is criticised for the simulation of emotion with little heightening of language.[3] Yet in 1892 Dr MacDiarmid wrote: 'Niall is probably the best known and most popular poet living,'[4] and John N. MacLeod, addressing the Gaelic Society of Inverness in 1917, described Niall's collection, *Clàrsach an Doire,* as 'co-chruinneachadh cho binn blasda tomadach 's a chaidh riamh an clò' (*'as sweet, pungent and weighty a collection as has ever been printed'*).[5] At the time of his death in 1913, Donald

MacKinnon, professor of Celtic at Edinburgh University, referred to Niall as one of the three foremost Gaelic writers of his time:

> Since Duncan McIntyre died, no Gaelic poet took such firm hold of the imagination of the Highlanders as Neil Macleod was able to do ... There is a happy selection of subject. The treatment is simple, unaffected. You have on every page evidence of the equable temper and gentle disposition of the author – gay humour or melting pathos; happy diction; pure idiom; exquisite rhyme ... and the melody of versification.[6]

Derick Thomson has said 'Niall Macleòid would seem to be the example *par excellence* of the popular poet in Gaelic, and he more than any other became part of the pop culture of his time.'[7] It may be easier to try to account for Niall's popularity in his own time than to give a final assessment of the worth of his poetry.

The social conditions which Niall encountered in the Lowlands were very different from those of the ceilidh house in the townships of the Highlands. For the first time Gaelic speakers from all over the Highlands were meeting socially at dances in the cities of the Lowlands. While traditional songs had alluded to specific communities and places, a new sort of song was required for the Lowland gatherings that would evoke a common background and identity through some sort of generic neighbourhood and landscape. The new urbanisation of the Gaels made new demands on their poets: pieces were required for the annual gatherings of Gaelic societies, and after 1893 for singing at the Mod, for encouraging the Gaelic language, and for historical pieces, arising from a new self-consciousness about being a Gael.[8]

While the characters and places of Niall's father's and brother's songs were known to the people of Glendale, in Niall's songs characters and place become every community and every place. This accounts in large measure for the vagueness of Niall's verse, so different from the traditional exactitude of Gaelic verse.[9] His songs were required to entertain, to be easily memorable and immediately understandable, without the length, complexity of argument or of vocabulary, or the specificity of emotion seen in the work of his father and brother and other traditional poets.

Niall's father, Dòmhnall nan Òran, was born in 1787,[10] his life therefore overlapping with Uilleam Ros's and Dùghall Bochanan's, while Mac Mhaighstir Alasdair and Donnchadh Bàn were only a couple of generations older. He escaped the press-gang by working as a road-tax collector, which took him all over Skye. Like Robert Burns and Alexander Carmichael, his work allowed him to collect poetry and stories. Some of these he published with his own poetry in *Orain Nuadh Ghaeleach* in 1811, with the financial help of four MacLeod tacksmen.[11] He emigrated to America, perhaps as a result of the death of his sweetheart at the age of twenty-one and his boredom with fishing as a livelihood, but returned fifteen years later. In 1839, when he was fifty-two, he married Anna MacSween of Glendale and they had a family of ten. He published another book at the end of his life in 1871, but we are to understand from mention of manuscripts in the possession of his widow that a lot more of his work has been lost.

Dòmhnall is a traditional poet: he acts as a clan poet in praising the chief and in evoking a bird, in the traditional manner, to recount the past glories of the clan. He uses satire as a means of social control, sometimes to mock but sometimes to marshal righteousness to correct wrongdoing. He is highly literary and moves easily between genres, whether comic village verse, praise, satire, love, nature or religious verse. Sometimes he composes to entertain, but equally he composes to caution and exhort. Most of his poetry is passionate and personal with a range of metre, diction and vocabulary.

Niall was the oldest surviving child of Dòmhnall's and Anna's offspring. He moved to Edinburgh in the 1860s to join the tea firm of his cousin Roderick MacLeod, for whom he worked as a travelling salesman. In 1889 he married Katie Bane Stewart, a schoolteacher and daughter of a schoolteacher of Kensaleyre, Skye,[12] and they settled and raised a family at 51 Montpelier Park in Bruntsfield, Edinburgh.

MacKinnon spoke of Niall's 'equable temper and gentle disposition', and it seems he was different from his father and his brother, both in outlook and personality. Dòmhnall and Iain both had a strong streak of nonconformity; Niall on the other hand was essentially a conformist. It should be noted, though, that an early poem, 'Còmhradh eadar Òganach agus Oisean', composed when he was twenty-five, demonstrates a forcefulness and anger at the state of the Gaels rarely seen in his later work:

> Tha na Gàidheil air claonadh om maise
> Is air aomadh gu laigse ann am mòran:
> Thug iad riaghladh an dùthcha 's am fearainn
> Do shluagh do nach buineadh a' chòir sin ...[13]

> *The Gaels have declined in their fineness*
> *and have yielded to weakness in many matters:*
> *the rule of their land and country*
> *they have handed to a people with no right there ...*

Anne Loughran has suggested the wider family background might account for the difference between his youthful poetry and his songs of middle-age. His aunt, Dòmhnall nan Òran's sister Marion (Morag), married Iain Bàn MacLeod of Geary in Waternish, and the couple were noted for their piety. One of their sons reached the rank of major in the army and was very active in the Free Church, while his brother Roderick was the tea merchant for whom Niall went to work in Edinburgh. The circumstances of Niall's life, as well as his own inclinations, perhaps meant he had more in common with his cousins' family than with his father and brother.

Iain Dubh was Niall's younger brother by three years, and unlike his father and brother he never published his poems. The contradistinctions between the two brothers may have been exaggerated in local folklore. He was married twice and spent much time away from home as a seaman. In Glendale it was said that he was 'dubh air a h-uile dòigh' (*'black in every way'*), in hair, skin colour and even in deed. This last comment probably relates to his skills as a conjuror and his powers of hypnosis which would be demonised by the church, but all evidence is that he was a kindly man whose poetry John MacInnes describes as 'strong, realistic, compassionate'.[14] We know of only sixteen poems by Iain, but it is widely held that Niall saved some for posterity by publishing them under his own name in *Clàrsach an Doire*. Ailean Dòmhnullach (former headmaster of Staffin primary school) can be seen making the case for 'A' Bhean Agam Fhìn' being Iain's on YouTube,[15] and certainly its irreverent humour is atypical of Niall. Iain Dubh died of uraemia at the age of fifty-eight and is buried in Montreal, the grass that grows on his grave denying the mythology that it would not.[16]

Though Iain does not have the same range of diction or the productivity as his father, he likewise composes from his own experience, describing his life at sea and on land, the landscape of Glendale and situations that arose in his neighbourhood. He does not show the same moral seriousness as his father, but still praises the praiseworthy and satirises the misguided.

*

A sense of the difference in tone between the three poets can be shown in excerpts from poems each made on the subject of sea-faring: 'Rann Fìrinn do Sheann Bhàta' (*A True Verse to an Old Boat*) by Dòmhnall nan Òran, 'Gillean Ghleann Dail' (*'The Boys of Glendale'*) by Iain Dubh, and 'Duanag an t-Seòladair' (*'The Sailor's Song'*) by Niall. Dòmhnall's poem purports to be a faithful account of a decrepit ship that he had fulsomely praised in the mock-heroic poem preceding it in his 1811 publication. The boat is compared to a beast and a carcase into which the crew venture at their peril, standing hip-deep in water however fast they bale her out. The planks are badly planed, the nails rusting; she contains nests of slaters and enough grass to feed a cow; her mast is like a piece of charcoal, her sails like wet paper and her ropes like rushes:

>   Bha i sgallach breac mar dhèile
>   Air dhroch lochdradh,
>   Bha sruth dearg o cheann gach tàirne
>   Mar à Chorcur;
>   Mar a bha mheirg air a cnàmh,
>   'S a làr ga grodadh,
>   Bha neid na Corruichin-còsag
>   Na bòird mhosgain.
>
>   An fhàrdach is aognaidh 's as measa
>   Chaidh fo aodach,
>   An fhàrdach as truim' 's as tric ultach
>   Air fear taomaidh;
>   Rachadh an eultaidh air h-iteig
>   Ro gach taobh dhith,

> 'S ghearradh tu dh'fheur innte na dh'itheadh
> Mart san Fhaoilleach.[17]

> *She was bald and pitted like dealboards*
> *planed badly,*
> *there was a red stream from every rivet*
> *as if from crimson dyestuff;*
> *just as the rust had consumed her*
> *and her floor was rotting,*
> *there were nests of woodlice*
> *in her musty planking.*

> *The worst and most dismal of lodgings*
> *under sailcloth,*
> *the heaviest and most frequent of burdens*
> *to the baler;*
> *birds could take to wing*
> *through her planking,*
> *and in her you could cut enough fodder*
> *to feed a cow in winter.*

The poem (rather than song, for we are told that Dòmhnall spoke his work)[18] was composed about a real event, concerning a local man. However, a certain amount of intertextuality is involved, not only with the preceding praise of the old boat, but also with Mac Mhaighstir Alasdair's sea-faring poem, 'Birlinn Chlann Raghnaill', whose language and metrics it echoes, and perhaps also with the boat satires in the Book of the Dean of Lismore.[19] All this very much declares Dòmhnall nan Òran as an eighteenth-century poet himself, deeply conversant with the older culture.

'The Boys of Glendale' is probably Iain Dubh's best known song. It is said he composed it spontaneously, sitting in Pàdraig MacFhionghain's shop in Glendale, as a response to the local lads' questions about life at sea. He gives a realistic and frank account of his experiences of being sworn at by other sailors, of the unpleasantness of the heat, storms, rationing, of burials at sea, and the dangers of women and drink in port.

If he had a half of what he had spent on drink, he would sooner be at home in Pollosgan.

>Nuair thèid thu òg 's tu aineolach
>   A-mach air long nan seòl,
>Bidh cùisean dhut cho annasach
>   Gus am faithnich thu gach ròp;
>Gur tric a thèid do mhionnachadh
>   'S do sgrios chun an Fhir Mhòir,
>'S gus an tèid thu dha na cruinn aice
>   Cho aotrom ris na h-eòin.
>
>Gur iomadh rud a chì thu
>   Mun till thu far do chuairt,
>Gun toir droch lòn do neart asad
>   'S a' mhaise bha nad ghruaidh;
>Chì thu daoine bàsachadh
>   Gun bhàigh riutha no truas,
>Ach slabhraidh mun sliasaidean
>   'S an tiodhlacadh sa chuan.[20]

>*When you set out young and innocent*
>   *on a ship of many sails,*
>*everything will seem so peculiar*
>   *till you get to know the ropes;*
>*often will people swear at you*
>   *and curse you all to Hell,*
>*till you can climb into her masts*
>   *as lightly as the birds.*
>
>*There's many a thing you'll witness*
>   *before you return from your trip,*
>*bad food will take your strength from you*
>   *and the bloom from your cheeks;*
>*you'll see people dying*
>   *shown no tenderness or care,*

only chains around their thighs
for their burial at sea.

Niall's 'Sailor's Song' is in marked contrast to the other two. It is not written from personal experience, but is a sentimental set-piece on the separation of a sailor and his sweetheart as the boat sails.[21] They part with pain and tears and she gives him a lock of her hair to remember her by. While she sleeps in her warm bed, he must climb the masts to rig the sails. Though life is hard at sea, the hope of winning her gives the sailor renewed strength. He asks the wind to convey a message to the girl that, should she wait for him, she will gain her reward. The notion the wind can speak is new to Gaelic, coming through English songs, and perhaps ultimately through Macpherson's Ossian.

Guma slàn don rìbhinn òig,
Tha tàmh an eilean gorm an fheòir,
'S e dh'fhàg mo chridhe trom fo leòn
    Nach fhaod mi 'n còmhnuidh fuireach leat.

An àm dhuinn dealachadh Dimàirt,
Gun fhios an tachair sinn gu bràth,
Gun d' iarr mi gealladh air mo ghràdh,
    'S a làmh gum biodh i fuireach rium.

Ach thusa, ghaoth, tha dol gu tuath,
Thoir leat mo shoraidh seo gum luaidh,
Is innis dhi, ma bhios mi buan,
    Nach caill i duais ri fuireach rium.[22]

Farewell a while to the lovely maid
who dwells in the green grassy isle;
what left my heart wounded sore
    is that I can't always bide with you.

When on Tuesday we did part,
not knowing if we'll meet again,

> *I asked my love to make a pledge*
> *that she would keep her hand for me.*
>
> *But you, O wind, that travels north,*
> *take my greetings to my love,*
> *and tell her that, if I survive,*
> *she won't lose out if she waits for me.*

Many further comparisons could be made between the poets in songs about love and nature.[23] Again and again we see Dòmhnall and Iain composing from personal experience for a community of which they were a recognisable part, in the same way that Iain Lom, Donnchadh Bàn or Uilleam Ros are recognisable in their songs. By contrast, Niall addresses a generalised Gaelic audience with poems from which he is largely absent as himself. Rather he is a ventriloquist, producing songs to express different sorts of people, often as part of an emotional set-piece. He speaks for an emigrant leaving Skye, for a widow burying her only child, and a man burying his sweetheart – none of his own experience nor closely imagined.[24] Niall is the generic poet, a figure in his own fantasies. In 'Màiri Bhaile-Chrò' for example, the speaker gets lost in the mist in the heights and meets a girl who offers him a bed for the night in her humble dwelling. He swears his undying love for her, yet there is no expectation of their meeting again. It is an idyll evoked by cows, birdsong, flowers and dew, and should perhaps be read as a fantasy of escapism – even of virginity. As the walled garden was to the European medieval love-lyricist, so is the girl by herself in a remote sheiling to the Victorian, yet in reality the sheiling was a place for communal activity. The most palpable part of Niall's personae is his nostalgia.

Not only is the poet a generic, so also are the characters who appear in his songs – the old maid and old bachelor, the sailor and the sweetheart, the drunk, the widow burying her only child, the man and his wife, Anna. Of necessity, Niall's Lowland Gaelic community is largely imagined, but for a few prominent individuals such as John Stuart Blackie, the professor of Greek who raised money for the first chair of Celtic, or Dr Morrison, who had a shop in Edinburgh where Gaels were wont to meet. How interesting it would be to get more of a picture of the experiences of nineteenth-century Gaelic communities in the Lowlands. If it is to be found anywhere, it is in the periodicals of Caraid nan Gàidheal, and later in the songs of Dòmhnall Ruadh Phàislig (Donald Macintyre, 1889–1964). Apart from a few poems for Highland gatherings, Niall's main purpose was to provide songs of escapism, of evocation of the homeland. He lacked Gaelic models for depicting city life and we should probably look for English language models for what urban scenes he does depict (e.g., 'Taigh a' Mhisgeir' and 'Dòmhnall Cruaidh agus an Ceàrd'): Victorian idylls and sentimental verse, the songs of Robert Burns (Niall uses the Scotch Standard Habbie stanza), Chartist songs and the literature of the Temperance Movement,[25] of which Niall was himself a member.[26]

As his brother, Iain Dubh, spoke of his own experience at sea, it is also he who suffers pangs of homesickness in 'Mo mhàthair an Àirnicreap'; he, whose shoes are eaten by his mother's heifer, he who has to carry home a drunken publican.[27] To underline his presence in his songs, six of his surviving songs include his name to vouch for their truth.[28] As he is a real personality, so too are the characters who appear in the songs: his wife who worries about his drinking, ('O Anna na bi brònach'), Ruairidh Chaluim Bhàin and Calum Ros in 'Oran A' Cheannaiche', who take more than their share of ling, crabs, and lobsters (see vv. 5–6); Dòmhnall Grannd, whom he satirises in 'Aoir Dhòmhnaill Ghrannda' for cutting boughs from a tree in the graveyard, and whose sister Catrìona he must then mollify in 'Òran Catrìona Ghrannda.' Iain's songs are quirky, closely observed and risk unusual flights of the imagination. His portrayal of the drunken Edinburgh publican in 'Tost Dhòmhnaill an Fhèilidh' is a good example:

> Ged ghabh mi fhìn air spraoi gun chiall,
>   Bha d' ìomhaigh a' cur eagal orm,
> Nuair a laigh thu air a' *charpet* sìos
>   Mar chearc ag iarraidh neadachadh,
> Thuit an sgian a bha gad dhìon
>   Le d' shliasaid a bhith cho leibideach,
> Do dhà dhòrn bheag a-null 's a-nall
>   A' sealltainn dhomh mar bhogsaiginn.[29]

> *Though I went myself on a senseless spree,*
>   *your own appearance frightened me,*

> when you lay down on the carpet
> like a hen wanting to nest,
> the knife fell that protected you,
> as your thighs had grown so shaky,
> with your two fists going back and forth
> showing me how I ought to box.

If Dòmhnall nan Òran sometimes fulfilled the role of praise poet to Macleod (in 'Smeòrach nan Leòdach' and 'Marbhrann do Chaiptean Alastair MacLeòid, ann a Bhatain'), he was also a village poet, making poetry to commemorate events, to entertain, and to commend and chastise. Rob Donn makes an obvious comparison with Dòmhnall from the same century. Dòmhnall's earliest extant poem, composed when he was fifteen, 'Rann Molaidh do Thaigh Ùr', is a satire on an ostentatious house built by one of his father's friends, whose splendour, the young poet suggests, will have the effect of overwhelming the guests and frightening them away.[30]

Much more serious is his satire against the church elders of Lonmore who refused to baptise his infant on the grounds that he was not himself converted ('Chan eil thu iompaichte dhà sin'). Dòmhnall vents his anger by correcting what he sees as the pharisaic power of the elders. It was said that he knew most of the Bible by heart[31] and, in an overwhelming array of biblical citations, he gives examples of those who have withheld God's grace, among them the foolish virgins, Balaam, and the prodigal son's brother. The elders are named, and he says they look as if they have been kissed by death. They should be careful that they do not get caught out by their own judgementalism, like Haman in the book of Esther, who was hanged on the gallows he had built to kill Mordecai.[32] This shows Dòmhnall at the height of moral indignation, with a complexity of allusion and argument never encountered in the work of his sons.

That Niall deals in generalities while Dòmhnall and Iain deal in specifics is as true of their handling of people as it is of place. Niall's famous song, 'An Gleann san Robh Mi Òg' (*'The Glen Where I Was Young'*), is about a beautiful but generalised place that could evoke the homeland of any Gael in the Highlands. Dòmhnall and Iain are more typical of the tradition in evoking a specific landscape through placenames familiar to a local audience. It is the specific sight of Àirnicreap seen at a distance from his ship that awakens Iain's longing; and it is playing with the concepts of the strangely named headland, An t-Àigeach (*The Stallion*), and the stack, An Ceannaiche (*The Merchant*), that provides the material of a further two songs.

While the humour in Dòmhnall's and Iain's poems arises from the situations in which they find themselves, Niall's humour is that of the music-hall and its stock characters. John N. MacLeod and Professor MacKinnon, quoted at the beginning of this paper, praise Niall for his delicacy of sentiment and exquisite humour, which, they say, differentiated him from other poets.[33] By today's standards of political correctness, this same humour can sometimes seem in poor taste. The old maid is a figure of fun, desperate for any man, poor, blind or coloured ('Oran na seanamhaighdinn'); the teuchter, Dòmhnall, makes a trip to Glasgow, and under the influence of drink, is decoyed by a pretty girl to a den of thieves ('Turus Dhomhnuill do Ghlascho'); while a poor drunk dies from his wounds and a cold after being set upon by a demonic crew of tinkers, men, women and children ('Dòmhnall Cruaidh agus an Ceàrd').

But Niall's father's humour is full of social comment. One poem mocks a local cottar for acting above his station when he got a loan of a horse to take him home.[34] In another, the potato is personified as a cheerful fellow in a jacket, and praised for its ability to feed both rich and poor and to clean the ground, and that it doesn't need chewing and is a good missile to throw at a thief.[35] Iain's song for Catrìona Ghrannda is so specific to the circumstances that produced it that its humour would be lost on an audience who lacked the background knowledge that Catrìona was neither beautiful nor a good singer.

There are marked formal contrasts between the three poets. Niall produced a standard product – almost two-thirds of his poems are between six and nine verses long.[36] This is considerably shorter than the average length of his brother's and father's work, and of traditional song-poetry in general. The city ceilidh with a structured list of performers perhaps had greater time pressures than the ones in the Highlands. Niall's regularity of rhyme and rhythm also makes for easier memorisation and execution than the more conversational rhythms of Iain's and Dòmhnall's poetry. Niall's metres were praised by Sorley Maclean as being 'exquisite in modulation and even in general technique', but were criticised by Derick Thomson who made a connection between their rhythmic regularity and their lack of surprise, shock, and tension.[37] In his thinking too, Niall follows simple formulas. Very often he describes the land, then the nostalgia it awakens, and closes with a rallying call for recovery, or with a didactic message on the fragility of life. All of Niall's poems are rounded off with some clear message or conclusion, but because Iain's songs were aimed at a known audience, they are often not self-explanatory, as was seen in the case of Catrìona Ghrannda above, and end abruptly. 'Mo Mhàthair an Airnicreap' describes Iain's dangerous life at sea and his longing for home. His audience would have understood what lay behind his envy of Finlay who had stayed at home.

> Nach sona dhuts', a Fhionnlaigh,
> Gun do dh'ionnsaich thu cur is buain.[38]
>
> *Weren't you lucky, Finlay,*
> *that you learnt to sow and reap.*

The three have a distinctly different tenor to their language. Dòmhnall's poems can have an eighteenth-century density and exuberance of language. We saw this in his seafaring poem above. His poem to a grassy hillock in Glendale called Tungag is typical of Mac Mhaighstir Alasdair's nature poetry – and even quotes from it – while his 'Dàn a' Bhreitheanais' on the Day of Judgement brings Dùghall Bochanan to mind. In Niall there is a limited centralised vocabulary and a new Victorian prettiness combined with the influence of MacPherson. Love swims in the face of Màiri Bhaile-Chrò (v. 6); the sun dries a daisy's tears ('Do Neòinean'); the wind laments lost warriors and the departed population ('Fàilte don Eilean Sgitheanach' and 'Muinntir a' Ghlinne Seo' v. 5). This is quite different from the rocks, An t-Àigeach and An Ceannaiche, speaking to Iain Dubh, because the wind had never spoken in Gaelic before James Macpherson's time, while the rocks had been talking since the Lia Fáil.

However, for all his advocacy of non-violence in the Land Wars, for all his lack of understanding of Highland history, and his unwarranted hope for the restoration of the population and their language in the Highlands, Niall was more politically aware than either his brother or father who, I think, make no mention of the Clearances. Sorley MacLean has written in this regard:

Niall MacLeod ...had no deficiency in intellect, and his fine sensitive nature reacted keenly to the tragedy of his people, but he was incapable of expressing a militant ardour ... incapable of bitterness and incapable of the adequate expression of strong indignation, and he saw human life as sad whether the sorrow was of a particular or universal nature.[39]

MacLean points out that 'Poetic sincerity is not the same thing as moral sincerity,' so although Niall wrote poetry in which he expressed indignation at the treatment of the Highlanders, Sorley felt that they were not as convincing as his poems of nostalgia.

In conclusion, though Niall might be said to have created a new genre of emigré verse, it is important to recognise those places where he still worked within the Gaelic tradition. In writing elegies for prominent city Gaels, Niall fulfilled the traditional role of the Gaelic poet, by commemorating the dead and holding up their virtues to others. Just as his father had used tree imagery in his Lament for Captain MacLeod, and Iain had satirised his neighbour for cutting branches from a tree growing in Cille Comhain cemetery to protect his kale patch from sheep, so too does Niall use tree imagery to praise not a warrior but the academic, Professor Blackie:

> Ghearradh a' chraobh bu torach blàth,
> 'S a dh'àraich iomadh meanglan òg,
> Bu taitneach leam a bhith fo sgàil,
> 'S mo chàil a' faotainn brìgh a lòin.[40]

> *The tree of fruitful blossom has been felled,*
> *which nurtured many a young shoot,*
> *it was my delight to be in its shade,*
> *my appetite nourished from its fruit.*

Niall seeks seclusion to enable him to experience the beauty of the Highland landscape without the evidence of the Clearances (e.g., in 'Ri Taobh na Tràigh'). The idyll of seclusion and of finding comfort and companionship in nature is at least as old in Gaelic as the hermetic poetry of the sixth to the ninth centuries, and the traditions of Suibhne Geilt of the ninth to the twelfth centuries. However, the emptiness of the Highlands is itself a sign of Clearance, so the beauty of the Highlands becomes at once synonymous with their sadness.

Judging by the number of people who knew the eighty-eight poems in *Clàrsach an Doire* by heart,[41] and by the demand for this book, which has run to six editions, it is clear that the Gaels have relished Niall's songs, whatever late-twentieth-century critics may say. People appreciate their shortness, their easy performance owing to their simple language and rhythms, their availability in book form and their ability to stand alone without explanation. They were a mass-produced product for the Gaels working in the industries of the Lowlands when they came together socially. In such a situation they would not want the songs of protest and anguish that were part of land league rallies; rather they wanted a balm to heal the wounds of recent history, of Clearance and war.[42] The social function of Niall's poetry was to give people, who historically would have felt little commonality, a group identity, based on a shared Highland upbringing, a shared language, and a shared nostalgia and concern for their homelands. Niall's songs expressed, and were shaped by, the closeness and affection that were the glue of such gatherings. But without their music, the words of songs live only a half-life.[43] We should be careful about judging Gaelic song as poetry, nor should we forget that Niall's work may have worked all the better for its relative simplicity. The fusion of melody with easy-flowing versification in the evocation of an idyll would have given thousands a sense of pride in their past, a sense of common purpose and optimism about their new lives.

Notes

1. I. MacAonghais, 'Bardachd Iain Duibh Mac Dhomhnaill Nan Oran' in *Gairm* 82 (1973), pp. 113–21 (p. 113) and D. Thomson, *An Introduction to Gaelic Poetry* (London: Gollancz, 1974), p. 233.
2. Ian MacLeod in D. S. Thomson (ed.), *The Companion to Gaelic Scotland* (1983), p. 183–84.
3. Donald Meek, 'Gaelic Poets of the Land Agitation' in *TGSI*, 49:309–376 (1974–76), pp. 312–15; and D. Thomson, *An Introduction to Gaelic Poetry*, pp. 224–233.
4. R. C. MacDiarmid, 'Donald MacLeod, the Skye Bard – His Life and Songs', *Transactions of the Gaelic Society of Glasgow* (Glasgow: Archibald Sinclair, 1888), vol. 1, pp. 18–33 (p. 22).
5. John N. MacLeod, 'Dòmhnull nan Òran: Am Bàrd Sgitheanach', *TGSI*, 29 (1917), pp. 119–33 (p. 125).
6. Donald MacKinnon: 'Neil MacLeod', *Celtic Review*, vol. 9 (1913–1914), pp. 151–56 (pp. 153–54).
7. Thomson, 1974, p. 232.
8. See *A' Chòisir-Chiùil*, parts 1–4, for songs by Niall Macleòid prescribed for the Mod.
9. See for example Sorley MacLean, 'Realism in Gaelic poetry' in *Ris a' Bhruthaich*, ed. W. Gillies.
10. R. C. MacDiarmid states that he was born in 1/8/ (*TGSG*, 1.18).
11. A comparison can be made here with Iain MacIllEathain, Bàrd Thighearna Cola (1787–1848), a contemporary of Dòmhnall's, who also collected songs and published them with his own in 1818 before leaving for Canada (my thanks to Rob Dunbar for this information).
12. Listed in the 1889 Register of Marriages for the District of Blythswood in the Borough of Glasgow.
13. Neil MacLeod, 'Còmhradh eadar Oganach agus Oisean', *Gailig* (*An Deò-Gréine*) 18 (1922–1923), pp. 58–59, and 77–78, vol. 18.
14. John MacInnes, quoted by Ian MacLeod (Dingwall) in Thomson (1983), *The Companion to Gaelic Scotland*, p. 183.
15. www.youtube.com/watch?v=dRp4oAdhoGU (accessed 12 February 2014).
16. Ross, James, 'Iain Dubh mac Dhòmhnaill nan Òran', BBC Radio, 3:2:64.
17. Domhnul MacLeòid, *Orain nuadh Ghaeleach; maille ri beagain do cho-chruinneachadh urramach na 'n aireamh* (Inbhirnis: Eoin Young, 1811), p. 151, vv 3–4.
18. R. C. MacDiarmid, 'Donald MacLeod, the Skye Bard – His Life and Songs', *Transactions of the Gaelic Society of Glasgow* (Glasgow: Archibald Sinclair, 1888), vol. 1, pp. 18–33 (p. 23).
19. See A. MacDonald and A. MacDonald, *The Poems of Alexander Macdonald (Mac Mhaighstir Alasdair)* (1924), pp. 370–401, and W. J. Watson (ed.) *Scottish Verse from the Book of the Dean of Lismore*, SGTS 1937, p fol 218 and 224.
20. MacAonghais, in *Gairm*, 82 (An t-Earrach, 1973), pp. 114–15, vv. 2 and 5, libcat.uhi.ac.uk/search%7ES14?/c891.63+GAI/c891.63+gai/-3,-1,,E/browse
21. It should be noted that Aonghas Dubh MacNeacail thinks that this is one of those poems by Iain Dubh published under Niall's name.
22. N. MacLeòid, *Clàrsach an Doire* (1975), p. 28.
23. A comparison of love poems could be made between 'Litir Ghaoil ga Freagairt' by Dòmhnall, 'O Anna, Na Bi Brònach' by Iain, and 'Màiri Bhaile-Chrò' by Niall; and of

nature poems between 'Òran do Thullaich Ghlais ris an Abrar "Tungan"' by Dòmhnall, 'Òran an Àigich' by Iain, and 'An Gleann san Robh Mi Òg' by Niall.
24. See 'Cumha Eilean a' Cheò', 'Bàs Leinibh na Bantraich' and 'Cumha Leannain'. A different sort of ventriloquism is evident in 'Tobar Thalamh Tholl' which he wrote for a specific old woman when moving away from the well that had served her for many years.
25. Dòmhnall Meek, 'Gaelic Poets of the Land Agitation' *TGSI* 49, 1974–76, pp. 309–76 (p. 316).
26. Dòmhnall Meek, 'Gaelic Poets of the Land Agitation'.
27. 'An Gamhainn a Tha aig Mo Mhàthair' and 'Tost Dhòmhnaill an Fhèilidh'.
28. His name appears in 'Anna Nic Leòid', 'Gillean Ghleann Dail', 'Mo Mhàthair an Àirnicreap' and 'Oran a' Cheannaiche' and he vouches for the truth of 'Oran do dh'Fhear Hùsabost' and 'Tost Dhòmhnaill an Fhèilidh'.
29. Source: www.tobarandualchais.co.uk/en/fullrecord/9862/8 sound file, v. 5 (accessed 12 February 2014).
30. Domhnul MacLeòid, *Orain nuadh Ghaeleach; maille ri beagain do cho-chruinneachadh urramach na 'n aireamh* (Inbhirnis: Eoin Young, 1811), p. 173.
31. John N. MacLeod (1917), p. 127.
32. D. MacLeoìd (1871), p. 3.
33. John N. MacLeod (1917), p. 125, and MacKinnon (1913), p. 155.
34. 'Oran Mhurchaidh Bhig' (*ONG*, p. 42).
35. 'Òran Molaidh a' Bhuntato' (*ONG*, p. 96).
36. Though they vary in length between three and twenty-two verses (the latter in couplets), the vast majority (59/88 – almost two-thirds) are between six and nine verses long, six being the commonest.
37. MacLean (1985), p. 69 and Thomson (1974) p. 232.
38. Cairistiona Mhàrtainn, *Òrain an Eilein* (An t-Eilean Sgitheanach: Taigh na Teud, 2001). p. 19.
39. MacLean (1985), p. 68.
40. MacLeòid (1975), p. 187.
41. A note in Malcolm MacFarlane's handwriting among his papers says that there are many who know all Niall's songs, and that he had never written or set a poem to music that wasn't executed with finesse:

> Is dìomhain a bhi leughadh eiseimplir air bàrdachd Niall. Cha'n urrainn da bhi nach eil moran dibh a tha eolach oirre air fad. Cha d' rinn e ordu-seinn no dàn nach eil math agus tha cuir fìor ghrinn. Nam b'fhear seinn mi sheinninn òran. *(NLS Acc 9736/65: miscellaneous notes and fragments in red ink on a strip of paper 6 x 1 inch)*

42. I must thank Mairead Bennett for this point.
43. The phrase comes from Gerda Stevenson, a singer-songwriter herself.

Bibliography

References are given below to sources at time of writing, but all the poems by Niall, Dòmhnall nan Òran and Iain Dubh mentioned in this paper are now available in Meg Bateman with Anne Loughran (eds), *Bàird Ghleann Dail/The Glendale Bards: a selection of songs and poems by Niall MacLeòid (1843-1913), his brother Iain Dubh (1847-1901) and father Dòmhnall nan Òran (c.1787-1873)* (Edinburgh: Birlinn, 2014).

Budge, Rev. Domhnull, 'Bàird an Eilean Sgiathanaich: Domhnull MacLeòid, "Domhnull nan Oran"' (*TGSI*, 47: 1972), pp. 392-403.

Loughran, Anne, 'The Literature of the Island of Skye: A bibliography with extended annotation' (University of Aberdeen M Litt thesis, 1986, two volumes); vol. 1, pp. 218-37, on Donald, Iain and Niall Macleod; available online at: www.apjpublications.co.uk/skye (accessed 12 February 2014).

MacAonghais, An t-Urr. Iain, 'Bardachd Iain Duibh Mac Dhomhnaill nan Oran', *Gairm* 82 (1973), pp. 113-21.

MacDiarmid, R. C, 'Donald MacLeod, the Skye Bard – His Life and Songs' (*Transactions of the Gaelic Society of Glasgow* (Glasgow: Archibald Sinclair, vol. 1 (1888), pp. 18-33.

MacKenzie, John, *Sàr-Obair nam Bàrd Gaelach: or, the Beauties of Gaelic Poetry and Lives of the Highland Bards* (1841; Edinburgh: MacLachlan and Stewart, and London: Simpkin, Marshall & Co, 1872).

MacKinnon, Donald, 'Neil MacLeod', *Celtic Review*, vol. 9 (1913-1914), pp. 151-56.

MacLean, Sorley, 'Poetry of the Clearances' in W. Gillies (ed.), *Ris a' Bhruthaich* (Stornoway: Acair, 1985).

MacLeod, John N., 'Dòmhnull nan Òran: Am Bàrd Sgitheanach', *TGSI*, 29 (1917), pp. 119-33.

MacLeod, Neil, 'Còmhradh eadar Oganach agus Oisean', *Gailig* (*An Deò-Gréine*), 18 (1922-1923), pp. 58-59 and 77-78.

MacLeòid, Domhnul, *Orain nuadh Ghaeleach; maille ri beagain do cho-chruinneachadh urramach na 'n aireamh* (Inbhirnis: Eoin Young, 1811).

MacLeòid, Domhnull, *Dàin agus Orain* (Glascho: Mac-na-Ceardadh, 1871).

MacLeòid, Niall, *Clàrsach an Doire* (6 eds, 1883-1975: edition used Glasgow: Gairm, 1975).

Mhàrtainn, Cairistiona, *Òrain an Eilein* (An t-Eilean Sgitheanach: Taigh na Teud, 2001).

Meek, Donald, 'Gaelic Poets of the Land Agitation' (*Transactions of the Gaelic Society of Inverness*, vol. 49 (1974-1976), pp. 309-76).

Ross, James, 'Iain Dubh mac Dhòmhnaill nan Òran', BBC Radio 3:2:64.

Thomson, Derick, *An Introduction to Gaelic Poetry* (London: Gollancz, 1974).

Thomson, Derick (ed.), *The Companion to Gaelic Scotland* (Oxford: Blackwell, 1983).

Thomson, Derick (ed.), *Gaelic Poetry in the Eighteenth Century* (ASLS: Aberdeen, 1993).

12. Robert Louis Stevenson's Highlanders

CHRISTOPHER MacLACHLAN

This paper was originally called 'Robert Louis Stevenson: The Lowland Highlander' and under that title it was listed in the programme for the Skye conference. The title stemmed from a vague idea that it might be possible to discuss Stevenson's expression of a romantic desire to be a Jacobite clansman. This turned out to be impossible, but it led to looking again at just how Stevenson portrays the Highlands and Highlanders, and to wonder if the usual idea of this is altogether correct. If it is not workable to try to say that Stevenson the Lowlander really wanted to be a Highlander, it is I think common to suppose that he might have done, or at least that he is one of the chief sources, after Scott, of the idea of the Highlands as exciting and glamorous, and of Highlanders as heroic adventurers. How far is this so?

Let us start with a Highland gentleman who is a main character in one of Stevenson's novels, a soldier and an adventurer, mixed up in the politics of Scotland after the '45, a slightly mysterious figure who inspires loyalty and suspicion, who becomes a fugitive and an exile, one who must live by his wits and his powers of persuasion, a risk-taker and a gambler, a character who, without being the narrator or even the centre of the action, still dominates the plot of the book he appears in. No, not Alan Breck, but James More, or James MacGregor Drummond, as he styles himself, the father of Catriona, the girl who marries David Balfour in the sequel to *Kidnapped*, though you will see from the previous sentence that there are strong parallels between the two characters.

James More is a neglected character. Indeed *Catriona* itself, published in 1893, seven years after *Kidnapped*, is a neglected novel, perhaps because of the unattractiveness of James More. We see him first in Chapter 1, when David Balfour, just come into his fortune after asserting his rights against his Uncle Ebenezer, has left his Edinburgh bank and is passed by a group of soldiers escorting a prisoner, 'a tall man in a greatcoat [who] walked with a stoop that was like a piece of courtesy, genteel and insinuating: he waved his hands plausibly as he went, and his face was sly and handsome' (p. 217).[1]

Immediately after this David encounters three Highlanders, a girl and two 'ragged gillies'. He overhears the argument between the girl and her followers about the loss of the small piece of money needed to buy snuff for her father, who is the prisoner being brought to the house of Lord Advocate Prestongrange. Even from the start we wonder what kind of man, imprisoned for treason, would be so concerned about his 'sneeshing'. If he does not get his snuff, Catriona says he 'will think his daughter has forgotten him' (p. 222). This reflects better on her than on him, surely.

David Balfour no doubt thinks the same for, when in Chapter 5 he meets James More in a small room in the Lord Advocate's house, as they both wait for interviews with Prestongrange, David's account is far from flattering about the father of the girl he has already fallen in love with. At James's reply to David's wish that his meeting with Prestongrange will be brief, he records that '[t]here came a kind of Highland snuffle out of the man that raised my dander strangely' (p. 249). It is hard to say what exactly a 'Highland snuffle' is, but it does not sound prepossessing. The two exchange names and James tries to connect David with a Balfour who 'marched surgeon in the year '45 with my battalion' (p. 250). David, a little too clever, say he knows who this was, and James insists that 'since I have been fellow-soldier with your kinsman, you must suffer me to grasp your hand', and he shakes hands with David 'long and tenderly, beaming on me the while as though he had found a brother' (p. 250). It does not much matter to James when David explains that he has never seen this other Balfour. The Highlander continues to declare that his '[meeting] in with the blood of an old brother-in-arms' heartens him 'like the skirling of the Highland pipes'. This leads James on to reflections on the contrast between the past and his present situation, and the fact that he lacks 'mere ne*cess*aries', since, to use his own words, 'the malice of my foes has quite sequestered my resources' (p. 251), which leads in turn, one feels inevitably, to 'I could have wished it was your cousin I had met, or his brother … himself. Either would, I know, have been rejoiced to help me; while a comparative stranger like yourself –' (p. 251). The sentence tails off but its meaning is obvious, as David's next makes clear: 'I would be ashamed to set down all he poured out to me in this beggarly vein'.

David's revulsion at 'the grossness of immediate falsity that clung about' James is well conveyed by the unctuousness of the dialogue Stevenson gives him: the formality of some of his language, his deployment of references to his home and his military career, and his appeal to both as links, however tenuous, with somebody he has only just met, links that he deems enough to justify appeals for money. These are to be the basis for James More's character in the rest of the novel. We shall not meet him again for another twenty chapters, but he is never far from our minds. He is behind the fact that David is dogged by Highlanders for the rest of his time in Edinburgh and the Lothians, until they catch up with him and transport him to the Bass Rock. Then, in Chapter 18, comes the suspicious story of James More's escape from Edinburgh Castle, slipping out in the disguise his daughter brings to him, a romantic episode that David suspects was a ruse of the Lord Advocate's to rid himself of James's embarrassing presence. But with all that out of the way Stevenson turns back to the love affair between David and Catriona.

By a series of accidents they find themselves awkwardly living together in Holland, where James More finds them. He appears suddenly at the door early one morning. His re-entry to the story is quite typical:

> 'Ah,' said he, 'I have found you, Mr Balfour.' And he offered me his large, fine hand [...] 'It is a remarkable circumstance how our affairs appear to intermingle,' he continued. 'I am owing you an apology for an unfortunate intrusion upon yours, which I suffered myself to be entrapped into by my confidence in that false-face, Prestongrange; I think shame to own to you that I was ever trusting to a lawyer.' He shrugged his shoulders with a very French air. 'But indeed the man is very plausible,' says he. (p. 424)

The 'unfortunate intrusion' on David's affairs referred to here is his imprisonment on the Bass Rock.

David has to invite James More into the apartment, and so begins an embarrassing conversation, in which it must come out that he is sharing the two rooms with James More's daughter. This 'very unusual circumstance' (p. 425), as James describes it, needs an explanation, which, despite some bluster from David, does not go entirely his way, until he raises the question of his expenditure in looking after Catriona. There is 'a change in [James's] manner [...] as soon as the name of money fell between us' (p. 427). This prompts David to suggest that James regard himself as his guest, and he offers him his room in the apartment. This wins James over rapidly:

> 'Sir,' said he, 'when an offer is frankly made, I think I honour myself most to imitate that frankness [...] I am an old soldier,' he went on, looking rather disgusted-like around my chamber, 'and you need not fear that I shall prove burthensome. I have ate too often at a dyke-side, drank of the ditch, and had no roof but the rain.' (p. 428)

When, however, David explains that breakfast, brought in from a nearby tavern, will be accompanied by water only, James warns that 'that is fair destruction to the stomach, take an old campaigner's word for it. Our country spirit at home is perhaps the most entirely wholesome; but as that is not come-at-able, Rhenish or a white wine of Burgundy will be next best' (p. 429). David agrees to see that that is supplied. A few pages later we find David also supplying James with additional furniture, which he did not need himself. As David explains, '[b]efore twelve hours were gone he had raised a small loan of me; before thirty, he had asked for a second and been refused. Money and refusal he took with the same kind of high good nature' (p. 435). David then sums up James More: 'To me, after my first two interviews, he was as plain as print: I saw him to be perfectly selfish, with a perfect innocency in the same; and I would hearken to his swaggering talk (of arms, and "an old soldier," and "a poor Highland gentleman," and "the strength of my country and my friends") as I might to the babbling of a parrot' (p. 436).

He adds, however, that '[t]he odd thing was that I fancy he believed some part of it himself, or did at times', often 'break[ing] forth in pitiable regrets for his own land and friends, or into Gaelic singing' (p. 436):

> 'This is one of the melancholy airs of my native land,' he would say. 'You may think it strange to see a soldier weep, and indeed it is to make a near friend of you,' says he. 'But the notes of this singing are in my blood, and the words come out of my heart. And when I mind upon my red mountains and the wild birds calling there, and the brave streams of water running down, I would scarce think shame to weep before my enemies.' Then he would sing again, and translate to me pieces of the song, with a great deal of boggling and much expressed contempt against the English language. (p. 436)

James ends an attempt to translate one of his songs with the assertion that 'it is mere mockery to tell you it in English', to which David as narrator responds: 'Well, I thought there was a good deal of mockery in the business, one way and another; and yet, there was some feeling too, for which I hated him, I think, the worst of all' (p. 436).

This passage at the end of Chapter 26 of *Catriona* is surely one of the most extraordinary in Stevenson's work, and perhaps in any Scottish writing about a Highlander after the Waverley novels. David adds to it the thought that 'I was sure that one half of his distress flowed from his last night's drinking in some tavern' (p. 437), joining drunkenness to mendacity, sentimentality and hypocrisy in the portrait of James More, a portrait that includes most of the iconic features, or if you prefer the clichés, of the image of the literary Highlander created in the nineteenth century and still evident today: such things as his pride, his courtesy, his soldierly honour, his love of his native land, its language and its music, and his feelings for comrades and family. One can surely hear the echo of Macpherson's Ossian in the quotation above, or at least of the Highland tourists, in the reference to the 'red mountains and the wild birds calling there, and the brave streams of water running down', and the weeping over them. But when David says James More 'was so false all through that he scarce knew when he was lying' (p. 436), Stevenson opens up a very dark view of the romantic idea of the Highlands.

In the next chapter David receives news of the death of his Uncle Ebenezer and the fact that he is now the full owner of the estate of Shaws, and James More makes an instantaneous change of tack. He revives the business of finding David living alone with Catriona, mentions the danger this means to her reputation and presents David with two alternatives: 'either that I should cut your throat or that you should marry my daughter' (p. 440). David replies that he will marry Catriona, but only if she agrees, to which James responds: 'I will engage for her acceptance' (p. 441). This is not enough for David, however, who insists that Catriona should herself freely consent. When she does not, James is forced to accept her decision, and father and daughter must leave Holland.

Before they go, David unwisely makes an arrangement with James to send him money for Catriona's upkeep As a result he finds himself in correspondence with James. At the start of Chapter 29 Stevenson includes one of the letters from James More. It is an anthology of all the traits in his character, and worth quoting in full:

> My dear Sir,—Your esteemed favour came to hand duly, and I have to acknowledge the inclosure according to agreement. It shall be all faithfully expended on my daughter, who is well, and desires to be remembered to her dear friend. I find her in rather a melancholy disposition, but trust in the mercy of God to see her re-established. Our manner of life is very much alone, but we solace ourselves with the melancholy tunes of our native mountains, and by walking upon the margin of the sea that lies next to Scotland. It was better days with me when I lay with five wounds upon my body on the field of Gladsmuir. I have found employment here in the *haras* of a French nobleman, where my experience is valued. But, my dear Sir, the wages are so exceedingly unsuitable that I would be ashamed to mention them, which makes your remittances the more necessary to my daughter's comfort, though I daresay the sight of old friends would be still better.
>
> My dear Sir,
>
> Your affectionate, obedient servant,
>
> JAMES MACGREGOR DRUMMOND.

To which Catriona adds a postscript, 'Do not be believing him, it is all lies together,—C. M. D.' (p. 453), the first clear indication that she has turned against her father.[2]

James More, learning that Alan Breck is on a visit to David, invites them both to come and visit him and Catriona in Dunkirk, saying he has something he wants to tell them. They cannot guess what he means and rather foolishly decide to go to Dunkirk to find out. It is of course a trap, by which James has plotted with the British government to betray Alan. Alan escapes, of course, James's double-dealing is revealed and he flees, leaving Catriona with David once more. He takes her to Paris, to the exiled chief of her clan, who promptly arranges their marriage, and then reveals that James More too is in the city, although ill enough that he is near to death. The newlyweds visit him, and are liberally forgiven:

> 'I have been never understood,' said he. 'I forgive you both without an afterthought'; after which he spoke for all the world in his old manner, was so obliging as to play us a tune or two upon his pipes, and borrowed a small sum before I left. (p. 473)

The idea that a man on his deathbed could play the bagpipes is amazing, and this final scene of James More 'propped in a pallet', amusing his French neighbours with his playing as he dies, seems to owe more to Smollett or Dickens than to realism. Of course, Stevenson's description of the death of James More is part of his ending. The tricky business of how to rid David Balfour's married life of a disreputable father-in-law requires a lightening of tone to make it acceptable to the reader.

James More seems a less attractive version of another Stevenson rogue, Long John Silver. James is as loquacious and posing as Silver, and as treacherous, and has a similar difficulty in confronting his own weaknesses, but James is less amusing and, crucially, he is not given the chance to establish himself in the reader's affections, and he does not show the resourcefulness of Silver, though he has the same ability to survive. Though the comparison with a pirate does not flatter the Highlander, it does show that he is one of Stevenson's gallery of mixed or split characters, not quite a Jekyll and Hyde, but still a combination of outer respectability and inner self-indulgence. Selfishness is one of the main accusations David voices against him.

He is not, however, Stevenson's only mixed character of a Highlander. A further example, this time from *Kidnapped*, is Cluny Macpherson. The contrasts in Cluny's character in Chapter 23 of *Kidnapped* are very obvious. He is both the chief of his clan and an outlaw, living in his 'cage' on Ben Alder more like a boy in a den. There is a strong division between the formalities of his station and his domestic arrangements. When his servants enter, '[w]ith each of them [...] he ceremoniously shook hands, both parties touching their bonnets at the same time in a military manner' (p. 151), but on the other hand 'cookery was one of his chief fancies, and even while he was greeting us in, he kept an eye to the collops' (p. 150). Though, given his circumstances, it seems harsh to blame him for his stay-at-home idleness, his interest in cooking and gossip is hardly masculine, and his enthusiasm for playing cards makes him seem childish. When he wins all of Alan Breck's money, and David's too, and then has to give it back so that they can continue their journey, he is much put out, and it needs an appeal from David to him as a son to a father to make Cluny face his responsibilities. As with James More, the heart of the matter seems to be money, and as with the characterisation of More, that of Cluny hovers between the romantic (the fugitive chieftain in a greenwood hide-out still supported by his loyal clan) and a debunking of it, with the indications of the boredom and inconvenience of being a permanent camper, and the futility of a leader with nowhere to go.

James More and Cluny therefore indicate some complications in Stevenson's idea of the Highlands, and this is also the case with another story by Stevenson with a Highland, or to be more accurate an Island setting: *The Merry Men*, written in 1882, before *Kidnapped*. Because this story is less well known here is a brief outline. It is told by a first person narrator, Charles Darnaway, a recent graduate from Edinburgh University, and set on the island of Aros, which is off the Isle of Mull and is, as Stevenson later admitted, in fact the island of Earraid, used again by him as the place where David Balfour is washed ashore in *Kidnapped*. In *The Merry Men* the island is much bigger, in fact nearer its actual size, and not only habitable but habited, for there Charles's uncle Gordon Darnaway lives, with his daughter Mary and an old servant, Rorie, on a croft where Charles, having lost his parents, has spent his vacations. The period of the story is the late eighteenth century; Charles remarks that he has been assisting 'our then Principal in Edinburgh College, the famous writer, Dr Robertson' (p. 9).[3] The key feature of the setting is not perhaps Aros itself but the seas around it. The many rocks and the racing tidal currents make it a trap to unwary shipping. In particular there are the fierce currents off the south-west of the island that, when there is a high tide and storms from the south-west, create such breakers in the sea that the water splashes up high in the air with a roaring that sounds like wild laughter and gives the spouts their name, 'The Merry Men', the title of the story.[4]

The story opens with Charles's return to Aros for another vacation. As Rorie brings over the boat to ferry Charles to the island, he notices that the old servant keeps leaving the oars to go to the stern and peer over into the water as though looking for something. He does this while rowing back to Aros with Charles, but when asked what is wrong he says only 'It will be a great feesh' (p. 11). On reaching the house Charles finds it contains many rich additions and learns a ship has been wrecked on the south side of the island, almost intact though its keel is broken. The excitement of his uncle Gordon about the wreck seems to Charles frantic and worrying, as though he has something to hide. These forebodings are not reduced by the talk over dinner of sea-monsters and portents, including whatever it was Rorie was looking for behind the boat:

> 'Was it there?' asked my uncle.
> 'Ou, ay!' said Rorie.
> I observed that they both spoke in a manner of aside, and with some show of embarrassment, and that Mary herself appeared to colour, and looked down on her plate. [...]
> 'You mean the fish?' I asked.
> 'Whatten fish?' cried my uncle. 'Fish, quo' he! Fish! Your een are fu' o' fatness, man; your heid dozened wi' carnal leir. Fish! it's a bogle!'
> (p. 17)

Later, when Charles goes across the island to look at the wreck, he discovers a fresh grave nearby and begins to wonder what happened, and why he has heard no mention of a burial after the shipwreck. Who is in the grave and who put him there?

Charles, in his work for Principal Robertson, has come across a document relating to the legendary wreck of a Spanish Armada galleon on Aros and he sets out to find it, diving down into the bay where the recent wreck lies beached, but his finding of a human bone so disgusts him that he soon gives up. He is not, however, the only one looking for treasure and he watches as a group of strangers begin exploring the bay where he himself has been searching. As he rushes back to warn his uncle of these intruders the weather changes and the strangers row back to their ship hurriedly, leaving, as it transpires, one of their number behind. They are, however, too late. Against the wind the ship cannot escape from the bay. Uncle Gordon, knowing it is doomed, rushes out into the storm to a vantage point to watch the coming wreck. Fearful for his mental state, Charles and Rorie join him, hoping to restrain the manic glee with which the old man looks on the disaster, as the ship is driven into the Merry Men and torn apart.

Even then, Gordon Darnaway does not calm down. He insists on circuiting the island to find what may have been washed ashore. Charles goes with him, more and more concerned for his uncle. When they come to the grave Charles attempts to make his uncle face facts by asking him how the man who is buried there died, but before he can get an answer his uncle catches sight of the sailor left behind by the treasure hunters. He is standing on the upraised stern of the previous wreck, and he is black. For a moment even Charles is disturbed by imaginings of who this man is and where he comes from, but as he waves to him to approach his uncle begins 'swearing and praying in a mingled stream' (p. 53) and when Charles tries to draw Gordon Darnaway nearer to the black man his uncle 'felled me to the ground, burst from my grasp, leaving the shoulder of his jacket, and fled up the hillside towards the top of Aros like a deer' (p. 54). The rest of the story is about the frustrated attempts of Charles and Rorie, and the stranger, to recapture the madman, who clearly sees the black man as a figure of retribution from some sinister realm.

Gordon Darnaway is no Highlander. He speaks broad Scots and, from what Charles says about his family, comes originally from the Lowlands. His talk is full of Biblical and Calvinistic language, and his mental breakdown is partly the result of the conflict between his own belief in sin and judgement and the guilt of his actions after the shipwreck. Lurking behind this character is, I think, James Hogg's Justified Sinner. *The Merry Men* is mainly a story about how a believer in divine retribution punishes himself by imagining a perfect stranger is the devil incarnate. What is relevant about the story to this essay is its setting, and the way the landscape, or to be more precise, the seascape, is made the haunt of the supernatural. The business of the thing like a giant fish that Rorie sees behind the boat is a good example of this. So great is Gordon Darnaway's fear of it that he refuses to leave the island, except when he can wade across to the mainland at low tide. His references to the Merry Men increasingly treat them as beings. As he watches the ship being wrecked he calls out to the Merry Men and even offers them a drink from his whisky-bottle: '"Ha'e, bairns!" he cried, "there's your han'sel. Ye'll get bonnier nor that, or morning"' (p. 47). In an earlier passage, Charles and his uncle look out over the bay in the calm before the storm, when 'there appear certain strange, undecipherable marks – sea-runes, as we may name them – on the glassy surface of the bay' (p. 20). Gordon Darnaway asks his nephew if he can see some of these marks as letters, to which Charles answers yes, though the letters he sees, a C and an M, that he links with himself and his cousin Mary, mean nothing to his uncle. He reads the C as a reference to the *Christiana*, the ship wrecked on the shore. Both men are reading some sort of meaning into the waves, and relating it to themselves. Though neither character is a Highlander, once again Stevenson draws on a cliché of the idea of the Highlands and Islands, that it is a place of the uncanny, where the landscape itself has messages for humans, if we could make them out.

The next question to ask, however, is what Stevenson is doing with this kind of material. There are two opposite possibilities. One is that, despite his high literary reputation, Stevenson in fact belongs to the range of nineteenth-century exploiters of the Highlands for romantic glamour, that in some sense he sees Highlanders and the Highlands with some of the clichés that are common from the Victorians onwards (this is perhaps where the original, discarded idea for this essay began). Another and more attractive possibility is that he is certainly aware of these clichés, and uses them, but in ways that undermine them. *Kidnapped*, *Catriona* and *The Merry Men* are all told by first-person narrators, and not by the author himself. We ought not simply to transfer to Stevenson what his characters say and believe. Starting from that position, we could argue that James More is a kind of ironising of the figure of the Highland Jacobite warrior and gentleman, and Cluny Macpherson is a debunking of the clan chieftain. And we could also argue that *The Merry Men* is a story that takes the conventions of the haunted Gaelic landscape and tries to rewrite them as a psychological study, not unlike Hogg's suggestions, in the *Private Memoirs and Confessions*, that Gil-Martin and much else of the supernatural exist mainly in Robert Wringhim's mind.

The sticking point to this line of argument is the character not yet dealt with, Alan Breck. He has been deliberately left out so far in order to look round him to other characters, but a brief word about him is now needed. Approaching Alan after considering James More and Cluny Macpherson tends to draw attention to the very mixed way Stevenson presents him. Almost every fine quality in Alan Breck is balanced by something less so, and almost every reference to him combines the attractive with the off-putting. Take for instance his first appearance in the novel:

> He was smallish in stature, but well set and as nimble as a goat; his face was of a good open expression, but sunburnt very dark, and heavily freckled and pitted with the smallpox; his eyes were unusually light and had a kind of dancing madness in them, that was both engaging and alarming; and when he took off his great-coat, he laid a pair of fine silver-mounted pistols on the table, and I saw that he was belted with a great sword. His manners, besides, were elegant, and he pledged the captain handsomely. Altogether I thought of him, at the first sight, that here was a man I would rather call my friend than my enemy. (p. 50)

Notice the balancing of one thing against another, at first around the word 'but', a sentence structure that sets the tone for the rest of the paragraph and alerts us to the ominous details later: the 'dancing madness' in his eyes, which is 'both engaging and alarming' and his production of both two pistols *and* a 'great sword'. The reader is then ready to find Alan's elegant manners and his pledging the captain (the piratical Hoseason, remember) 'handsomely', as somehow suspicious. David Balfour's summing up, 'that here was a man I would rather call my friend than my enemy', leaves us poised like him between admiration and apprehension.

This essay begins by suggesting parallels between Alan Breck and James More, each the Highlander who dominates the novel he is in (and perhaps the difference in their appeal to the reader is one reason *Kidnapped* is more loved than *Catriona*). Balancing the two novels and the two characters against each other gives some support to the idea that Stevenson is critically exploring the idea of the Highlands and Highlanders, not just purveying it, as he has often been thought to do.[5] In this respect *Kidnapped* and *Catriona* are indeed a matched pair of novels, and Alan Breck and James More are two sides of Stevenson's Highlander,[6] and the superstition and twisted passion of Aros in *The Merry Men* are part of Stevenson's critical view of the Ossianic realm of the supernatural and portentous.

Notes

1. Quotations from *Kidnapped* and *Catriona* are taken from the World's Classics combined edition of the novels, edited by Emma Letley (Oxford: Oxford University Press, 1986).
2. The French word 'haras' that James uses to refer to the retinue of the nobleman means, as far as I can discover, nothing more nor less than a stud-farm; perhaps one of Stevenson's jokes, but if so a fierce one.
3. Presumably the historian William Robertson (1721–93), Principal of Edinburgh University from 1762, and friend of David Hume. Quotations from 'The Merry Men' are from *The Merry Men and Other Tales & Fables* (London: Macmillan, 1928).
4. It is of course on these very rocks that the brig *Covenanter* is wrecked in the thirteenth chapter of *Kidnapped*, depositing David Balfour on the island, the starting-point for his journey through the Highlands back to Edinburgh.
5. Recall, for example, the romantic stereotype of the Alan Breck who figures in the fantasies of Sandy Stranger in Muriel Spark's *The Prime of Miss Jean Brodie*.
6. There is a sign of the connection between the two in James More's letter to David Balfour, quoted above, in which he refers to the wounds he received 'on the field of Gladsmuir', another name for the battle of Prestonpans, 1745, where, according to himself, Alan Breck began on the government side before he 'deserted to the right side' (p. 71), an act that does not impress David Balfour, though he does not say so out loud.

13. Art, the Highlands and the Celtic Revival

MURDO MACDONALD

The indigenous visual culture of the Gàidhealtachd has, from the days of the Book of Kells and before, right up to the present, always worked through networks rather than through centralisation.[1] That must be borne in mind when we look at landscape paintings of the Highlands produced in response to such urban needs. As industrial cities began to dominate economies in the eighteenth and nineteenth centuries, images of landscape found a market amongst those desiring to experience the land not directly but by proxy from within the city itself.

The interaction of conventional landscape painting with the predominantly non-urban Gàidhealtachd is, therefore, an uneasy one. Indeed landscape images can be considered, at least in their origins, the most psychologically urban of all art forms. With respect to the Gàidhealtachd that is something of an irony when one notes that many early landscape paintings of the Highlands were made by mapmakers and artists who were assisting in the military suppression of the Highlands in the Jacobite period and its aftermath.[2]

That irony has not be lost on artists of the present; for example, in 1987 Louise Scullion commented concisely on the surveillance aspect of this map-making tradition. The title is to the point: *Objective: to aid in the pacification of the Highlands*.[3] However, the paradox is that whilst landscape painting may have started off as something external to – and indeed threatening to – the Scottish Gàidhealtachd, it was in due course fully absorbed into it. Indeed by the late nineteenth century a significant proportion of the urban demand for Highland landscapes would have been from those who had strong links to the Gàidhealtachd themselves. This reappropriation by the Gàidhealtachd of landscape art finds clear expression in the fact that the artist who revolutionised Scottish painting in the second half of the nineteenth century, William McTaggart, was himself a Gaelic speaker, born near Machrihanish in 1835.[4] McTaggart made works that were both meditations on the everyday life of the Gàidhealtachd and at the same time radical experiments in the use of paint. As a native Highlander he knew his spectacular environment not as an artist-tourist but as an artist aware of places within which people live and work.

McTaggart is not of course the only painter of Highland landscape to have strong links with the Gàidhealtachd. Consider, for example, Horatio McCulloch, that key Scottish landscape painter of the generation before. McCulloch was not a native Gaelic speaker like McTaggart but he had strong Gàidhealtach links.[5] He married Marcella McLellan in 1847. She was born near Ord on the western side of the Sleat peninsula, and it is reasonable to assume that she was a Gaelic speaker. McCulloch's commitment to his wife's birthplace is shown in the 1850s, when he painted a number of pictures looking towards the Cuillin ridge. A good example is *The Cuillin from Ord*, in which that serrated ridge is shown rising behind the intervening peat of the Strathaird peninsula.[6] Viewing that work today it is easy to think of it as a kind of advertisement for a mountaineering destination.[7] But of course it wasn't that, because it predates most documented mountaineering, so the point here is that McCulloch was making an innovative image that prefigured future perceptions of the significance of the Highlands. And it is crucial to note that he was doing so in the full consciousness of the pioneering Scottish science of the day, geology.[8]

But what of the inhabitants of the Highlands? McCulloch was painting the very ridge that in Sorley MacLean's reference to the Clearances rises 'on the other side of sorrow'. When McCulloch was painting at Ord in the mid-1850s he was directly across from Suishnish, the very place to which MacLean refers, an area that had just suffered clearance of its people as a result of Lord MacDonald's attempts to make money from the land he controlled. What did McCulloch know of this through his wife? Was he just an artist for the potential mountain tourist with no thought for the inhabitants? What did he think? I can't answer those questions, but one can get some insight into this via the writer Alexander Smith, who was married to McCulloch's wife's cousin. Smith's writing gives an indication of the equivocal attitudes of the day.[9] In *A Summer in Skye*, a book in which he describes a visit to the island in the early 1860s, he has empathy for those who face clearance but uneasily supports the landlord's right to clear them. I quote what may be the understatement of all time: 'to have your house unroofed before your eyes, and made to go on board a ship bound for Canada, even although the passage-money be paid for you, is not pleasant.' Indeed not. He goes on:

> An obscure sense of wrong is kindled in heart and brain. It is just possible that what is for the landlord's interest may be for yours also in the long run; but you feel that the landlord has looked after his own interest in the first place. He wished you away, and he has got you away; whether you will succeed in Canada is matter of dubiety.[10]

All this is somewhat equivocal, if sympathetic, but at least Smith is getting the issues into the public domain. We can take it that Smith and his cousin-by-marriage McCulloch were part of the groundswell of disquiet that led to the Napier Commission twenty years later. In that context it is important to stress that McCulloch was no advocate of deserted wilderness, for it is often assumed that he is just that. Take his famous image of Glencoe, painted in 1864. It is true that no people appear but their presence is in fact strongly implied. A road, the forerunner of the A82, is clear in the foreground. That road leads on to Ballachullish, Oban and Fort William. It leads back to King's House at the top of Glen Etive and then, as part of what is now the West Highland Way, across Rannoch Moor, past Duncan Bàn McIntyre's birthplace at Druim Liaghart and on, via Inveroran, to Bridge of Orchy.[11] Bearing in mind McCulloch's marriage into the Gàidhealtachd, one wonders whether Duncan Bàn McIntyre was an influence on him, just as were Burns and Scott. He would certainly have been aware of the major monument to the bard that had been designed by J. T. Rochead, whose next monument would be none other than the National Wallace Monument at Bridge of Allan. The monument to Duncan Bàn was constructed above Dalmally in 1858, not long before McCulloch painted his image of Glencoe. The road would simply not appear in his *Glencoe* had the artist been after a conveniently cleared 'wilderness' view of the Highlands. Instead it is a crucial part of his composition and it implies the inhabited rather than deserted nature of the landscape. It indicates both geography and history.

I now want to link the Celtic Revival as a kind of parallel strand, for at the very same time that McCulloch was painting, an art based on the early art of the Gàidhealtachd was developing in Scotland. The pioneering archaeology of Daniel Wilson is crucial to understanding this development.

In 1851, shortly before McCulloch painted his *Cuillin from Ord*, in the heart of the period of the Clearances, Wilson made a major visual contribution to recording the art of the Gàidhealtachd in his *Archaeology and Prehistoric Annals of Scotland*. Wilson was both artist and academic, and many of the images in his book originate from his own hand, including the frontispiece, which shows the Hunterston Brooch. The cover of the first edition, perhaps also designed by Wilson, is a very early example of Celtic Revival design. Furthermore, in his text, Wilson takes the trouble to identify what he calls 'Celtic arts' as a stylistically distinct current of art.[12]

Turning from Wilson's archaeological motivation to the needs of the applied artist, five years later in 1856 *The Grammar of Ornament* by Owen Jones was published. That book further propagated the notion of 'Celtic' as a visual category. Its wider aim was to be a comprehensive visual source, and it helped to order the ornamental pluralism of the Victorian age. Owen Jones gathered examples from all cultures and all periods available to him and categorised them in an accessible way. One of Jones's categories of ornament was 'Celtic'. It was explored in three pages of images that range from details of Celtic manuscripts to Pictish cross slabs. The accompanying essay by J. O. Westwood should also be mentioned.[13] Leading on from this, the outstanding folklorist John Francis Campbell uses *The Grammar of Ornament* to support his own use of the description 'Celtic art' in volume four of his *Popular Tales of the West Highlands*, published in 1862. He writes: 'It may be new to many to hear of "Celtic art", but nevertheless it is classed [as such] in the Grammar of Ornament by Owen Jones, who is an acknowledged authority on such matters.'[14]

Campbell's book also contains some significant illustrations of this newly defined Celtic art, one of them drawing directly on a facsimile of an initial letter 'T' made for the 1805 Report on the Authenticity of the Poems of Ossian published by the Highland Society of Scotland. This source of Campbell's imagery demonstrates how the controversy around Macpherson's work helped to drive the Celtic Revival in the visual arts by making available good facsimiles of Celtic material as early as 1805, although it was some fifty years later before artists began to make serious use of the material. Campbell redraws the image for West Highland Tales, and uses it as the conclusion of the entire work. Campbell would of course also have been aware of Daniel Wilson's discussion of Celtic arts in 1851, but I think his foregrounding of Jones reflects his understanding that *The Grammar of Ornament* had put Celtic art firmly on the international map.[15]

It is worth noting that, like Wilson's *Archaeology and Prehistoric Annals of Scotland*, Campbell's *Popular Tales of the West Highlands* has an important Celtic Revival cover. These works thus both help to define Celtic art as a historical category, while at the same time pioneering the revival of that art. However, where Wilson's cover takes as its model an Iona cross of the eighth century, Campbell takes a work of the West Highland School of Sculpture, from the fourteenth or fifteenth century. Thus already, in these two seminal works by Wilson (from 1851) and by Campbell (from 1860 to 1862), we have a kind of visual manifesto, which implies the significance of reviving Celtic art as well as simply taking an antiquarian interest in it. In addition, through Owen Jones, from 1856 we have an internationally propagated definition of Celtic art that can be the basis of this revival.

Another key work published in 1856 was volume one of John Stuart's *Sculptured Stones of Scotland*. That work not only includes analysis of Celtic art, mainly Pictish, but, as with Wilson's cover, it begins to use the inspiration of that art for the purposes of Celtic Revival decoration, this time in the decorative initial letter of the main text.[16] That was the work of Andrew Gibb, who – with his co-workers in the lithography firm of Gibb and Keith – took over the illustrative project in its entirety for Stuart's second volume, published in 1867.

Gibb's significance as visual analyst was recognised in his election as a Fellow of the Society of Antiquaries of Scotland.[17] He, and his colleagues, were much more accurate in drawing than their predecessors and sympathetic to the subject matter. For example, the images of St Martin's Cross and the Kildalton Cross, as well as being fine examples of lithography, are much more useful than any preceding work for both the scholar and the artist.

While Gibb's images contribute to the visual research that made Celtic Revival art possible, his illuminated initial letter to Stuart's second volume is a highly significant work of Celtic Revival art in its own right, drawing on and transforming a letter 'Q', presumably from the Book of Durrow, and presenting it as a letter 'P'. It is because of Gibb's work that Stuart's second volume, published in 1867, attains its extraordinary value as a visual source, not least for Mary Carmichael in her decorations for *Carmina Gadelica*, published in 1900. Thus, while the publication of Jones's *Grammar of Ornament* may have facilitated the wide use of the category 'Celtic Art', it was Stuart's second volume of the *Sculptured Stones of Scotland* that made this art a reality for nineteenth-century artists and designers.

From that time Celtic crosses, most often based on Iona and Islay designs, began to populate the cemeteries of Scotland. There had, however, been a few examples of Celtic Revival crosses before the publication of Stuart's second volume. Notable is what almost amounts to a Celtic obelisk designed in 1860 by William Bell Scott for his brother, the painter David Scott. It is to be found in Dean Cemetery in Edinburgh. This monument has the added interest of supporting a bronze relief of David Scott by the Inverness-born, Pre-Raphaelite sculptor Alexander Munro. Another presumably pre-1867 example is the monument designed for Alexander Nasmyth's grave in St Cuthbert's churchyard beneath Edinburgh Castle. This was the work of the sculptor John Rhind and was made at the behest of Alexander Nasmyth's engineer son, James; indeed the design is adopted again for James's own burial place in the Dean Cemetery. Alexander Nasmyth died in 1840, so the date when his grave was marked in this way is uncertain, but the 1860s would be consistent with the date of another important Celtic Revival monument in the same cemetery, also by John Rhind. That cross has Celtic interlace decoration carved into its shaft and it marks the grave of the influential artist William Borthwick Johnstone, Keeper of the National Gallery of Scotland, who died in 1868. It will be noted that these works deriving from the Gàidhealtachd were regarded as the appropriate way of marking the passing of the leading Scottish artists of the day, at a time when such imagery was still rare. Thus during the 1860s the relationship between imagery deriving from the classical tradition and imagery deriving from the Celtic tradition was rebalanced in favour of the Celtic. I would argue that the Celtic Revival in Scotland gets into full swing with these works.

Another important example dates from 1861. This is the monument to the 78th Highlanders (a predecessor regiment of the Seaforth Highlanders) erected on the esplanade of Edinburgh Castle to mark the regiment's involvement in the suppression of the Indian Mutiny. It was designed by the Scottish Arts and Crafts architect Robert Rowand Anderson. All these monuments show substantial knowledge of Celtic art, and the last mentioned also has text in Gaelic. In due course the graves of other artists and writers are marked in this way, including that of Horatio McCulloch in Warriston Cemetery in Edinburgh, erected in 1872. It incorporates reference to two Iona crosses; one is Maclean's cross, a work of the West Highland school dating to the fifteenth century, and one from an earlier tenth century cross-slab. A touching addition is a carving of McCulloch's favourite dog on one side the base, balanced by his artist's palette on the other. The design is by James Drummond, who through his art did more than anyone else to draw attention again to the West Highland School of Sculpture, in his book *Sculptured Monuments in Iona and the West Highlands*, eventually published after his death in 1881. In 1867 Drummond had designed a Celtic cross in the same cemetery for the grave of Alexander Smith. Where McCulloch has his palette, Smith, the poet, is given the clarsach of a Bard. It will be recalled here that Smith and McCulloch were related through their marriages to Gaelic-speaking cousins from the Sleat peninsula in Skye.

In due course, such crosses became a commonplace in the cemeteries of Scotland. For example Charles Rennie Mackintosh's first executed design, dating from 1888, was for a Celtic cross in Glasgow's Necropolis.[18] The achievement of stone carvers such as Peter Smith who sculpted that design by Mackintosh has not yet been properly recognised. Smith worked for the firm of Mossman in Glasgow. The equivalent firm in Edinburgh was McGlashan. We take the contribution to the Celtic Revival of such firms for granted. We should not. Their work is a crucial indicator of the wide recognition of the significance of the revived art of the Gàidhealtachd from the 1860s onwards. For example, a fine Celtic Revival cross by McGlashan was erected to mark the grave of the Bard of the Gaelic Society of Inverness, Mary Mackellar, who died in 1890.[19] It is loosely based on an eighth-century Iona original, with a nod to Pictish cross design, and it is situated in the old Cameron graveyard at Kilmallie near Corpach.[20] In 1891 a monument deriving, loosely, in style from the later Gàidhealtachd tradition of the West Highland School of Sculpture was erected in honour of the seventeenth-century Macdonald Bard, Iain Lom, at Cille Choirill (St Cyril's Church) in Glen Spean. It was designed by the architect John Rhind (not to be confused with his near contemporary the sculptor John Rhind who, as noted above, designed the Celtic memorial for Alexander Nasmyth in Edinburgh). Iain Lom's monument is inspired by West Highland work of the fourteenth or fifteenth century rather than by the Celtic ring cross, but it takes its place in this Highland setting as an outlier of an impressive group of late nineteenth- and early twentieth-century Celtic Revival ring crosses of the highest quality. A telling aspect of this cemetery is that those who commissioned and erected these monuments were Lochaber Gaels who had reclaimed their Celtic visual tradition, after centuries of neglect – even as their kinsfolk were scattered, many to Nova Scotia.[21] By contrast, the influence of the West Highland School is evident also at the heart of the early twentieth-century Scottish Establishment, for example, in a monument erected in 1900 in memory of Caroline Campbell of Blythswood at St Conan's Kirk, Loch Awe. This tall free-standing cross, with a Gaelic inscription, is related in form to the fourteenth-century West Highland School cross which still stands outside the church at Keil Church near Lochaline in Morvern. It is presumably to the design of Walter Campbell, Caroline's son, who also designed the church. A strong current of Celtic Revivalism runs through Walter Campbell's conception for St Conan's. For example, the organ screen is carved to reflect an elegant interlaced cross design, probably fourteenth-century, from a West Highland slab in Iona.[22] Just as Stuart's second volume drove the passion for the ring cross, here we see, very probably, the influence of James Drummond's lithographed version of this design as published in his book of 1881.

The persistence of such interlace designs in the art of the Gàidhealtachd from the seventh century to the present is significant, for such long-term continuities are by no means common in the history of art. In 1851 Daniel Wilson noted: 'the unchanging character of Celtic arts is to be found in the fact that the ornamentation, not only on many of the old Highland brooches and drinking horns, but invariably employed in decorating the handle of the Highland dirk and knife, down to the last fatal struggle of the clans on Culloden Moor which abruptly closed the tradition of many centuries, is exactly the same interlaced knot-work which we are familiar with on the most ancient class of sculptured standing stones in Scotland.' To make his point he illustrates a seventeenth-century powder-horn in the collection of James Drummond. An image of this was also published in Drummond's *Ancient Highland Weapons* thirty years later.[23]

Such subtly interlaced panels and borders have become something of a stereotype of the Celtic world, so much so that we may tend not to give them the attention they deserve. As Wilson points out, such decoration continues in artefacts of the Jacobite period and, indeed, after. Despite gaps in the evidence consequent on the usual vagaries of the history of any visual tradition, that is to say – in the case of the Scottish Highlands – invasion, iconoclasm, emigration and neglect, one might suggest that this is a continuous tradition rather than a set of revivals, and that it begins in the seventh century at the latest and continues, at least in the decoration of objects, into the nineteenth century. At that point, via the efforts of antiquaries such as Henry Mackenzie, Daniel Wilson and John Stuart, this tradition begins to underpin the art of the Celtic Revival. Such attention to, revival and transformation of earlier visual insights is, of course, the lifeblood of art. The very word 'renaissance' implies it. But the fact that the living tradition of Gàidhealtachd art is actually continuous with the Celtic Revival is of considerable interest, not least because that Celtic Revival art is then reappropriated by the Gàidhealtachd, as I have noted at Cille Choirill.

One of the most important of all Celtic Revival works, the first edition of Alexander Carmichael's *Carmina Gadelica*, is another example of such reappropriation of its own visual language by the Gàidhealtachd. Published in 1900, it contained initials and other decorations by the Alexander Carmichael's wife Mary.[24] It is worth noting in passing that one of the initials that Mary Carmichael re-appropriated appears on the frontispiece of the 1805 Ossian report, again, as for J. F. Campbell, indicating the usefulness of this document as a visual source.

Patrick Geddes expressed the wider cultural importance of the Celtic Revival when he wrote in 1913 of the restoration of Iona Abbey as being 'of far more importance than Scotland has yet commonly realised'.[25] Geddes' point was that the restoration had the potential to become a cultural driver for the future, and he was of course correct. Furthermore it is reasonable to argue that it was Geddes' knowledge of the Gàidhealtachd that drove his passion for cultural revival, not only in Scotland but internationally, not least in India. It should be remembered that Geddes, who probably had a little Gaelic himself, was the son of a Gaelic-speaking father and the father of a Gaelic-learner son.[26]

Geddes' friend and colleague, the artist John Duncan, was the most well-known of all artists of the Celtic Revival in Scotland, and I want to note his significance here, not least with respect to how he links in not only with Geddes but with Alexander Carmichael. One can regard Duncan's interest in Bride as strongly mediated by Carmichael's translations in *Carmina Gadelica*; indeed Duncan later wrote about the book.[27] In Duncan's *St Bride*,[28] painted in 1913, the outline of the restored Iona Abbey can be seen in the background. In the later *Coming of Bride*, from 1917, Bride's role is as pre-Christian Celtic goddess and herald of spring.[29] Duncan's approach to Bride in these two works is as Christian saint and pre-Christian Goddess respectively. This view is encapsulated in Anne Ross's comment that 'Bride was ultimately a pagan Goddess who became a Christian saint, as was so often the case'.[30] Duncan balanced his Bride works with a number of works relating to Saint Columba in Iona, for example, in 1904, *St Columba on the Hill of Angels*.[31] This has a particular interest, for the original drawing was owned by Ella Carmichael, Alexander Carmichael's daughter.[32] Ella was a highly influential figure in Celtic studies in her own right and had a key role in making sure that her father's *Carmina Gadelica* was published. Duncan's *St Columba on the Hill of Angels* includes a dedication which reads 'To my Celtic Muse in homage' and it seems more than idle speculation to suggest that the 'Celtic Muse' in question was Ella Carmichael herself. Further indication of this close link is the fact that, some years earlier, Ella's features had provided the physical model for the central figure of Duncan's drawing *Anima Celtica*, which was published in Patrick Geddes' *Evergreen* in 1895.[33] There is so much of interest in this image, including strong reference to Jacobite symbols and to Macpherson's *Ossian*. It is also interesting to note that William Sharp (aka Fiona Macleod) was very critical of this image, and I have speculated elsewhere that the basis for his dislike is that he did not want the flesh and blood Ella Carmichael to occupy the role of the 'soul of the Celt' that he had reserved for the imaginary Fiona Macleod.[34]

Looking further, John Duncan's work can be used as the starting point to explore key issues such as authenticity and cultural colonialism, not least by exploring links between the art of the Celtic Revival and other cultural revivals, in particular those in India and Finland. Indeed these are generic issues for any cultural revival.

To conclude: any consideration of art and the Scottish Highlands in the nineteenth century is of interest in its own right, but its real importance for us is the way it informs our present. Any analysis reminds us how academically ill-served this area has been, except as a source of discussion

ART, THE HIGHLANDS AND THE CELTIC REVIVAL

of stereotypes. And yet the figures involved, from the anonymous illustrators of the 1805 *Ossian* report, and visually-literate antiquarians like Daniel Wilson, Andrew Gibb and John Francis Campbell, through the great landscape painters Horatio McCulloch and William McTaggart, to the intriguing Celtic Revival artists Mary Carmichael and John Duncan, lie at the very heart of Scottish cultural activity in the nineteenth century. We should treat them with the respect they deserve, and acknowledge that such respect entails properly admitting the Gàidhealtachd as a key dimension in our discussions of them.

Notes

1. This paper reports, *inter alia*, research from the AHRC-funded *Window to the West* project, a collaboration between the University of Dundee and Sabhal Mòr Ostaig. Key to the project throughout have been Meg Bateman and John Purser of Sabhal Mòr Ostaig, so I was delighted to be able to present this paper at the ASLS conference at Sabhal Mòr Ostaig.
2. One of these was the English artist Paul Sandby. See, for example, J. Bonehill and S. Daniels, (eds), *Picturing Britain* (London: Royal Academy of Arts, 2009). Other early landscape paintings were driven by landowners wishing to display their holdings, often in a map-like way, e.g., James Norie's *Taymouth Castle*. See, e.g., M. Macdonald, *Scottish Art* (London: Thames & Hudson, 2000), p. 52.
3. Full title: *Objective: to aid in the pacification of the Highlands (For Major-General William Roy, 1726–1790)*. Private collection. Reproduced on page 136 of F. Macleod (ed.), *Togail Tìr: Marking Time – The Map of the Western Isles* (Stornoway: Acair, 1989).
4. In the same period prints of Highland landscapes by artists such as John McWhirter became common in homes throughout the Gàidhealtachd. Research by Eleanor MacDougall at Sabhal Mòr Ostaig is currently exploring such landscape images as part of the material culture of the late nineteenth-century Highland home.
5. He was named Horatio in honour of Nelson's victory at Trafalgar, which occurred in the year of his birth, 1805. His name is a reminder of the major Scottish contribution to that battle. About thirty per cent of the men in the British fleet were Scots.
6. This is an enduring view of the Cuillin. For a twentieth-century interpretation from almost the same viewpoint (Tokavaig rather than Ord) in different light conditions, drawn in watercolour at three times during one evening, see M. Hedderwick, *An Eye on the Hebrides* (Edinburgh: Canongate, 1989).
7. See, for example, the caption to McCulloch's image, reproduced in the plate section between pages 84 and 85 of Ian Mitchell, *Scotland's Mountains before the Mountaineers* (Edinburgh: Luath, 1998). One can even see the pinnacle that forms the highest point of Sgurr Dearg, famous to mountaineers the world over and now reclaimed for the Gàidhealtach by the film *Seachd: The Inaccessible Pinnacle*. It is therefore remarkable that at the time McCulloch was painting, most of that ridge had not been climbed, or rather not recorded as climbed, and much of it had not been named either. It is thus a painting very much of its time with respect to the development of mountaineering. It

is very much of its time in a related respect also, for at that time the study of rocks in the Highlands was driving the development of geology as a discipline throughout the world. The fact that he shares his last name with a pioneer of Scottish geology, John Macculloch, who was also an accomplished artist, is a somewhat confusing bonus.
8. McCulloch's close contemporary William Dyce was also acutely aware of such scientific developments; indeed one of his geologically-inclined works of the south coast of England, *Pegwell Bay*, is regarded as a representative work of pre-Raphaelite 'truth to nature'. Dyce also made remarkable Highland works, in particular his *Christ as the Man of Sorrows* and *David in the Wilderness*, both of which show an impressive understanding of the minutiae of Highland landscape.
9. The two cousins who became their wives were Gaels of middle status in the social hierarchy, related to the tacksman Charles MacDonald of Ord, who appears as 'McIan' in Smith's book.
10. A. Smith, *A Summer in Skye* (London: Strahan, 1865).
11. His birthplace is not in Glen Orchy as many accounts suggest.
12. D. Wilson, *Archaeology and Prehistoric Annals of Scotland* (Edinburgh: Sutherland & Knox, 1851), pp. 220–21.
13. It is interesting to note that Westwood in his later book from 1868 ignores the term Celtic (except in reference to his earlier essay) and uses the terms 'Anglo-Saxon' and 'Irish' instead, thus introducing a slack terminology which takes no account of either Scotland or Wales, and attributes all Gaelic speakers, by implication, to Ireland. See J. O. Westwood, *Facsimiles of the Miniatures and Ornaments of Anglo-Saxon and Irish Manuscripts* (London: Quaritch, 1868).
14. John Francis Campbell, *Popular Tales of the West Highlands* (Edinburgh: Edmonston and Douglas, 1862), vol. 4, p. 382.
15. D. Wilson, *Archaeology and Prehistoric Annals of Scotland*, pp. 220–21.
16. Stuart reuses some images made a few years previously for Patrick Chalmers' *Ancient Sculptured Monuments of the County of Angus*, published by the Bannatyne Club in 1848. Notable precursors of Chalmers are the images in John Stuart of Inchbreck's 'An Account of some Sculptured Pillars in the Northern Part of Scotland', *Archaeologica Scotica* (1822), vol. 2, pp. 314–23, and Charles Carter Petley's 'A Short Account of some Carved Stones in Ross-shire, accompanied with a series of Outline Engravings', *Archaeologica Scotica* (1857), vol. 4, pp. 345–52. Some of the images in Chalmers are less than accurate and new images were made where necessary by the Aberdeen artist and lithographer Andrew Gibb. See also J. N. G. Ritchie, *Recording Early Christian Monuments in Scotland* (Rosemarkie: Groam House Museum, 1998).
17. Note that the young George Reid (later Sir George Reid PRSA) worked for Gibb, and may have made a significant contribution.
18. This has been severely damaged and, as of writing, has been partially restored. It was intact in the early 1990s.
19. Complementing the style of her memorial, in 1916 her work was included in a publication with a cover decorated with Celtic interlace, Malcolm Macleod's *Modern Gaelic Bards*.
20. Mary Mackellar was herself a Cameron. My thanks to Ian Abernethy for information about this remarkable woman. See I. Abernethy, 'The Sweet Singer of Locheil', *Oban Times*, 23 January 1969.

21. Many Gaels from Glen Spean settled in Mabou, Cape Breton Island, Nova Scotia.
22. The carving is by Walter Campbell himself. The same Iona cross slab was to inspire the cover design by the Ritchies for Frances Balfour's biography of Dr Macgregor of St Cuthbert's.
23. Plate 20.
24. These, and related, initials, were quite widely used, for example in the newspaper *Canada Scotsman* in 1903 (thanks to Michael Newton for this information) and by Edward Dwelly on the title page of his Dictionary.
25. P. Geddes, *The Masque of Ancient Learning and its Many Meanings, a pageant of Education from Primitive to Celtic Times devised and interpreted by Patrick Geddes* (Edinburgh: Patrick Geddes and Colleagues, 1913), p. 51.
26. His father was also in the Black Watch, so the young Patrick would have appreciated both the realities of linguistic decline and the glories and ironies attendant on the transmission of Celtic culture via the military.
27. J. Duncan, 'Carmina Gadelica', in J. MacDonald (ed.), *Voices from the Hills / Guthan o na Beanntaibh* (Glasgow: An Comunn Gàidhealach, 1927), pp. 25–30.
28. National Gallery of Scotland.
29. Versions can be found in the municipal collections of both Glasgow and Dundee.
30. A. Ross, *Druids* (Stroud: Tempus, 1999), p. 160.
31. Made in aid of the building fund of the Church of Saint Columba, Blackhall, Edinburgh. See W. B. Stevenson (ed.), *The Saint Columba Scrip* (Edinburgh: St Columba's Church, 1904; reprinted in V. Branford, *St Columba: A Study of Social Inheritance and Spiritual Development*, Edinburgh: Patrick Geddes and Colleagues, 1912).
32. SUA TGED 12/3/31. John Duncan to Patrick Geddes, written from 29 St Bernard's Crescent, nd, probably spring 1912.
33. This was pointed out to me by Abigail Burnyeat of the Department of Celtic, University of Edinburgh, after I had shown an image of *Anima Celtica* at an Edinburgh University Fine Art research seminar in April 2006. She noted the similarity to images of Emma Carmichael, including one signed 'Mackie' (presumably Charles Mackie) in the Department of Celtic.
34. M. Macdonald, 'The Visual Dimension of *Carmina Gadelica*' in D. U. Stiubhart (ed.), *The Life and Legacy of Alexander Carmichael* (Port of Ness: The Islands Book Trust, 2008), pp. 135–45.

14. From Celtic Revival to Scottish Renaissance?

DOUGLAS GIFFORD

In his essay 'Arcades', in *The Edinburgh Companion to Twentieth Century Scottish Literature,* Cairns Craig argued that there is probably no period in Scottish cultural history more complex and requiring reconsideration than that transitional half-century from Stevenson to MacDiarmid, 1870–1920.[1] I agree – and it is in the light of this argument that this chapter explores the contribution of the Irish Revival, and the work of Fiona Macleod particularly, to the Scottish revival after the Great War, so often termed 'Renaissance' and so associated with MacDiarmid. I then thought that for this conference it might be relevant (if provocative) to go on to suggest that we need to revisit our notions of 'Scottish Renaissance' as well as our cultural maps of the 1870–1920 period, from the Celtic Revival on, emphasising what I increasingly see as continuity from the mid-nineteenth century till the Second World War.

I begin with Celtic Revival, very briefly in Ireland, and then in Scotland with Patrick Geddes and Fiona Macleod. Thereafter – what was its legacy?

Celtic Revival in Ireland begins in the second half of the nineteenth century with the great Irish historians like William Lecky, strong on Ireland's terrible grievances, but light on its lost cultures, but then followed in tradition, literature, arts and translation from Irish by Douglas Hyde, Daniel Corkery – and then Lady Gregory, George Russell (Æ), Yeats, Joyce, Synge and O'Casey.[2] Celtic Revival begins with the recovery of the great epic cycles like the Three Sorrows of Ireland's story-telling – the children of Lir, the sons of Usnach, and Cuchulain, Deirdre and Finn. Celtic Twilight haunts the early poetry of Yeats, and the epic cycles inspire him and the Abbey Theatre right through to his last and deeply complex play *The Death of Cuchulain* in 1939. That said, Celtic Twilight and respect for epic evaporate in Joyce's stringent Dublin stories, in Synge's savage rural satires, and the violence of O'Casey's Dublin tenements. Certainly from this reader's perspective, however impressive the pantheon of Sidhe, Danaan, Milesians, Fomorian intruders, and the vast array of endlessly slaughtering heroes and fickle heroines, the sheer lack of any consistent moral codes other than vague obligations to ritual vengeance becomes overwhelming – and may help explain the later Revival's movement away from exploitation other than for parodic and satiric effect.

In terms of Scotland, Celtic revival is too conveniently labelled as 'Twilight' – and blame for this is recurrently attached to the strange case of Fiona Macleod – and the impact of Patrick Geddes in Edinburgh in the 1890s. But some questions need to be asked about these assumptions. Is the Scottish Celtic Revival of Geddes, with his movement's magazine, *The Evergreen*, and his lieutenant Macleod, to be seen as a pale shadow of its Irish original? Does it owe its origin entirely to Ireland?

Arguably, setting aside Macleod for the moment, Geddes, for all his encouragement of the arts, was, as the art historian Duncan Macmillan, and Murray Pittock, more recently have argued, primarily a visionary whose visions were of an all-inclusive renaissance in everything from botany to biology to sociology, and following Ruskin and Morris in seeing crafts and town planning and economics as a total whole. Ahead of his time and immensely gifted, it does seem to me, however, that the colossal and Utopian range of his ambitions, his obsession with theorising everything from the way we think to promoting his ideas world-wide from his base, 'the world's first social laboratory', in his Outlook Tower at the head of Edinburgh's High Street, he saw the arts as a branch, and hardly the entire tree of his ambitions; and literature a branch of a branch.

Duncan MacMillan discusses him at length in *Scottish Art 1460–1990* – and it's significant that this fine critic, who constantly interweaves the visual arts with their literary counterparts, sees Geddes as primarily aiding *painters*, like John Duncan, and Phoebe Traquair, emphasising the flourishing links between Geddes's Edinburgh and Mackintosh's Glasgow. Arguably the real Celtic revival was in the arts and crafts – and certainly Neil Munro, looking from Glasgow at the cultural scene around 1900, had no doubt that a revival *across* the arts was in progress.[3]

Despite Geddes's engagement with life sciences and city planning, the *Evergreen*'s seasonal and rural bent meant that it hardly led towards the future. Four swallows hardly make a summer, let alone a renaissance; and to foreground the four issues of *The Evergreen*, Macleod and the notion of Celtic revival is I believe misleading, when real revival was flourishing around it in literature, art, architecture and collections of folk-lore. We need to recognise the variety and interweaving of the arts and literature in the period, and question the over-facile creation of discrete areas with terms like 'Celtic Revival' – or 'Twilight', which I believe are as unhelpful as 'Kailyard' – or even 'Scottish Renaissance'. For example, so-called Kailyarder S. R. Crockett was a contributor to Patrick Geddes's 'Evergreen' – and yet his best historical novels like *The Raiders* (1894), *The Men of The Moss Haggs* (1895), and *The Grey Man* (1896) are part of that robust tradition of Scottish historical fiction carried on from Scott by Stevenson, Lang, Munro and Buchan – thus yet again breaking the superficiality of Celtic or Kailyard categories.

Any Scottish 'Revival', Celtic or otherwise, was bound to be greatly influenced by related 'movements'. Nearly all the major Scottish writers of the nineteenth century enjoyed close relations with London, and English (and Irish) writers from even before the obvious connection with the Irish revival to turn of the century. Macleod's Celtic visions draw liberally from other and English movements, from Neo-Medieval fantasy, as early as Tennyson's 'The Lady of Shalott' (1852), *Idylls of the King* (1859) and his version of the voyage of Maelduine (1880), William Morris, with his Icelandic-Celtic influenced *The Well at the World's End* (1896) and *The Water of the Wondrous Isles* (1897), the Pre-Raphaelites, the Symbolists, the Decadence movement's *Yellow Book* (to whose decadence *The Evergreen* was seen as antidote). When Irish Revival reached Britain, and Scotland, it was particularly via Sharp/Macleod who was just as much at home in London's Cheddar Cheese tavern, with Yeats's Rhymer's Club, with Dowson and Davidson, as he was in Scotland – or Italy, for that matter, where his gravestone, a Celtic Cross, is on Mount Etna.

*

So how do we reassess the strange cases of William Sharp/Fiona Macleod (1855–1905)?

> A doomed and passing race. Yes, but not wholly so. The Celt has at last reached his horizon. There is no shore beyond. He knows it. This has been the burden of his song since Malvina led the blind Oisin to his grave by the sea. 'Even the children of light must go

down into darkness.' But this apparition of a passing race is no more than the fulfilment of a glorious resurrection before our very eyes. For the genius of the Celtic race stands out now with averted torch, and the light of it is a glory before the eyes, and the flame of it is blown into the hearts of the mightier conquering people. The Celt falls, but his spirit rises in the brain of the Anglo-Celtic peoples, with whom are the destinies of the generations to come ...[4]

This is from the Dedication of *The Sin Eater* (1895) to 'The Prince of Celtdom', George Meredith. Yet more explicitly, in *The Spiritual History of the Gael* (1910), he tells us that the dream of independence for Scotland and Ireland is 'a perilous illusion', and that the genius of the Gael lies in 'a more ardent longing, a more rapt passion in the things of outward beauty and in the things of spiritual beauty'. In the passing of the Gael, for Macleod, there is only 'the serene sadness of a great day's end ... in the tragic lighting of torches of beauty around its grave'.[5] Is it not intriguing that in both Ossian and Macleod we find the same distorted picture of noble savagery declining into decadence, and that Macleod exemplifies a view of the Gael, which, for all its apparent dignifying of its subject, can be read as supporting political and social neglect of Gaelic economy and culture?

Yeats thought that Sharp/Macleod was 'the most extraordinary psychic' he had ever met. Certainly this dual personality exemplifies vividly the divided loyalties of so many Victorian and turn of the century Scottish writers, so many of whom, like Stevenson, Macdonald, Oliphant, Thomson, Davidson, Barrie and Buchan sought success in the south – but a success premised, like Joyce's, on re-working native experience.

Sharp was born in 1855 in Paisley; his mother was of Swedish descent, his father a wealthy textile manufacturer. He went to Glasgow Academy and Glasgow University (never sitting his degree exams). Money supported his wayward life as a would-be gypsy, as a runaway child, as a failed banker, in Australia studying Aborigines, visiting America and Whitman, all his life continually travelling. For all he consistently places himself (as Fiona) as the thoroughly embedded and accepted Celt at home in the places of his Celtic stories and sketches, from Loch Long, to Arran, to Iona, to Barra, to Uist, speaking for the spiritual mysteries of the Gael through his continual '*we* of the islands/mountains/oceans' (my emphasis), the claim is based on long holidays from wealthy childhood days, whereas he spent his winters as an unhealthy adult in England, France, Africa, and particularly in Sicily.

Sharp discovered 'Fiona Macleod', his essential feminine Celtic spirit, when he was forty. It's worth remembering that by then Sharp was a highly respected London author, with respected biographies of Browning, Heine, Rossetti and Shelley, studies of Arnold and Swinburne's poetry, and substantial travel sketches and fiction under his own name – all of which was to fade away when he found his alter ego. The scandals and innuendos which circled around Sharp's elaborate pretence that Fiona was a cousin, and not to be publicly revealed, far from mattering to us now, simply recede into recognition of the habit of so many Scottish writers to find an alter ego, from Scott to Gibbon/Mitchell, Munro/Foulis, Macdonald/MacColla, and surely now, as with Gibbon and MacDiarmid, simply allow legitimate discussion of 'Macleod's' fiction, without any gender innuendos, to be judged solely on its intrinsic merits. And setting aside our suspicion of Sharp's interpretation of Gaeldom, from a Lowland and holiday perspective, the time is right that we should re-assess the work, simply in terms of its value and influence. We have, I believe, underestimated the cultural impact of Sharp/Macleod; not only as man of letters, but as President of the London Stage Society, following the ideas of Yeats in presenting ambitious, spiritual and non-commercial drama. His/her play-cycles around Maeve, Conchubar and the House of Usna were written before the stage reforms of Gordon Craig, which might well have placed his Yeats-like mythic dramas alongside those of Yeats on similar Celtic themes. And likewise the fiction of Fiona Macleod, usually condemned as twilight pseudo-celebrations of the Scottish Gaels and their culture, in novels like *Pharais: A Romance of the Isles* (1894), and *The Mountain Lovers* (1895), with their portrayals of beautiful simpletons as doomed children of the mist, last remnants of an ancient poetic race, now brain-fevered and dying into their Western oceans.

Macleod himself saw his fiction as being in three categories: Spiritual Tales, Barbaric Tales (he was also proud of his (tenuous) Scandinavian descent) and Tragic Romances. I speculate that it was that spiritual side of his vision and poetry which has cost his reputation dear. Its characteristic vagueness, mysticism (close to the weakest side of Yeats?) and sheer verbosity of natural description, together with his inflated claims for his quintessential Gaelic identity, have placed him in direct antagonism to the authentic traditions of Gaelic poetry and culture as emphasised by Derick Thomson and Sorley MacLean, and in the great folk collections of Campbell and Carmichael.[6] And here it's important to understand that Sharp/Macleod, for all the attempt to 'belong' to Gaeldom, quite consciously – and to their collective mind rationally – felt that Gaeldom had reached its terminus, and that there was no shame in accepting absorption into the dominant Anglo-Saxon culture. This view was not unusual; at the same time, another Scot, of the Rhymer's Club, John Davidson, for example, in an important but little known essay-letter to the House of Lords, puts forward the radical suggestion that Ireland, Wales, and Scotland should all yield to the evolutionary inevitability – and honour – of being supporting players to a superior race in a Westminster-and-English dominated Britain.[7]

Yet many of Macleod's stories, if taken out of this paradoxical political context, often create their own dark power and atmosphere – which, I suggest, had real influence on later Scottish writers like Munro, Cunninghame Grahame, and Neil Gunn. There are three novels – *Pharais, The Mountain Lovers* and *Green Fire* – and well over sixty short stories, moving from a vague West Highland modernity to timeless mythology, drawn from Ireland, Scotland, Wales and Brittany. The quality is uneven; that indulgent luxuriating in moody and over-spiritualised descriptions of natural setting which is Macleod's bane is threaded throughout – but this should not hide the real poetry and mythic power of Macleod's best work. He categorised his stories in the three groups – Barbaric, Dramatic and Spiritual – I've referred to. Arguably, however, Macleod, while recognising contrasting types and modes in his fiction, was not the best judge or arranger of his work, which appeared in too many confusingly-overlapping editions, so that the types of his stories become bewilderingly intermingled.

I would suggest no less than *five* differing categories of fiction which deserve much fuller analyses than Macleod has received so far. Firstly, there are the three 'contemporary' novels (probably the weakest of his fiction) and many of the short stories (often only recognisable as modern from the fleeting appearance of the odd steamer from Tobermory or Greenock!). These 'modern' and heavily spiritualised tales of brain-fevered, *dubhachas*-haunted and second-sighted relics of Gaeldom are portrayed in a very personalised and moodily subjective West Highlands, centred on Iona but randomly moving from Arrochar to Uist, Oban to Barra – and often betraying a confused topography (at one point he places the Quirang near Oban!) and with very little realisation of actual place as opposed to a kind of timeless repetitive sea, croft and sky setting. Here are doomed yet somehow inhuman eternal loves; somehow, too, Macleod manages to combine darkest tragedy with a vague hint of resurrection – perhaps in weather, trees, or through transmogrification as seals or birds. (Macleod was a pagan-Christian, and the strain shows.) This category, probably the most popular in its day, seems weakest now, with its endlessly indulgent natural description, and its sense of an animate and haunted landscape. Perhaps the novel form simply allowed Macleod to over-indulge his mysticism, while many of the more straightforward supernatural short stories, my next category, benefited from their relative compression, like the powerful and atmospheric 'The Sin Eater' or 'The Ninth Wave', stories comparable to the best of Munro and Buchan (MacDiarmid thought Macleod and Munro to be the finest Scottish short-story writers). Then there is a large group, which Macleod's 'Barbaric' category certainly fits – the many stories where he recreates with real savagery the world of the Norse raiders, anticipating Eric Linklater and George Mackay Brown. These, published separately, would surprise Macleod deniers; just as would another group, his book-length interconnected stories of the blighted Achanna family, exiled from Galloway to the Highlands, and carrying with them a destiny as bleak as that of the fall of the house of the Gourlays in *Green Shutters*. They all come under the title *Under the Dark Star* in later editions; and the overall story is that of the warped loves and tragic dispersal of the Achannas, and Gloom Achanna, the sinister master of evil music who brings about the doom of his brothers and enemies. (He anticipates Munro's magnificent and manipulative flute-playing spy, Sim MacTaggart, factor to Argyll, the charismatic villain of *Doom Castle*, 1901). Macleod's fiction can often be light years away from sentiment or whimsy. And I find a last category which carries real poetic power in that group of stories in which he recreates, and, like Ossian, liberally adapts, his powerful versions of Irish, Scottish, Welsh and Breton epic myths.

Overall, Macleod's over-indulged Highland pessimism and Celtic poetry regarding the Highlands had a profound effect, I believe, on writers like Munro and Gunn. Munro may have hated Celtic Twilight, but I see correspondences in his work, in his amendment of Macleod's synthetic Gaelic syntax to a more forceful, yet related non-standard English to fit his

West Highlands. Again, Munro too accepted the inevitable decline of the older Highlands, and great stories like 'Castle Dark' or 'Boboon's Children' draw from Macleod's sense of a terminal destiny for older Gaeldom, Munro, however, with a far finer historical awareness and astringency. But the inspiration is there – outstandingly in the way, for example, 'The Lost Pibroch' develops Macleod's haunting use of music, song or story as carrier of timeless or supernatural meaning, a meaning which can be sinister, signifying a baleful influence. As so often in Macleod, in Munro's story the playing of the Lost Pibroch signifies an ending for community and family.[8]

And the influence is there on Gunn, who, in the longest of his short stories, 'Half-Light', in *Hidden Doors* (1929), reveals that he – in the persona of a tormented Highland writer – has wrestled long and hard, in love and hate, with the influence of Macleod, finally admitting that the influence is profoundly there.[9] Some of the early novels, especially *The Grey Coast* (1926) and *The Lost Glen* (1932), are directly in line of descent from Macleod's fatalistic acceptance of Highland decline, adapting and refining Macleod's excessive natural description. Here in Gunn too is the use of song, story and music as uncanny epiphanies, their ancient meaning and experience communicating with the present. Gunn would of course go on to re-create a sense of regeneration for the Highlands in his great epic cycles – but the debt is there, yet to be fully explored.

Finally, though, it seems crucial to me to realise that for all Macleod's involvement with Geddes's arts and crafts 'renascence', he has been looking at Scotland from an utterly different perspective – a perspective which saw Gaeldom accepting decline. But were they alone in this? Or can we now see that all around them serious Scottish writers, while not accepting inevitable decline, at the very least were interrogating the reasons for what they accepted was Scottish and Highland decline?

*

More generally, what did Irish and Scottish Celtic Revival give to Scottish writers? For me there seem to be three high waves of inspiration from the Irish revival.

Some would begin with an obvious effect – that of the wave of political incitement to national assertion – and of course that's true, though home rule had been on the agenda since John Stuart Blackie, Gladstone and 1914.

I certainly accept the charge it gave to MacDiarmid with his Renaissance poem/slogan 'Scots steel tempered wi' Irish fire' – but going beyond him for now, it seems to me that if we widen the idea of Renaissance, there were many differing shades of derivation, and sometimes none, many writers relying on indigenously Scottish reasoning for their commitment to their nationalism.

There is, as I have argued, the immediate influence of Yeats and his Celtic Twilight. Beyond that, both Neil Gunn and Sorley MacLean work, in different ways, in this tradition. Gunn's early and very bleak fiction of the 1920s like *The Grey Coast* can be seen to be a more effectively stripped-down version of Macleod's fiction – though of course Gunn later rallies in his epic fiction to create an affirmative message diametrically opposed to Macleod's. Comparably, it seems to me (from reading Christopher Whyte's magisterial editions) that Sorley MacLean first exploits the Celtic epics with a kind of bleak despair, as reason combats aspiration, so that the *Eimhir* cycle evokes associations with Cuchulain and Eimhir, but with MacLean's utter honesty working in such a way as to contrast his feelings of inadequacy with ideal heroism and beauty unattainable by himself – but then in the *Cuillin* cycle rising above human despair.[10]

And of course there is MacDiarmid taking inspiration from his meeting in 1929 with Yeats, whom he called 'my kingly cousin'. Alan Riach argues that it was simultaneously the aristocratic loneliness of Yeats and Irish political rebellion since 1916 that inspired MacDiarmid – 'Scots steel tempered with Irish fire / Is the weapon that I desire'.[11] Yet MacDiarmid valued Macleod. In the 1920s, in *Contemporary Scottish Studies*, MacDiarmid early on praises Macleod's amazing powers of word-painting and of spiritual insight, actually placing him higher than Stevenson! – although in later chapters talking less highly of 'the mongrel work of Ossian or Fiona Macleod'. More significant for MacDiarmid's relationship with Celtic and Gaelic ideas was MacDiarmid's meeting with MacLean, leading to his translation (via MacLean's literal translations) of 'The Birlinn of Clan Ranald' and 'In Praise of Ben Dorain', all part of his grand vision of the Gaelic Ideal and a Pan-Celtic Union of Socialist Soviet Republics in Britain.

The second wave of Celtic inspiration is that of Joyce, Synge and O'Casey – and especially Synge. But now Joyce is ironic, parodic and reductive in his attitude towards the folk epics of Ferguson, Hyde, Gregory and Yeats in *The Portrait, Ulysses,* and *Finnegan's Wake*. (I recall the last pages of *The Portrait* and Stephen's mythic fear of the old man in the mountain cabin in the West of Ireland, who, uninterested in learning of universe and stars, spits, saying that 'there must be terrible queer creatures at the latter end of the world'.) This is taken further in Synge's parody of heroic epic in *The Playboy of the Western World* (1907), and, I think even more subtly, in his play-portrait *Deirdre of the Sorrows* (1907) of a Deirdre who talks unromantically as she condemns her lover and his brothers to an avoidable death so that *her* story, rather than that of her lover and his brothers, will live on. This is clearly parodic mockery of the values of the epics as passed on by Lady Gregory, Yeats and the Abbey Theatre, and Synge's formative experience of his Aran Islanders was shortly to reject Yeats's 'purely fantastic [...] ideal [...] of a Cuchulanoid National Theatre'. He realised – as Fiona Macleod unfortunately never did! – that the necessary balance to the dreamy romance of Celtic and Yeatsian revival 'was always reached where the dreamer is reaching out to reality, or when the man of real life is lifted out of it'.[12] If Macleod did not hear this, Neil Munro, throughout his life deeply antipathetic to Sharp/Macleod, certainly did, yet without losing the poetry of his stories of Highland tragedy and self-betrayal, from *The Lost Pibroch* of 1896 to his elegy for the passing of the old Highlands in *The New Road* of 1914. And after Synge, O'Casey's urban satire on feckless men and enduring women in *Juno and the Paycock* (1926) surely leads directly into the plays of Joe Corrie, and outstandingly, Ena Lamont Stewart's *Men Should Weep* (1947), as well as Bridie's later drama of urban disillusion in *Mr Gillie* (1950).

The third inspiration coming from Ireland is arguably derived from Yeats's concept of 'The Great Memory', which was to merge creatively with Jung's notion of 'Collective Unconscious' and deeply affect writers like Muir, Mitchison, Gunn and Gibbon outstandingly, giving them new cultural strategies. Consider the moments of realisation of ancient kinship of identity in Gunn and Gibbon, Mitchison and Linklater, when protagonists realise their re-enactment of roles of thousands of years ago – for examples, Finn of *The Silver Darlings* (1941) re-enacting his namesake's role of heroic Celtic leader, or Rob Galt of the story 'Clay' realising his essential kinship with the Pictish farmer who worked the croft of Pittaulds ('the croft of the old Picts'?) thousands of years ago. Such supra-rational moments are not just continuation of the traditional 'either–or' or mutually exclusive interpretations of Scottish literature, but also a political and cultural strategy, an assertion of the Scottish writer's hidden resources. Is it not being suggested that these writers have a sensitivity to 'Great Memory' perhaps denied to English literature? (Or, more dubiously, that they are asserting the validity of racial essentialism?)

*

The second part of my discussion is complementary to my suggestion that we need to review Celtic Revival – in that I suggest that we also need to review 'Scottish Renaissance'. In recent years new histories and guides have significantly and positively revalued individual writers and groups in what Cairns Craig described as one of the least understood periods of Scottish literature – the radical poets rescued by Tom Leonard, Davidson and Geddes, Neil Munro; Barrie and Buchan are being seriously reassessed. In the light of all this, I believe it is time to remap 1870 to 1920.

As early as 1959 Kurt Wittig argued for a revival in 'Scottish literature' with Stevenson in his chapter 'Heaving Again'. Recent reassessment of a whole range of Scottish writers within the period of 1870 to 1920, together with a fuller exploration of what we mean by 'Kailyard' writing and culture, and what was really going on behind the guise of the 'Celtic Twilight', is revealing a greater richness than hitherto thought. I argue for the need to reconsider the achievement of writers previous to MacDiarmid and his contemporaries, bearing in mind that MacDiarmid himself had his own reasons for undervaluing his predecessors, while his self-centred genius all too often judged the worth of his contemporaries in terms of their closeness to his ideals and achievement, irrespective of the quality of their work, or sometimes even, one suspects, because they came too close to stealing his leading light. The MacDiarmid map of Scottish writing before him is first substantially represented in his *Contemporary Scottish Studies* (1926). His priorities quickly appear; poetry is the premier literary genre, while the novel form is a low second, 'alien to Scotland'! Dismissing Violet Jacob's now highly regarded *Flemington*, he sees the novel as 'a bastard form, never rising above the bar sinister'. Unlike modern criticism, which recognises thematic and formal linkage among Scott, Galt, Hogg, Stevenson, Brown and MacDougall Hay, he does not discern any tradition in 'unexciting' nineteenth-century Scottish fiction, a verdict modern criticism would find bizarre.[13] And as MacDiarmid had experienced the horrors of the Great War, so it is somewhat shocking to realise that fine poets of the calibre of Ewart McIntosh or Charles Hamilton Sorley, whose range of comment on the agonies of actual war far exceeds that of MacDiarmid, are never mentioned.[14] I simply contend that MacDiarmid (and, for other reasons, Edwin Muir) were great poets but inadequate literary mapmakers, whose opinions have clouded the real territory. What emerges from this is the importance and influence of cultural mapmaking. Arguably, neither MacDiarmid or Muir (or even Grassic Gibbon) should have been mapmakers, since they had so many axes to grind, Muir like Gibbon making Scotland scapegoat for his personal displacement and unhappiness.

*

I believe that at this point we must review the development of literature in Scotland after the deaths of Scott, Hogg and Galt in the 1830s. Scottish culture indeed languished for a time thereafter. This is the period T. C. Smout too readily restricts in *A Century of the Scottish People 1830–1950* (1986), refusing to discuss culture at all.[15] This is also the period when Scots and Gaelic and Scottish culture became systematically ignored in schools and universities. Thus 1835–1855 (with the Disruption of the Church of Scotland in 1843 at its heart) seems to me to be the real nadir of the uneasy century. Industrialisation, Clearance, Scottish celebration and participation in British Imperialism, Anglicisation of our educational institutions – all dissipate celebration of national culture. The most popular novelists of the period, like James Grant, William Black, and Victoria's chaplain Norman Macleod, celebrants of Highlands, soldiers and Empire, are surely the real developers of that pseudo-mythology which we too readily term 'Kailyard'.

But beneath the surface of fashionable Britishness something was stirring. The 1850s saw the foundation of The Society for the Vindication of Scottish Rights, led by John Stuart Blackie, himself a poet and essayist. And although doomed to failure due to the Irish crisis involving Parnell and Kitty O'Shea, Scottish Home Rule was once more back on the agenda.

I turn again to the pioneering German critic Kurt Wittig, who argued as early as 1959 that with Stevenson a spring tide was running for Scottish literature – perhaps unfortunately (if metaphorically appropriately) expressed in his chapter-heading 'Heaving Again'.[16] Recent revaluation has worked along broadly three lines, seriously reassessing writers like Stevenson, MacDonald, Oliphant, and Davidson and poets of the Great War period. Revaluation has rediscovered lost voices – 'City of Dreadful Night' Thomson, James Young Geddes of Dundee, the radical tradition, and Violet Jacob and Marion Angus, the unacknowledged lyric predecessors of MacDiarmid. The serious historical fiction of Munro, Crockett, Jacob and John Buchan so obscured by the shadows of the crew of The Vital Spark and Richard Hannay, is increasingly recognised as forming a post-Stevenson school, while the profound underlying seriousness of Barrie's drama, including *Peter Pan*, has been marvellously recovered by critics like Ronnie Jack and Andrew Nash.[17]

I cannot here back up my claim that this roll-call represents major achievement before 1920. Yet I make the assertion anyway – that we should not dismiss as trivial the revival of literature in a small country which can, between 1880 and MacDiarmid, offer writers of such stature – with many others being reassessed – such as William Alexander, Douglas Brown, S. R. Crockett, the Findlater sisters, Buchan, Jacob, Cunninghame Graham, Campbell Hay (not to mention Fiona Macleod), and in poetry Young Geddes, Robert Buchanan, Thomson, the war poets. Here is richness in English and Scots; and the period gains added richness in Gaelic, from poets like William Livingston, the unfulfilled John Smith of Iarsiadar, and Big Mary MacPherson of the Songs, bard of the 1880s land movement. This is hardly a literature in decline – indeed, it may rightly be described – with certain qualifications – as being in a state of revival from at least the 1870s onwards.

Let me return to Wittig's 'heaving again' in the light of what we might expect a mature national literature to achieve. Arguably, a full and mature national literature would represent, explore and criticise its social and historical contexts, not necessarily celebrating national historical achievement and certainly no longer seeking essential national identity, but rather expressing the uncertainties, dilemmas, and challenges of its age. It would seem to me that in a postmodern age we should appreciate the diversity of our older voices, and rather than blaming them for their uncertainties of subject, perspective and identity, read them as articulating their fragmented and displaced situations and times. Just because so many – arguably most – of Scotland's major writers left Scotland in the second half of the nineteenth century does not mean that they do not speak of Scottish issues and predicaments, or cease being Scottish as they look wider afield. And far from being insulated from Europe, there is abundant evidence that nineteenth-century writers were in touch – MacDonald with Boehme and Novalis, Stevenson with Henry James and Western fiction, Young Geddes with Whitman, Davidson and Macleod – and Barrie! – with Darwin and Nietzsche, as well as all these in touch with *fin-de-siecle* English writing, as Holbrook Jackson showed in his seminal survey, *The Eighteen Nineties* (1913).

We have to admit, however, that they speak with mainly negative voices, to the point that they could be seen as pretty sickened with what Scotland had become. And wrestling with their ideas of Scotland and identity, they express themselves in terms of clearing out old ideas, old values, old sacred cows of community and culture. 'Heaving again' takes on a new and purgative connotation.

I am of course arguing that, prior to any manifestation of 'Scottish Renaissance', in the period from Stevenson to the Great War and just after there was an impressive revival of Scottish literature. What are the principal features of the best writing of the period? Not, admittedly, industrialisation or urbanisation, Clearance or emigration – but, I suggest, in their own way equally significant issues, relating to what is almost universally perceived by the major writers as social, religious and cultural damage to Scottish character and community. I have elsewhere gone into far greater detail regarding the principal features of which I now briefly give details in the numbered points below. I suggest that these characteristics do indeed show that the major writers, far from following Celtic or Kailyard inspiration, were undertaking a radical and generally negative review of Scottish cultural history and cultural achievement (my list merely indicates the principal features, together with the prominent writers who illustrate that negativity in their work; the interested reader may find the categories extended in the two essays referenced in footnote 18):

1. *personal alienation, unsureness of identity, a feeling of being imaginatively stifled:* Oliphant, Brown, Munro, Barrie, Davidson, Campbell Hay, Findlaters, Carswell.
2. *sickness in rural community:* MacDonald, Alexander, Stevenson, Brown, Munro, Barrie, Hay, Findlaters, Jacob, Buchan.

3. *antipathy towards dogmatic and secularised religion:* Stevenson, Geddes, Thomson, Buchanan, Davidson, MacDonald, Brown, Crockett, Hay.
4. *reassessment of Scottish history and culture:* Alexander, Stevenson, Crockett, Munro, Davidson, Brown, Buchan, Jacob.
5. *an awakening sense of gender and of the limitations and predicaments of women:* Stevenson, Oliphant, Findlaters, Barrie, Hay, Jacob, Angus, Carswell.
6. *a surprising degree of international awareness:* MacDonald, Stevenson, Geddes, Buchanan, Thomson, Davidson, Findlaters, Cunninghame Grahame, Buchan, the war poets, Carswell.
7. *a wide range of innovatory methods and attitudes, including parody and pastiche, a willingness to cross genres, to use symbolic fantasy and allegory:* Macdonald, Stevenson, Oliphant, Geddes, Munro, Davidson, Barrie.[18]

By the 1890s Neil Munro (who hated the Kailyard movement, and had a most uneasy relationship, still not fully understood, with the Celtic Revival) could argue, as one of Scotland's foremost commentators on arts and culture, that Scottish art and industry was in the middle of a great revival.[19] With the Scottish Colourists, the Glasgow Boys, Whistler, and the Rennie Mackintosh Circle in art and the work of Brown, Davidson, Buchan and Munro himself, together with the Patrick Geddes and Celtic Revival movement in literature, clearly at least Glasgow and the West felt that something big was going on, right across the range of Arts and sciences. Munro's own cross-journalism at the turn of the century captures this mood well, as he mixes art and engineering, memory and modernity. This was Glasgow's time as Second City of the Empire; witness the many major national and international exhibitions (outstandingly in 1888, 1901 and, the most ambitious, that of 1911).[20] Significantly, this Exhibition simultaneously celebrated Glasgow in science and art as central to Empire, but presented Scottish customs and traditions on a lavish scale, even down to an entire Highland village at its heart – and used its profits to found a Chair of Scottish History and Literature at Glasgow University. This was also a period when momentum was moving towards presenting a bill for home rule to parliament in 1914 – not the most opportune moment. This was the Glasgow and Scotland Carswell remembered in *Open the Door!* and a case can be made for seeing this novel of 1920 – a few years before MacDiarmid's own wonderful early lyrics appeared – as answering, before MacDiarmid, his requirements for modernism in approach and awareness of European trends in literature, such as symbolism and structure, together with intellectual rigour.

*

In the light of this claim I turn to the post-1920 literature. There is no doubt that emphases changed, and new elements came in. Most critics would agree that after 1920 there was a return to roots in terms of language and respect for tradition; a search for an essentialism of racial inheritance; and a resurrection of national consciousness and – single – Scottish identity. As I have argued, the ideas of Frazer, Freud and Jung became a powerful influence in stressing the importance of subconscious, dream, legend and myth – adding to the influence of Yeats's 'Great Memory'. Much of the literature, fiction outstandingly, foregrounds mythic protagonists, suprarational epiphanies, the Jungian concept of the 'collective unconscious', producing in these protagonists coexisting moments of ancient time with time present (outstandingly in the work of Gibbon and Gunn), and an underlying use of the Wasteland ideology of Jessie Weston (*From Ritual to Romance*, 1920), with its emphasis on protagonists who become symbols of the decline of the Land and its culture, as in *Sunset Song* (1932) and its sequels, or even as martyrs, scapegoat corn kings and spring queens who die for their people and the process of regeneration of the land (as in Mitchison's *The Corn King and the Spring Queen*, 1931).

Yet isn't there something of a paradox in the idea implicit in the term 'Renaissance' for the major literature of the inter-war years? Do not the later writers continue the principal characteristics I have listed of their predecessors, in their presentations of the cultural decline or sunset of old traditions and language, the negative effects of Highland Clearance, the malicious gossip of small communities, the warping effects of severe religion? This seems to me to be the recurrent subject matter of so many of the major writers. Consider the implications of Gibbon's title, *Sunset Song*. Doesn't it seem strange that our most well-known and popular native novel is hardly about rebirth, but – and in its sequels even more so – about loss of tradition, song, community? Gunn likewise, although his great trilogy concludes with a very temporary rebirth in *The Silver Darlings* – but most of his 20s work, like *The Grey Coast* (1926), *The Lost Glen* (1932), and *Butcher's Broom* (1934), is about decline and loss, like McColla's *And the Cock Crew* (1945) or even Linklater's wonderful Orkney Renaissance satire, *Magnus Merriman* (1934).

After the war, the more affirmative Renaissance aims and values, deriving from a focus on what was essentially a rural Scotland, were dramatically dispersed with post-war scepticism. Yet if we allow my qualifying remarks regarding the underlying pessimism of Renaissance writers, we can see that this negativism, adopting the tone and perspective of Edwin Muir's grim journey around Scotland, in *Scottish Journey* (1935), became the hallmark of major Scottish literature – with the outstanding difference being that urban, rather than rural, issues, came to the fore, until the mid-1960s and the new work of writers like Crichton Smith, MacCaig, Mackay Brown and Edwin Morgan. The immediate post-war disenchantment is most vividly seen in the novel and the 1950s and 1960s work of writers like George Blake, Edward Gaitens (*The Dance of the Apprentices*, 1948), Dorothy Haynes (*Winter's Traces*, 1947), the novels of Robin Jenkins, 'Fionn MacColla' and James Kennaway. Their themes are almost always tragic, set in Scottish decay, and urban blight, with rural tradition often mocked for its irrelevance to present stagnation, just as in drama, with the plays of McLellan and Corrie, and particularly in James Bridie's last play, of urban and ideological blight, *Mr Gillie*, in 1950. Even MacDiarmid had turned away from his early and wonderfully humane poetry of community and tradition in Scots to a bleak and distanced poetry of impersonality and overpowering fact.

Wherein lies the reason for the paradox, and the oxymoron of Renaissance and elegy? Surely we must look to the earlier effects of the Great War, the decimation of the big men of communities, the impact of depression, the decline of Gaelic and Scots? The most powerful statement of this is surely Sorley MacLean's, in his fiercely pessimistic (and, thanks greatly to his poetic achievement, inaccurate) assessment to Douglas Young in 1943:

> The whole prospect of Gaelic appals me, the more I think of the difficulties and the likelihood of its extinction in a generation or two. A highly inflected language with a ridiculous (because etymological) spelling, no modern prose of any account, no philosophical or technical vocabulary to speak of, no correct usage except among old people and a few university students, colloquially full of gross English idiom lately taken over, exact shades of meaning of most words

> not to be found in any of its dictionaries and dialectically varying enormously (what chance of the appreciation of the overtones of poetry, except among a handful?). Above all, all economic, social and political factors working against it, and, with that, the notorious moral cowardice of the Highlanders themselves ...[21]

And with this in mind, can we deny the paradox, that the main achievement of 'Renaissance' is principally the powerful articulation of an intense criticism of, and even disgust for, a Scotland which has lost so much, in MacLean's Gaeldom, but also in similar echoes across the whole of Scotland, from MacDiarmid to Muir in *Scottish Journey*, or from George Blake's prophetic elegy for Glasgow shipbuilding in *The Shipbuilders* (1934) or Linklater's mocking laughter at the pretensions of Scotland in *Magnus Merriman*?

Outstandingly, of course, the most negative poetic voice is that of Edwin Muir in poems like 'Scotland 1941', and 'Scotland's Winter'. Yet even MacDiarmid's Drunk Man is unsure about whether the thistle rising is a positive or a negative feature, and the end of his drunk man's odyssey and his reflections on the state of Scotland is to take the matter to *avizandum* – stalemate. And reading through MacDiarmid's principal fellows, one is struck by their muted zeal – Goodsir Smith more hung up on his lost lemans and his eccentric personal life than a Renaissance programme, and Sorley MacLean, with devastating honesty, preoccupied with his lost love, whether for actual woman or Gaelic tradition, and his own weakness in the face of international injustice and war, William Jeffrey in love with ancient mythology rather than present redefinition, and Robert Garioch unable to conclude any representation of modern Scotland without the concluding last-line sting of his inimitable reductive idiom – 'I wisht I hadnae worn my MA goun'! This is not to deny that there are many examples of affirmative writing, in the work of Gunn, MacDiarmid, MacLean, Mitchison especially – indeed Wittig praises Gunn's fiction as outstandingly 'embodying all the ideals of the Scots Renaissance'. But for every *The Albannach, Highland River, Silver Darlings* or *The Bull Calves* there's *a Sunset Song*, a sceptical *Quair*, a bleak insistence on rural and urban despair as in *The Land of the Leal*, or *And the Cock Crew, The Shipbuilders,* or hilarious satirical send-up of so-called Renaissance as in Linklater's *Magnus Merriman*, or exposure of meanness of average Scottish small town as in Willa Muir's *Imagined Corners* (1931).

Even drama, from Unity Theatre to early Citizen's, reflects this, in the angry early work of Joe Corrie, Paul Vincent Carroll, and Ena Lamont Stewart; and movement towards disillusion can be seen as well in McLellan's preoccupation with internecine history, as in *Jamie the Saxt* 1937 – or disillusion with the present, as in *The Hypocrite* (1967); or in the work of James Bridie, from *The Anatomist* and *The Holy Isle* in the 1930s to the urban disillusionment *of Mr Gillie* in 1950.

I have come far from 'Celtic Revival'; but, to sum up, I argue that 'Celtic Revival', while important in itself in Scotland in the 1890s, and for the 'Renaissance' of Scottish writing, is in the end a distraction – as is the 'Kailyard' movement – from what I argue is a steady revival of Scottish literature from the 1870s. Allowing for a much wider and more inclusive 'Renaissance' than MacDiarmid's, 'Scottish Renaissance' can be seen to have been a phase, an organic part, of a revival which had been happening from the time of Stevenson on.

Notes

1. Cairns Craig, 'Arcades – The Turning of the Nineteenth Century', in Ian Brown and Alan Riach (eds), *The Edinburgh Companion to Twentieth-Century Scottish Literature* (Edinburgh: Edinburgh University Press, 2009), pp. 15–24.
2. See Declan Kiberd, *Inventing Ireland: the Literature of a Modern Nation* (London: Random House, 2009).
3. Duncan Macmillan, *Scottish Art 1460–1990* (Edinburgh: Mainstream, 1990); see especially Chapter XIV, 'The 1890s', pp. 291–398.
4. 'Fiona Macleod', 'From Iona: To George Meredith', in *The Sin Eater* (Edinburgh, 1895), pp. 1–13.
5. William Sharp, 'Prelude to "For the Beauty of an Idea"', in *The Winged Destiny: Studies in the Spiritual History of the Gael* (London, 1904), pp. 89–94.
6. See 'Realism in Gaelic Poetry', in Somhairle Mac Gill-eain (Sorley MacLean), *Ris a' Bhruthaich: The Criticism and Prose Writings of Sorley MacLean*, ed. William Gillies (Stornoway: Acair, 1985) pp. 15–47; and Derick Thomson, *An Introduction to Gaelic Poetry* (London: Gollancz, 1974).
7. Davidson's essay-letter, 'To the Peers Temporal of the United Kingdoms of Great Britain and Ireland' (which is also the dedication to *The Testament of John Davidson*, 1908), can be found in *The Poems of John Davidson*, ed. Andrew Turnbull (Edinburgh: Scottish Academic Press, 1973), vol. 2, pp. 539–44.
8. Neil Munro, 'The Lost Pibroch', 'Castle Dark' and 'Boboon's Children', in *The Lost Pibroch and Other Sheiling Stories* (Edinburgh and London, 1896).
9. Neil Gunn, 'Half-Light', in *Hidden Doors* (Edinburgh: Porpoise Press, 1929).
10. Somhairle Mac Gill-eain (Sorley MacLean), *Dain do Eimhir (Poems to Eimhir)*, ed Christopher Whyte (Glasgow: ASLS, 2002); *An Cuilithionn 1939 (The Cuilinn 1939 and Unpublished Poems)*, ed. Christopher Whyte (Glasgow: ASLS, 2011).

11. Alan Riach, 'Arcades – The 1920s and 1930s', in Ian Brown and Alan Riach (eds), *The Edinburgh Companion to Twentieth-Century Scottish Literature* (Edinburgh: Edinburgh University Press, 2009), pp. 50–60.
12. J. M. Synge, *Collected Plays and Poems and the Aran Islands*, ed. Alison Smith (London: J. M. Dent, 1992), introduction, p. xvi.
13. MacDiarmid's judgements on the writers discussed here can be found in C. M. Grieve, *Contemporary Scottish Studies: First Series* (London: Leonard Parsons, 1926).
14. A sample of the war poetry of these writers can be found in Trevor Royle (ed), *In Flanders Fields: Scottish Poetry and Prose of the First World War* (Edinburgh: Mainstream, 1990); and more recently in David Goldie and Roderick Watson (eds), *From the Line: Scottish War Poetry 1914–1945* (Glasgow: ASLS, 2014).
15. T. C. Smout, *A Century of the Scottish People 1830–1950* (London: Collins, 1986).
16. Kurt Wittig, 'Heaving Again: From Stevenson to World War One', in *The Scottish Tradition in Literature* (Edinburgh: Oliver and Boyd, 1958), p. 257.
17. R. D. S. Jack, *The Road to the Neverland: A Reassessment of J. M. Barrie's Dramatic Art* (Aberdeen: Aberdeen University Press, 1991); Andrew Nash, *Kailyard and Scottish Literature* (Amsterdam and New York: Rodopi, 2007). See also Nash and Jack in *The Edinburgh History of Scottish Literature*, ed. Thomas Owen Clancy, Susan Manning and Murray Pittock (Edinburgh: Edinburgh University Press, 2007), vol. 2, chapters 34 and 36 respectively.
18. For fuller illustration of my headings see my essays 'Remapping Scottish Renaissance in Modern Scottish Literature' in Gerard Carruthers, David Goldie, and Alistair Renfrew (eds), *Beyond Scotland* (Amsterdam and New York: Rodopi, 2004), pp. 17–38; and 'Preparing for Renaissance; Revaluing Nineteenth-Century Scottish Literature' in Gerard Carruthers, David Goldie, and Alistair Renfrew (eds), *Scotland and the Nineteenth-Century World* (Amsterdam and New York: Rodopi, 2012), pp. 21–36.
19. Lesley Lendrum, *Neil Munro: The Biography* (Isle of Colonsay, Argyll: House of Lochar, 2004) p. 60 and *passim*.
20. For a fuller account of these great exhibitions, see Perilla Kinchin and Juliet Kinchin, *Glasgow's Great Exhibitions: 1888, 1901, 1911, 1938, 1988* (Dorchester: White Cockade, 1988).
21. Raymond J. Ross and Joy Hendry (eds), *Sorley MacLean: Critical Essays*, (Edinburgh: Scottish Academic Press, 1986) p. 34.

www.ingramcontent.com/pod-product-compliance
Lightning Source LLC
Chambersburg PA
CBHW050242170426
43202CB00015B/2890